Your Journey to Professional Project Management

How to Pass the APM Project Management Qualification (APMP)

Parallel Project Management Limited
Reading, United Kingdom

Published by
Parallel Project Management Limited
Company registered in England number 7036508
Davidson House, Forbury Square,
Reading, Berkshire,
RG1 3EU

First Edition January 2010

Second Edition May 2011

Third Edition January 2013

Fourth Edition December 2013 updated to reflect changes to the APMP syllabus and BoK 6

ISBN — 978-0-9927891-0-7

Printed and bound in the UK by PublishPoint from KnowledgePoint Limited, Reading

Cover design by Steve West.

CONTENTS

SECTION 1 INTRODUCTION **10**

1.1   About This Guide 10

1.2   Who's Who and What's What? 10

1.3   How This Guide is Organised 11

1.4   Terminology 12

1.5   So... Where to Start? 12

SECTION 2 ABOUT THE EXAM **13**

2.1   What Is In the Syllabus? 13

2.2   What is the Format of the Exam? 13

2.3   Answering questions 14

2.4   Marking Schemes and Pass Marks 16

2.5   Time Management 16

2.6   The Questions? 17

2.7   General Hints and Tips 19

2.8   Make Sure You Are Properly Prepared 19

2.9   Revision Tips 20

SECTION 3 CONTEXTS AND ENVIRONMENTS **21**

3.1   Distinguish Between Project Management and Business as Usual 21

3.2   Differentiate between project management and portfolio and programme management 25

3.3   Outline the characteristics of programme management and its relationship with strategic change 25

3.4   Explain the challenges a project manager faces when working in a programme 25

3.5   Describe where the use of portfolio management may be appropriate 25

3.6   Describe how environmental factors affect projects 33

3.7   Explain the tools and techniques for assessing a projects context 33

3.8   Explain the importance of relevant legislation applicable to projects 38

SECTION 4 ORGANISATIONS AND PROJECT STRUCTURES **45**

4.1   Differentiate between types of organisation structures 45

4.2   Explain the way in which an organisational breakdown structure is used to create a responsibility assignment matrix. 51

4.3   Explain the role and key responsibilities of the project manager 51

4.4   Differentiate between the responsibilities of the project manager and project sponsor throughout the project life cycle .51

4.5   Describe other roles within project management 51

4.6   Describe the functions and benefits of different types of project office. 57

SECTION 5   PROJECT LIFE CYCLES **62**

5.1   Define a project life cycle and project life cycle phases 62

5.2   Explain why projects are structured as phases 62

5.3   Explain the differences between a project life cycle and an extended life cycle 62

5.4   Outline the processes for sharing knowledge and lessons learned throughout projects62

5.5   Explain the benefits of conducting reviews throughout the life cycle 62

SECTION 6   ORGANISATION AND GOVERNANCE **69**

6.1   Describe the principles of governance of project management 69

6.2   Explain how project management methodologies can be used to support the governance structure 74

6.3   Explain the advantages of using standard project management methodologies across an organisation 74

SECTION 7   COMMUNICATIONS **77**

7.1   Describe the key contents of a project communication plan 77

7.2   Explain the benefits of a project communication plan. .77

7.3   Explain the importance of effective communication in managing different stakeholders77

7.4   Identify factors affecting communication. 77

7.5   Identify sources of conflict within the project life cycle 82

7.6   Explain how to plan and conduct different negotiations 82

SECTION 8   LEADERSHIP AND TEAMWORK. **87**

8.1   Describe typical leadership qualities. 87

8.2   Explain the principles and importance of motivation. .87

8.3   Explain the impact of leadership on team performance and motivation. 87

8.4   Explain the benefits of adopting a situational leadership approach within project management. 92

8.5   Describe the characteristics and benefits of effective teams and teamwork 94

SECTION 9 SCOPE MANAGEMENT **100**

9.1 Define scope in terms of outputs, outcomes and benefits 100

9.2 Explain how to manage scope through requirements management and configuration management. 108

9.3 Explain the different stages of change control 116

9.4 Explain the relationship between change control and configuration management. . 116

9.5 Explain the advantages and disadvantages of a change control process 116

SECTION 10 PLANNING FOR SUCCESS **124**

10.1 Explain the purpose of a business case and its importance during the life cycle. . . 124

10.2 Describe who has authorship and ownership of the business case 124

10.3 Explain benefits management 129

10.4 Explain the use of Payback, Internal Rate of Return and Net Present Value as investment appraisal techniques. 134

10.5 Explain an information management system 139

10.6 Explain a typical project reporting cycle 139

10.7 Explain the purpose of the project management plan and its importance throughout the project life cycle 145

10.8 Describe typical contents of a project management plan 145

10.9 Outline the authorship, approval and audience of a project management plan 145

10.10 Explain estimating techniques 151

10.11 Explain the reasons and benefits of re-estimating through the project life cycle and the concept of the estimating funnel. 151

10.12 Describe stakeholder management processes. 157

10.13 Explain the importance of managing stakeholder expectations 157

10.14 Describe advantages and disadvantages of earned value management. 161

10.15 Perform earned value calculations and interpret earned value data 161

SECTION 11 SCHEDULE AND RESOURCE MANAGEMENT **162**

11.1 Explain the process for creating and maintaining a schedule 165

11.2 Describe different techniques for depicting a schedule 165

11.3 State advantages and disadvantages of using software scheduling tools 165

11.4 Explain categories and types of resource. 179

11.5 Describe how resources are applied to a scheduling process 179

11.6 Differentiate between smoothing and levelling. 179

11.7 Explain budgeting and cost management. 188

11.8 Describe advantages and disadvantages of earned value management. 198

11.9 Perform earned value calculations and interpret earned value data 198

SECTION 12 PROJECT RISK AND ISSUE MANAGEMENT. **213**

12.1 Explain each stage in a risk management process 213

12.2 Compare the responses to risk in terms of risk as a threat or opportunity 213

12.3 Explain the benefits of project risk management 213

12.4 Distinguish between risks and issues. 222

12.5 Explain the benefits of the escalation process 222

SECTION 13 QUALITY. **225**

13.2 Define quality management 225

13.3 Define quality planning, assurance, control and continual improvement 225

13.4 Describe the benefits of the quality management process. 225

SECTION 14 PROCUREMENT. **233**

14.1 Explain the purpose and content of a procurement strategy 233

14.2 Distinguish between different methods of supplier reimbursement 233

14.3 Distinguish between different contractual relationships 233

14.4 Explain a supplier selection process. 233

SECTION 15 GLOSSARY OF TERMS **239**

SECTION 16 CASE STUDY **267**

SECTION 17 EXAM PAPERS **270**

SECTION 18 MULTIPLE CHOICE ANSWERS. **274**

SECTION 19 INDEX **285**

List of Figures

FIGURE 1 THE PROJECT BALANCE. 21

FIGURE 2 PORTFOLIO, PROGRAMME AND PROJECT RELATIONSHIPS. 26

FIGURE 3 THE BENEFITS OF PROGRAMME MANAGEMENT 29

FIGURE 4 ENVIRONMENTAL CONSIDERATIONS 42

FIGURE 5 THE RELATIVE AUTHORITY OF THE PROJECT AND FUNCTIONAL MANAGERS. . . 45

FIGURE 6 THE FUNCTIONAL ORGANISATION 46

FIGURE 7 THE PROJECT ORGANISATION 47

FIGURE 8 THE MATRIX ORGANISATION 48

FIGURE 9 THE SPONSORS RANGE OF INFLUENCE 52

FIGURE 10 THE MAIN ROLES RELATING TO A PROJECT 52

FIGURE 11 THE ROLE OF THE PROJECT OFFICE AND THE MAIN RESPONSIBILITIES 57

FIGURE 12 PROJECT LIFE CYCLE. 62

FIGURE 13 THE NATURE OF GOVERNANCE OF PROJECT MANAGEMENT 69

FIGURE 14 A SIMPLE NEGOTIATION PROCESS. 84

FIGURE 15 PROJECTS - OUTPUTS - OUTCOMES - BENEFITS. 101

FIGURE 16 A WORK BREAKDOWN STRUCTURE 102

FIGURE 17 A PRODUCT BREAKDOWN STRUCTURE. 103

FIGURE 18 AN ORGANISATION BREAKDOWN STRUCTURE (OBS) 104

FIGURE 19 A RESPONSIBILITY ASSIGNMENT MATRIX (RAM) CHART 105

FIGURE 20 THE V SHAPED MODEL FOR UNDERSTANDING AND TESTING REQUIREMENTS110

FIGURE 21 THE COST OF CHANGE CURVE. 117

FIGURE 22 STEPS IN A CHANGE CONTROL PROCESS 118

FIGURE 23 BUSINESS CASE DEVELOPMENT 124

FIGURE 24 A SIMPLE BENEFITS MANAGEMENT PROCESS. 131

FIGURE 25 THE PAYBACK METHOD 134

FIGURE 26 NPV DEMONSTRATED WITH A DISCOUNT FACTOR OF 10% 135

FIGURE 27 NPV DEMONSTRATED WITH A DISCOUNT FACTOR OF 20% 136

FIGURE 28 NPV VARIABILITY DEPENDING ON RATE 137

FIGURE 29 INTERNAL RATE OF RETURN 137

8 TABLE OF FIGURES

FIGURE 30 INFORMATION REPORTING PRINCIPLES 141

FIGURE 31 A REPORTING CYCLE 142

FIGURE 32 THE CONCEPT OF THE PROJECT MANAGEMENT PLAN. 146

FIGURE 33 THE WAY ESTIMATING ACCURACY IMPROVES OVER TIME. 151

FIGURE 34 AN EXAMPLE OF BOTTOM UP ESTIMATING 153

FIGURE 35 AN EXAMPLE OF THREE POINT ESTIMATING. 154

FIGURE 36 A STAKEHOLDER MANAGEMENT GRID. 158

FIGURE 37 THE CREATION OF A PRECEDENCE DIAGRAM FROM A WBS 165

FIGURE 38 FINISH TO START RELATIONSHIP 166

FIGURE 39 START TO START AND FINISH TO FINISH LINKS 166

FIGURE 40 A BASIC DIAGRAM TO USE AS AN EXAMPLE 167

FIGURE 41 NETWORK DIAGRAM SHOWING EARLY FINISH CALCULATION 168

FIGURE 42 NETWORK DIAGRAM SHOWING EARLY START AND EARLY FINISH 169

FIGURE 43 NETWORK DIAGRAM SHOWING LATEST START AND FINISH CALCULATIONS . 169

FIGURE 44 NETWORK DIAGRAM SHOWING TOTAL FLOAT CALCULATIONS 170

FIGURE 45 NETWORK DIAGRAM SHOWING THE CRITICAL PATH. 171

FIGURE 46 NETWORK DIAGRAM SHOWING FREE FLOAT CALCULATIONS 172

FIGURE 47 SHOWING THE EVOLUTION OF A NETWORK DIAGRAM INTO A GANTT CHART. 173

FIGURE 48 EXAMPLE RESOURCE HISTOGRAM 180

FIGURE 49 EXAMPLE OF RESOURCE SMOOTHING 181

FIGURE 50 CUMULATIVE RESOURCE CURVE 189

FIGURE 51 THE PROJECT BUDGET. 190

FIGURE 52 TWO TYPES OF CASH FLOW SITUATIONS 194

FIGURE 53 THE NEED FOR EARNED VALUE 199

FIGURE 54 EARNED VALUE ANALYSIS TERMINOLOGY 201

FIGURE 55 EARNED VALUE FOR THE EXAMPLE PROJECT. 203

FIGURE 56 EARNED VALUE GRAPH SHOWING ACTUAL COMPLETION. 204

FIGURE 57 GOOD NEWS OR BAD #1 205

FIGURE 58 GOOD NEWS OR BAD #2. 205

FIGURE 59 GOOD NEWS OR BAD #3. 206

FIGURE 60 GOOD NEWS OR BAD #4. 206

FIGURE 61 THE APM RISK MANAGEMENT PROCESS (ANNOTATED) 215

FIGURE 62 RISK IDENTIFICATION TECHNIQUES. **216**

FIGURE 63 PROBABILITY IMPACT GRID 218

FIGURE 64 ISSUE LOG 222

FIGURE 65 QUALITY IS NOT AN ISOLATED 'CAMEO' SUBJECT 226

FIGURE 66 TYPES OF CONTRACTUAL RELATIONSHIPS 234

FIGURE 67 TYPES OF SUPPLIER REIMBURSEMENT TERMS. 235

SECTION 1

INTRODUCTION

1.1 About This Guide

This guide has been written by experienced practicing project management professionals with years of experience of training project managers. It is for use by the reader when preparing for the APMP, and it is a fundamental part of the Parallel Learning System. Its content has been constructed with reference to the APM Body of Knowledge 6th edition which is used with permission. The Body of Knowledge is referenced by the APMP Syllabus which describes the learning outcomes and assessment criteria that delegates need to demonstrate to be awarded the APMP qualification. We have written the guide in a matter of fact way, trying where possible to cut through the jargon, providing examples and real hands on practical advice on how to better manage projects and pass the exam.

You should aim to undertake approximately 40 hours of study prior to undertaking the APMP exam. This study guide has twelve main sections including numerous questions, tests and opportunities for reflection. You could consider going straight on and sitting the exam after spending 40 hours reading and digesting this guide. However, experience shows that you will be better prepared after a period of reflection and interaction with a tutor to help ensure that your own personal approach is correct. You may need feedback on whether you are tackling the questions in the right way and writing sufficiently detailed and accurate answers. By spending about 45 minutes on each of the 62 Assessment Criteria and answering the associated questions, you will be as prepared as you can be; but we do recommend attendance at a tutor-led exam preparation event, such as the Parallel APMP Exam Preparation Workshop, where your exam technique can be honed in the company of an experienced tutor and other professionals.

1.2 Who's Who and What's What?

The world of project management is full of jargon (some people would argue there is too much). There are also numerous organisations that have an involvement in the determination of standards and processes for use by the project management profession. Briefly, in the UK, the following are the 'Key Players':

- The Association for Project Management, based in Princess Risborough in Buckinghamshire, has a significant role and presence in the definition of project management standards and is the primary project management association in the UK. It controls the syllabuses for a number of examinations; particularly relevant here, being the APMP. People always ask 'does APMP stand for anything' and the answer is no. It is a name that was adopted some years ago but the relevance of the letters has now been lost. The other qualification from the APM are; The APM Foundation Qualification, the APM Practitioner Qualification and specialist risk courses.

- Axelos is a joint venture company with the UK's Cabinet Office (government) that provides the infrastructure and oversight for a number of professional management disciplines including the main one familiar to the project management profession which is PRINCE2®.

- The British Standards Institute is the national standards body for the United Kingdom and publishes BS6079 (1–4) Project Management Guides standard. There are four of these guides; the first being the guide to project management. The others relate to a glossary, the management of risk and a guide to project management in the construction industry. The APM use these standards to help describe some of the main areas within their own Body of Knowledge.

- The International Project Management Association (IPMA®) actively promotes project management to businesses and organisations around the world. In order to increase the recognition of the profession, they certify project managers, award successful project teams and individuals, and provide a number of project management publications (www.ipma.ch).

- The Project Management Institute, based in the United States, broadly do the same as the APM in the UK, but the user base is significantly larger than that of the APM. The PMI have a rigorous process for their 'Credential' programme and have similarly stringent experiential requirements for delegates wishing to attend one of their examinations to gain either the CAPM or PMP credential.

1.3 How This Guide is Organised

Section 1	Describes the structure of this guide and puts it into the context of the syllabus and the exam.
Section 2	Details the exam; its structure, format and how you should approach it. It contains numerous references and hints and tips borne out of our experience and guidance from the APM.
Sections 3 to 14	Follow the same basic systematic approach as the APMP Syllabus, indexed by Learning Outcome with sub-sections of Assessment Criteria they consider the breadth of knowledge encapsulated within the Body of Knowledge Edition 6. Please note that this guide does not follow the strict order of the syllabus. We have done this so that we can propose a logical journey through a project using a case study. It is recognised that some may find this strange and unnecessary, however it is our experience that this works best.
Section 15	Is an abridged glossary of terms taken directly from the Body of Knowledge, with only those terms needed for the exam. Throughout this guide we have tried to keep things as consistent and concise as possible.
Section 16	The case study; designed to give you something to work with when contemplating the various subjects and their practical ramifications. If you have your own project then this is even better. Along with the case study there are also sample templates for you to complete for your case study or this sample one, whichever you choose. These templates can be used for any project and you are free to copy them as you wish.
Section 17	Contains the APMP sample exam questions taken straight off the APM website, which you can 'have a go at'. The paper should take you 180 minutes (each question about 15-18 minutes).
Section 18	Contains the answers to the Quick Quizzes posed throughout the book
Section 19	Index

1.4 Terminology

There are numerous publications on project management. A quick web search will reveal hundreds of thousands of entries for project management and related topics. If you tried to read them all though you would a) take an enormous amount of time and b) probably have so many competing views that you would become confused. So, which are important and which are not? A key benefit of this guide is to help you sort the good from the bad. We have been able to draw on multiple sources and experience to do that for you. This guide uses a consistent form of words so that there is no confusion about terms.

1.5 So... Where to Start?

This guide contains most of the things you need to know to pass the APMP. The Body of Knowledge 6th edition, can be obtained also and this will provide some detail over and above what is included here if the delegate feels it necessary but you don't need to be completely familiar with the BoK or read it cover to cover but it may be helpful for some to get a copy. The APM also produce two key supporting documents — The Association for Project Management Guidance Notes for Candidates and the APMP Syllabus. Some parts of these guidance notes are reproduced in this guide along with other hints and tips to help you deal with revision and the exam itself. The syllabus is a very useful document as it describes in clear detail all of those Learning Outcomes and Assessment Criteria that you need to be familiar with. These Assessment Criteria appear in this guide at the start of the section that addresses them.

You should obtain a copy of both of these documents (www.apm.org.uk) just to make sure that you have the latest information. If you have booked any of the Parallel distance or classroom based learning events then you will already have been provided with them.

If you do read the BoK, you will notice that at the end of each section of it there is a selected reading list. For example, when considering the role of the project manager, you will notice that BS6079 is referenced. However, as mentioned above, there are also a number of other publications from respected authors and organisations that will give a different (sometimes radically so) interpretation of the same subject. Both are right, but for the purposes of the exam you will not be faced with a question that asks you to compare and contrast different works. We have created this study guide to provide a consistent and usable compilation of the relevant material and information from a number of sources to provide a 'one stop shop' for your learning.

You are of course free to purchase or borrow any or all of the above publications and of course they will help to provide a greater level of detail in particular areas than this document ever would be able to.

SECTION 2
ABOUT THE EXAM

2.1 What Is In the Syllabus?

The Assessment Criteria that you will be tested on appear in Sections 3 to 14 of this guide. They are the areas that the APM consider to be pertinent to the modern project management role. You may of course already practice some or all of these, but recognise them with a different name or terminology. One of the key things to do is to make sure you adopt a consistent approach so that you are in line with the expectation of the APM with regard to the exam.

There are 12 main learning outcomes as follows:

- Structure of organisations and projects
- Project life cycle
- Governance and structured methodologies
- Communication
- Leadership and teamwork
- Scope management
- Planning for success
- Schedule and resource management
- Risk and issue management
- Project contexts and environments
- Quality management
- Procurement

Highlighted in these various sections are the Assessment Criteria that will be used to evaluate the APMP exam returns and whether the delegates have demonstrated sufficient knowledge of them.

2.2 What is the Format of the Exam?

The exam is a three hour, closed book, written paper, invigilated under exam conditions by an APM representative. When you arrive, you will usually be able to choose a desk (unless you arrive last and there are only just enough); you are not permitted to take anything into the exam room with you apart from pens, rulers and calculators and may take nothing away that was given to you for the purposes of the exam. You will also need some form of photo ID. The qualification is highly regarded and as such valuable. You should be proud to obtain it, and respect the need to maintain its credibility and confidentiality.

Exams are not perfect and the APM seek only to test knowledge, not experience or 'competence'. All you need to know to pass the exam can be found in the syllabus, exam notes and this document (as mentioned the BoK may also be helpful). The APM seek to ascertain the level of your knowledge by setting a series of 16 questions on a selection of the various Learning Outcomes referenced in the syllabus and this guide.

- You need to answer 10 of these questions;

- You need to score at least 55% across all of the questions;

- Each question carries a total of 50 marks;

- The mark you need to pass therefore is 275 out of a total 500 marks possible.

In theory you could just answer six questions and try to get the full 50 marks for each. This is not a recommended approach.

The APMP Assessment Specification includes advice on the use of certain 'keywords' in the questions you will encounter. Note these well as they will be significant and have very different connotations in the context of the exam. The following is a direct extract from the latest APM Guidance (October 2013). You should make sure you download a latest version from the APM website (www.apm.org.uk).

You should be aware that the APM offer considerable help for people with disabilities or medical conditions that interfere with their ability to engage fully with the standard exam. You should contact the APM if you feel you would like to discuss this with them or your training provider will be able to help.

2.3 Answering questions

Questions should be answered in full, in a legible form (decisions regarding legibility will be made by APM and will be final). You should start each answer on a new sheet of paper and each sheet should be clearly marked at the top with your candidate number, the number of the question you are covering and the number of the sheet. Questions that require calculations should include each formula used and show workings as well as the final answer. Full details are available in the latest Candidate Guidance document from www.apm.org.uk. Some extracts are provided here to help.

Candidates should:

- start each question on a new sheet of paper

- write the question number clearly at the top of each page

- write their candidate number clearly at the top of each page

- write only on one side of each sheet

- show formulae and workings clearly

- put a line through any notes that are not to be marked

Any notes on the examination paper itself will not be marked.

Please note: Candidates may answer from the perspective of the purchaser, supplier, project manager or any other legitimate stakeholder perspective. Other appropriate examples from industry or public projects are equally accepted and are marked according to the mark scheme provided.

Please take note of key words in each question:

List & describe	A list of words or phrases with a clear description of what is understood by words or phrases listed. Each description requires a short paragraph made up of 2 or more sentences.
State:	A coherent single sentence that answers the question, as posed.
Explain:	An explanation making clear the meaning and relevance of an idea or concept. Each point requires a paragraph made up of 2 or more sentences. It may be appropriate to provide examples or diagrams to clarify the explanation. If there are specific marks for examples or diagrams this will be explicitly stated in the question.

In answering a List and describe question, a candidate may choose to:

List the number of points needed first and then describe them in separate paragraphs

or

Use clearly defined sub-headings in the text to indicate the points listed.

Allocation of Marks

Please note: Questions ask for a specific number of answers, therefore marks can only be allocated to the requisite number in the question. Additional information will not be marked. For example if a question seeks 3 list and describe responses and the candidate lists 5 items, they can only score marks for the first three. EVEN IF THE SUBSEQUENT ANSWERS ARE CORRECT THEY WILL NOT ATTRACT MARKS.

Diagrams are typically not required/sought and therefore do not attract additional marks. The information within the diagram may be marked as 'list items' if appropriate to the question posed.

Where a number of answers are sought, for example in relation to a process, these can be presented in any order. Marks are neither deducted nor awarded for the order in which items appear.

APMP marking conventions

LIST and DESCRIBE: (10 marks per answer)

The typical styles for answering are:

A list of requisite items, followed by equivalent number of paragraphs (marking: each correct listed item 2 marks, each corresponding and correct description 8 marks).

or

A number of paragraphs with embedded headers (marking: each embedded heading 2 marks, with corresponding description 8 marks).

Descriptions without headings will score a maximum of 8 marks each.

STATE: (5 marks per statement)

5 marks for a good statement which demonstrates both understanding and breadth/depth of knowledge.

EXPLAIN: (10 marks per answer)

10 marks for a good paragraph or number of points which demonstrate both detailed understanding and breadth/depth of knowledge, potentially with examples.

Markers can only allocate marks for the number of answers required by the question, e.g. if the question asks for list and describe five... then marks can only be awarded against the first five list items provided, additional items will not be marked. This is true for state/explain and both list and describe items, presented individually as a set list, followed by a set of descriptions; or integrated with each list item and corresponding paragraph.

2.4 Marking Schemes and Pass Marks

There will be no marking schemes identified to you on the question papers in the exam, but the apportionment of marks between sections will be provided along with some other guidance. Please see the sample paper at Section 17 of this guide. There are some instances where specific names, terms or processes need to be conveyed with a fiar degree of adherence to the marking scheme in other questions there is not so much need. The markers do have discretion to award marks for things that have been described well and are relevant.

The total marks in the exam are 500 (10 questions @ 50 marks per question). The pass mark for the exam is 55%. You will need therefore to obtain 275 marks overall. It is worth remembering that even if you only score a few marks on an individual question it will still go into the total pot of marks awarded and contribute to you passing.

2.5 Time Management

Given the need to answer ten questions in 180 minutes (3 hours), you will need a strategy. Try this:

- When told to do so, open the paper and skip through all of the questions, ticking (on the question paper) those you think you can do.

- For those ticked, put a scale against each to indicate how comfortable you are with your ability to answer the question (10 might mean you know the subject inside out while 0 might mean you should pick another).

- Once you have all the questions prioritised in this way, take a piece of the exam script paper and write down the questions you want to answer in order. Leave at least 5 lines between each. You will now have a list of questions in order.

- For each question, read the wording carefully and write down the key distinct points that you think will fully answer the question as asked; if you are unable to, it means you may not be as good at that topic as you thought.

- When complete, review the percentage scores and remark them in a new order.

- Build confidence by taking your highest scoring one first.

These steps may well take you 15 minutes of your 180. **DON'T PANIC**. You do not want to get half way through a question only to find your points are merging together, you don't really know any features/benefits/advantages of the topic in question, or you have simply dried up.
PLANNING IS CRUCIAL TO SUCCESS.
YOU WILL BE LEFT WITH ABOUT 15 MINUTES TO ANSWER EACH QUESTION.

A lot of the questions will ask for four/five/six points in your answer. Do the maths. If it wants five points then this is three minutes per point. Three minutes equals about two long or three short sentences. To provide a proper answer for each question you are looking at about 1½ pages of standard A4 lined paper. This will equate to about 2 pages of exam script as the exam paper provided has margins either side and wide line spacing.

Some questions will have split marks (e.g. 20 marks for part i and 30 for part ii). These work the same as above with marks apportioned as necessary. It is not a numbers game but you will need to have a plan to answer the questions fully and within the time you have.

2.6 The Questions?

Only the examiners actually see the exam questions. However, there are sample questions on the APM website and these are used within this guide in Section 17. You will also find questions that have been prepared to mimic the style of the official ones, but tackle a wider range of topics and material, to give you more practice before facing the real ones.

A typical question could be:

Explain the terms success criteria, success factors and key performance indicators and explain two ways in which they can be used in the successful management of a project, giving examples.   (50 marks)

Take a good look at this question, it is split into five parts;-

NOTE WELL

- For a start, you will need to be able to distinguish between KPIs, success factors and success criteria.

- If you make six points the last will be ignored so remember to use the plan you have written.

- It wants three descriptions (10 marks each) and two uses (10 marks for each use).

Here is a sample answer for the question above. It is included here to give you a feel for the style and quantity that the examiners will be looking for. As with any model answer this will probably score highly, but individuals will all write things slightly differently.

> *Success criteria describe the objectives that the project is seeking to achieve in order to be considered a success. The most obvious success criteria are the time, cost and quality objectives for the project but there may well be others, such as those that relate to the actual operational use of the finished product.*

> *A key performance indicator (KPI) is used systematically during the project to determine whether or not it will achieve its success criteria. It is too late to realise that the project will not achieve its success criteria after it has finished. The KPIs will be closely linked to the success criteria and will represent 'way-points' on the way to achieving them.*

> *A success factor is something in the project environment that will help underpin the project and its likelihood of success. They can, in some ways, be viewed as assumptions. An example of a success factor might be the need for a motivated team, strong management support or realistic objectives. Some success factors are considered critical, in that their absence will cause the project to fail.*

> *During the early phases of a project the project manager will seek to clarify and document the success criteria. The stakeholders are able to agree these criteria so that there is general agreement about what success looks like. At the end of the project, the stakeholders can be asked to confirm that the criteria have been achieved, thus evidencing the successful outcome. For example, if we are building a new stadium one of the success criteria might be that it costs less than £200m when completed.*

> *The rate at which a project delivers its products may be a KPI, and therefore the rate at which these are being delivered will be recorded and tracked to help understand whether we will be able to deliver the remainder on time. These KPIs will be reviewed at regular intervals (probably during project evaluation reviews) to ensure that any corrective action can be identified and executed to keep the project on track. In the instance of the new stadium, we may wish to keep track of the number of seats installed to help us understand whether we are on track to finish on time or not.*

This answer is written in longhand. It is not essential to do this and each of the constituent sentences can in themselves be a bullet point. Bullet points are perfectly acceptable, but care is needed to ensure that the examiner is clear which question (or part) is being answered and the answer does not become too brief. Bullet point answers still need to comprise complete sentences and you will NOT score 10 marks for just a few written words.

If you have not sat a three hour paper recently, one of your major issues is going to be simply writing for that period of time. The only answer, regrettably, is practice. When you have a go at the sample questions in this guide, do not simply skip through, thinking to yourself what you might write. Get organised, sit down in private and actually answer the question by writing a long hand answer.

2.7 General Hints and Tips

The most important point about any exam is so obvious — make sure you read the question. If it is asking for benefits of something, give benefits; if the question asks you to describe a process then describe it. A lot of failures seem to stem from a poor relationship between the answer and the question as asked.

Start each question (or part) on a new page. You will feel like you are wasting paper with only a couple of sentences at the top of some of the pages, but it means you can go back and change things without making your paper look a mess.

The easier it is to mark, the better. You do not get more marks for neat handwriting, but if the marker cannot read it at all they are going to have difficulty marking it. Don't waste a lot of time dotting every 'i' and crossing every 't' though.

If you are answering any calculation question, make sure you show your workings, there may be marks awarded if the end result is wrong, but some of the logic and rationale made sense. It may not turn a fail into a pass, but all the marks go into the total.

Leave a big gap between bullet points so you can annotate and add things as you go. You can go back (remember to try and keep 15 minutes at the end to review what you have written). This way your answer is not all crammed into the available space and you will have no trouble adding anything or making it clearer later.

Ensure your graphs and diagrams are clear, with a title and scales clearly identified and explained. Please note that whilst delegates are free to write as they wish on the examination question sheet only the answer sheets will be marked.

Try to avoid too many acronyms and jargon, especially if it is very specific to a workplace example. You might know what you are trying to say, the examiner will not be so informed.

Candidates may use examples from public, professional or the media or indeed ones fabricated for the purpose of making a point, so long as their answers relate appropriately to the question as posed. Bear in mind the comment above about specific examples that may be too obscure for a general syllabus.

2.8 Make Sure You Are Properly Prepared

- In the run up to the exam, you might be nervous and stressed; it is easy to say but try not to let it get in the way;

- Avoid alcohol;

- Get a good night's sleep;

- Arrive early, select a decent seat near the window, out of the sun and not right under the air conditioning unit (noisy and cold);

- Read the exam guidance from the APM and make sure you have everything you need (coloured pens, writing pens, ruler, calculator and photo ID);

- Avoid last minute panics by arriving in plenty of time;

- There are concessions for previously advised medical conditions — check the latest guidance notes.

2.9 Revision Tips

- Make sure you have read the quick quizzes at the end of each section in this guide to be sure you know the basics (e.g. the difference between success criteria, critical success factors and key performance indicators).

- If you are not very good at remembering equations, try writing them on an index card, turning it over and writing them again. Check if you got them right. Keep doing this and hopefully, eventually it will stick. Just before the exam do it a few times, and when you get into the exam, before writing any plans or answers, write them again on a blank sheet of script paper. You have practiced and your memory will be fresh. Remember — you cannot take anything into (or out of) the exam room.

- Try and set yourself a reasonable revision plan — little and often, set a time frame for revising and stick to it.

- Try not to just keep revising the things you already know, try learning the things you don't know. Avoid the comfort of familiar territory. Push yourself to explore new areas that you may have considered too obscure or difficult. Some of the less popular subject areas can in fact be relatively straight forward with the right approach.

- If one Assessment Criteria is completely inaccessible to you, at a pinch you could leave it out of your revision schedule. Avoid leaving too many out though, there are 69 Assesemnet Criteria and you answer 10 from 16 questions. You might end up with a paper full of questions you have consigned to the 'too hard' bin and spend three hours twiddling your thumbs.

SECTION 3

CONTEXTS AND ENVIRONMENTS

 Assessment Criteria

3.1 Distinguish Between Project Management and Business as Usual

Overview

Before we can really go on and start to consider the APMP syllabus, there are a few basics that need to be established.

The Main Characteristics of Projects

- In order to derive benefit the project will be required to produce a planned set of deliverables (or products).

- Projects are transient, they have a finite time in which they will deliver those deliverables.

- They are of various sizes, there are overheads associated with any project and they are therefore normally a significant endeavour involving risk that must be managed.

- Directed at the achievement of benefits, We do not do projects merely because we can. We expect to derive some long-term benefit from them potentially way beyond the end of the project itself.

- They operate within a predetermined and planned budget (for the project).

- Projects are the vehicles of change in an organisation. They are not the repetitive static business as usual types of activity.

Projects are normally referred to by virtue of their various 'success criteria' the key ones of these appear as in Figure 1 below.

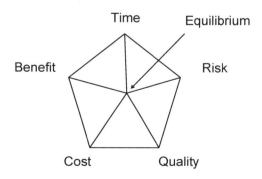

FIGURE 1 THE PROJECT BALANCE

Each of the vertices of the pentagon has a definite quantified criteria associated with it. These are called 'success criteria'. It is relatively common to hear the term 'quality' used instead of 'deliverables'. The broad term quality is interpreted as 'fitness for purpose' or to put it crudely, the products 'do what it says on the tin' (the tin being the specification). You may also often hear the word 'product' used. Use of the term 'Quality' though has advantages as it implies that it is not just any old deliverable but one that actually fulfils the stated requirement.

There is a point of equilibrium somewhere within the pentagon. The exact nature of the various success criteria is what the project manager has to balance throughout the project (after they have been agreed and documented in the business case and the Project Management Plan (PMP)). Some of these success criteria may not be compatible with each other. For example there may be situations where a particular end date (a big sporting event opening ceremony, for example) is absolutely paramount. It must be achieved almost at any cost, although what usually happens is that the scope (or Quality) is scaled back to fit within the time and the budget constraints.

There are usually trade-offs to be made between the resultant benefit of a project (saving 20% on our inventory costs, for example) and the costs of implementing a computer system to allow us to do so. A cheaper system may allow us to save 19% and it may be that the extra 1% comes at a too high price. We will consider success or failure of projects later, but suffice to say here that it is often the misunderstanding of the nature of the relationship between these criteria that causes projects to be perceived as failures.

The project sponsor is responsible for making and agreeing these trade-offs. They are the arbiter of the beneficial outcomes that may be achieved and the cost of achieving them. This is a fundamental aspect of a project sponsor's role and means they can create and own a viable business case. The business case will normally be 'approved' by the sponsoring organisation and the sponsor will own it through the life cycle.

The Scope of the project is loosely defined as all of those things that the project will do and all of those things that will be produced.

Projects Are Different from Business as Usual

Projects are formulated and undertaken in order to introduce a change to an existing status quo (e.g. a new computer system, a bridge, a new product launch, etc.). This distinguishes them from operational tasks. Consider the following examples:

- Open heart surgery, to the surgeon and the patient this may seem like a project, to the theatre nurse it may seem like a repetitive operation.

- A factory manufacturing 300 washing machines a day, the factory that makes the washing machines would have been the result of a project, each washing machine though is simply business as usual.

- Building a new footbridge over a major river, never been done before, this is a project.

- Manufacturing a new aircraft type, the first prototype is probably a project, as is the second and maybe third, eventually though even a large manufactured product becomes 'business as usual'.

- Implementing a prototype software system, never been done before, probably a project.

Which is the project? The table below helps to help identify the main key differentials that separate a project from other types of undertaking:

Project	Business as Usual
Seeks to introduce change.	Seeking to maintain a stable platform for efficient production.
Limited by time.	Repetitive and continues indefinitely.
Teams working with unique, bespoke plans and risks.	Highly procedural working practices to enable complex operations to be delivered in a consistent way.
Specified scope so we understand what the project work and products are.	The first few prototypes of a mass-produced item may be a project, once production is on-going they become business as usual.
Produce specific one off deliverables.	Produce specific deliverables, but repeatedly.
They have a discrete number of steps (delineated by the finite time), called a PROJECT life cycle.	Products go through a life cycle from build, through operations to disposal, called a PRODUCT life cycle.
Projects seek step change and transformation	Business as usual is seeking continuity, consistency and slow incremental improvement.
Requires a specific authorised business case	This is normally funded from Operational budgets rather than capital budgets. Business cases are less relevant.

 ## Quick Quiz (Answers In Section 18)

	Question	Options	Your Answer
1	The interaction between projects and business as usual is....?	a) Incidental b) Irrelevant c) Clearly identified to make sure projects deliver maximum benefit	
2	A project will require a business case	True or false?	
3	Projects can be undertaken many times in the same form	True or false?	
4	Projects have a distinct start / finish	True or false?	
5	Projects introduce slow incremental change	True or false?	
6	A project will only be justified if the benefits outweigh the costs.	True or false?	

	Question	Options	Your Answer
7	An example of a success criteria might be	a) The time a project takes b) How experienced the project manager is c) Assumptions made	
8	Which of these is a project	a) A prototype software system b) Making washing machines c) Running a finance department	
9	A key element of project management is the management of risk	True or false?	
10	The project sponsor approves the business case	True or false?	

Use this space to make some notes

What Kind of Questions Might There Be in the Exam?

1)	List and describe five key attributes of a project and how they differ from business as usual.
2)	List and describe five difficulties a project manager may encounter when running a project in a well established operational business.

	Assessment Criteria

3.2 Differentiate between project management and portfolio and programme management

3.3 Outline the characteristics of programme management and its relationship with strategic change

3.4 Explain the challenges a project manager faces when working in a programme

3.5 Describe where the use of portfolio management may be appropriate

It is difficult to differentiate between more than one concept without understanding what is meant by each one. We have sought to describe Project Management in the previous section and in this section we will look now at the two others (Programme Management and Portfolio Management).

The Context of Portfolio Management

Organisations face many challenges when running their projects. There are many key questions that they may feel they need to answer in order to make sure they are not only running the right projects but also that they are able to vouch for the fact that they are running them well. The term 'Portfolio Management' is used to describe this over arching form of governance exerted by the organisation over its projects and programmes. A portfolio in essence is the sum of all those projects and programmes. Portfolios therefore contain Programmes and Projects.

The portfolio manager may need to consider a number of things when deciding which projects and programmes should be within the portfolio, some of these considerations might be :

- Balancing the number and type of projects to suit changing strategic objectives

- The nature of the overall risk exposure - organisations could not take on too many risky projects

- Efficiency through 'weeding out' those projects and programmes not directly contributing sufficient value

- Effective use of scarce resources, making sure that the business is able to fund the entire workload

- Better focus on the achievement of a collective of benefits.

In Figure 2 we see that the 'Host Organisation' has choices about which projects, portfolios and programmes it will be running. In some organisations the overheads associated with portfolio and programme management may be unnecessary. In this case they may just run projects and any governance follows this path (the hatched arrow). As organisations become more and more mature with regard to their project management disciplines it may be appropriate to consider formal portfolio and programme management. This will assist with prioritisation, project control, risk management and reporting.

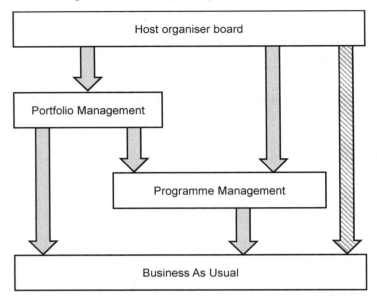

FIGURE 2 PORTFOLIO, PROGRAMME AND PROJECT RELATIONSHIPS

The role of managing the portfolio falls to the sponsoring organisation. They may choose to undertake the programmes and projects that best suit the strategic direction of the business. Each project will be commissioned in response to a specific business case; this is also true of a programme. It is these business case decisions that will be fundamental in deciding whether a project is in (or out) of the organisation's portfolio.

A portfolio manager has the job of ensuring that the whole range of projects and programmes that are underway represent the most appropriate mix of projects applicable to the organisations needs at any given time. They will need to:

- Screen projects to ensure they do in fact conform to the organisations needs at the time.

- Prioritise projects to make sure that they are optimised in terms of the available resource and return on investment.

- Continually re-assess throughout the accounting period, and add or remove some projects over time, because they may no longer be appropriate in changing business circumstances.

- Make sure that the considerations external to the portfolio are reflected and taken into account.

The area of governance (as we will see later) has a significant role to play in the management of a portfolio and therefore there are significant aspects of portfolios that overlap with those of governance.

A lot of students of the subject have significant problems with the concept of a portfolio. Very simplistically it is the organisations collection of everything to do with projects or programmes.

Where may Portfolio Management be appropriate?

- **Where the management of organisational risk is needed.** By having a holistic view of the whole workload, organisations can better co-ordinate all the different projects and programmes, enabling a better flow of risk information from senior management to project teams and vice versa. This means that contingencies can be transferred between different projects and programmes, providing a more efficient use of those funds and resources. Furthermore, the overall risk profile can be better understood. We may have one very risky project where our efforts need to be directed, whilst other less risky ones can manage their own risk exposure.

- **Where organisational capacity is a limiting factor.** With a global view of all the projects and programmes it is possible to avoid capacity bottlenecks, where multiple projects and programmes compete for the same resources. It is imperative that organisations are able to divert scarce resources quickly and seamlessly from one area to another so that delays and issues on one project, which can yield under-utilisation, can be diverted elsewhere.

- **Where standardisation and consistency of approach is needed.** Common methods and tools can be established and maintained at portfolio level, avoiding duplication and confusion. An organisation would not really want its project managers all coming up with their own way of doing things. A corporate project office might be instrumental in reducing these overheads.

- **Holistic view of the workload**. Here, senior management can make far more effective judgments on how to best ensure that investment resources are most appropriately allocated. The portfolio can be balanced to find a compromise between the desire to everything as soon as possible and actually making sure that the most beneficial projects are done first.

- **Co-ordination of the impact on business as usual.** When an organisation embarks upon a range of projects and programmes there is a need to make sure that these do not have a combined effect on the business that is so great so as to put the maintenance of business as usual at jeopardy.

Programme Management

We saw in the earlier section how a project is characterised by its:

- Uniqueness

- Introduction of change

- Constrained budget

- Specified schedule

- Differentiation from business as usual.

What are the implications for organisations that have more than one project on the go at any one time though? Some organisations will have literally hundreds of projects. What do these organisations need to do to control them? What organisational components need to be in place to help manage them?

Where an undertaking is so significant that it is introducing a large component of organisational change into the business, to a wider audience, perhaps even society in general, then the concept of a project does not have sufficient scope to allow these bigger challenges to be dealt with. For these circumstance we need to discuss programme management

Programme management can be summarised as being the co-ordinated management of a range of projects and change management initiatives. It is basically a wrapper that surrounds the projects and provides a framework of control that enables a more co-ordinated approach to a number of these associated and inter dependant projects.

- Programmes consist of multiple projects and an interaction with business as usual. Each of these is dependent on the others, the exact projects contained within a programme will vary with time, and some will start sooner than others and some later. Which projects exist within a particular programme is a result of their contribution to the overall programme objectives. If they are fundamental to the achievement of the strategic objectives, then they should be in the programme; if they do not, then they should be omitted.

- Programmes and projects have an impact on business as usual. This is because they clearly deliver products into the business and proper transition arrangements need to be made. A programme will have much clearer visibility of these issues and may also have a lot of them within its own scope.

- Large programmes may also have their own specialists drawn from the business dedicated to the programme itself. Projects need this support also but to much smaller degree and may well share resources rather than have dedicated long term commitment as in programmes. For example, a programme may well incorporate its own HR team to deal with staff issues. Other significant areas where this may happen is in the areas of procurement, risk management and financial services.

- Projects can exist in isolation not forming part of a programme. These will be single highly focused activities that have a relatively small or low impact on the organisation and its objectives. This is not to belittle projects not in programmes, but merely to acknowledge that programmes are in place to provide co-ordination and control of large multi-disciplinary endeavours of strategic importance.

- The layer of programme management control made possible through the use of the structure can add significant extra cost, but the better control of risk and focus on benefits makes it worthwhile.

Programmes and Strategic Benefits

- Interdependence of the component projects to each other - only by linking each project with each of the others in the programme can we be sure of having a consistent set of them, managed collectively. For example the relationship between the project to build the data centre needs to be managed tightly aligned to the the iT hardware project to equip it.

- They are normally associated with a 'vision' and a top-down approach. "We want to be the Worlds best employer". The vision set by the senior managers in the organisation will dictate which projects are in and which out of the programme. By definition this vision is the key cornerstone of intent. If projects contribute to the vision they are in the programme and if they do not they are not.

- They can adopt a flexible evolutionary model. Not all programmes have certainty over the outcomes, sometime in a multi-year programme complete predictability is impossible and delivery in tranches with the objectives continually evolving may be a preferred approach.

- They are strategic in nature - they are generated as a consequence of some larger organisational imperative. "We want to be the largest seller of XYZ in the World" may be the vision for the programme. This will yield overall strategic deliverables focussed squarely on the needs of the organisation in the broadest sense. This Vision is the highest level of intent applicable to the programme and needs to accurately reflect the strategic direction of the company.

- They focus on the overall benefits to be derived by the organisation - they are benefits focussed in that they are clearly reliant upon the needs of the end beneficiary to describe what success looks like in benefit terms. "We need to reduce a hospital waiting time because of XYZ..."

Benefits of Programme Management

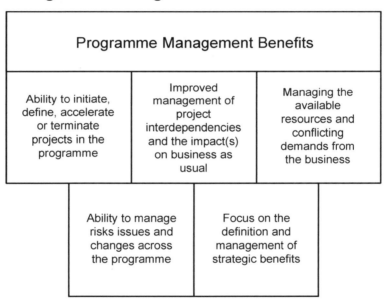

FIGURE 3 THE BENEFITS OF PROGRAMME MANAGEMENT

Projects Versus Programmes

Project	Programme
Constrained by specific objectives understood at the start.	Objectives evolve and can (to a degree) be modified as the programme matures.
Tactical single solution to single requirement.	Strategic in nature tackling large change programmes or major changes at an organisational level.
Projects deliver outputs which will subsequently deliver benefits after the end of the project.	Programmes will deliver benefits throughout their life cycle and have a highly developed benefits management focus.

Project	Programme
Focused teams with a systematic and structured approach with clearly defined roles and responsibilities.	Complex inter project relationships call for highly developed communication and influencing skills.
A project has a single customer defining the requirements and accepting specified products.	Programmes have multiple customers at different times through their life.
Satisfaction of a single tactical objective.	Top-down 'visionary' approach, projects assembled into a programme where they contribute to the vision.
A known scope means a clear view of the necessary tasks is possible.	Cyclical development means projects can come and go from the programme as necessary (but always to achieve strategic benefit).

Programme Management Roles

Project and programme managers share a number of attributes. They both need to be strong communicators, be able to manage resources and schedules, influence stakeholders and attend to detail.

Programme managers have a number of key attributes (and responsibilities) that are different in proportion than their project management counterparts. They need to be a strategic thinker, able to operate at the higher echelons of an organisation, able to juggle multiple projects, have a highly developed approach to risk and be comfortable with uncertainty.

The programme manager has to:

- Plan the programme including scheduling the projects trying to ensure early delivery of benefit
- Prioritise individual resources across projects
- Make sure that risks (and lessons learned) are communicated across the projects in the programme
- Make sure that all the programme processes are properly executed
- Support the project teams
- Ensure the business is ready to receive the outcome of the projects
- Ensure proper assurance is carried out.

In the same way projects have a project sponsor, the programme also has a programme sponsor, who has the job of making sure that the programme and the programme manager have support and guidance. Due to the overtly strategic nature of the programme, the programme sponsor has to be a senior individual, capable of 'paving the way' for the programme, providing an escalation route and also a source of communication in support of the programme. They need to have a high degree of political acumen, able to negotiate at board level.

Difficulties with Programme Management

Some of the problems a project manager may experience when working within a programme structure can be quite difficult to overcome. The Programme Manager will need to work closely with their project managers to ensure that they are supported in their endeavours.

Particularly a project manager may experience the following difficulties :

- They may need to recognise that the Programme Manager is their sponsor. This may not be the case when working in an isolated project but as part of a larger programme structure the programme manager will have control of their activities

- The programme will usually instil its own governance arrangements upon its constituent projects thus requiring the project manger to conform to these rather than have some autonomy over their own particular activities directly

- The project manger may not be trained on the specific method being used to govern the programme

- Working alongside other project managers may mean more reliance on managerial meetings and time spent co-ordinating activities with others.

- The project manager may feel distant from the end customer as the products as they are produced will be delivered to the client through the programme. This layer of translation opens up opportunities for misinterpretation and confusion unless managed well.

Work Based Exercise
What sort of programmes do you encounter?
Seek out your organisation's project or programme management office and see if they can point out examples of programmes.
Speak to colleagues about this.
See if you can think of areas where organisations (either ones you have worked in or those you are aware of) have used programmes to help deliver strategic change.
Some examples of programmes might be:
• A merger or acquisition in the financial service sector where one organisation merges its own people, processes and systems with those of another. Look for a key reason for this programme happening "We want to be the leading supplier of XYZ services".
• A car company developing a model through a number of key stages. This form of development programme is cyclical, the end result is never completely clear, but, for example, to satisfy a desire to be a market leader will lead the programme through a number of product launches and upgrades.
• Where there are a large number of diverse but complimentary activities, with products that are not always clear or tangible. Perhaps one project being that of lobbying governments to get support for funding a charity aid project.

Use this space to make some notes

_____
_____
_____
_____
_____
_____
_____
_____
_____

Quick Quiz (Answers In Section 18)

	Question	Option	Your Answer
1	Programme managers are just senior project managers.	True or false?	
2	Programmes are just big projects.	True or false?	
3	The interaction between portfolios and business as usual is....?	a) Incidental b) Crucial c) Where relevant to make sure projects deliver maximum benefit	
4	The scope of a programme is fixed throughout its life cycle.	True or false?	
5	Portfolio management has a linkage with corporate project office management and governance.	True or false?	
6	The words vision, benefits, focused and strategic are associated with portfolios.	True or false?	
7	Portfolios have a distinct start and finish.	True or false?	
8	Programme management and portfolio management are the same thing.	True or false?	
9	A portfolio manager would be interested in making sure that individual projects were initiated, mobilised and terminated in line with the strategic plans of the business.	True or false?	

	Question	Option	Your Answer
10	Which of these could be classified as a programme	a) The integration of two large financial institutions b) Installing a new computer network c) Building an estate of new houses	

What Kind of Questions Might There Be in the Exam?

1)	List and describe five key benefits of using a programme management approach.
2)	List and describe five benefits of running projects as part of a programmes instead of unconnected activities.

Assessment Criteria

3.6 Describe how environmental factors affect projects

3.7 Explain the tools and techniques for assessing a projects context

The Context of Projects

It is necessary to understand the context of a project for many reasons. The project can be affected in lots of ways simply because of its context and the environment in which it finds itself operating. The context of a construction project versus a project to implement an IT project will vary greatly depending on the bias and emphasis of some key factors. These are usually categorised according to the acronym of PESTLE.

PESTLE

	Construction Project	Implementing a Software System
Political	A large publicly funded capital programme will have a large number of politically motivated stakeholders and decisions on the strategic direction will be difficult to determine.	External political influences may be quite small, but internally bringing together a number of internal departments and gaining consensus across the supply chain of a company can be significant.

	Construction Project	Implementing a Software System
Economic	Funding a large capital project is usually almost wholly dependent upon public funds (either directly or indirectly). Quite often things like public finance Initiatives or private partnerships will be relevant. Long-term projects are much more susceptible to the uncertainty around interest rates for example.	An IT project to automate internal processes will have an impact over the whole investment case for the project. The benefits of the system are usually less measurable and they may well not occur until well into the future. The cost of the software and implementation will be offset against a more intangible business case.
Sociological	Projects need to be aware of, and may be constrained by, their position and impact on society in general. Power stations, bridges, railway lines, etc., require a deep understanding of the sociological trends surrounding the project; this will make the stakeholder identification process critical.	The interaction between the users of the system and the system itself will need to be understood. Understanding the needs of the society will mean more attention to ease of use and accessibility. Making it available to homeworkers or those with disabilities, for example, are areas where other projects may not need to tread.
Technological	If the project is in a safety critical area (e.g. replacing rail track outside a mainline station), it will require a much greater understanding of the technological specifications relating to the expected implementation time scales, specifications and anticipated through life reliability.	A software system requires some form of hardware infrastructure on which to operate. Typically computer related technology races ahead at high speed, so there needs to be consideration given to the availability of such systems and also the anticipated time before it becomes beyond 'end of life'.
Legal	Significant attention to health and safety and other critical safety issues will be needed. The nuclear and rail industries have a very high degree of regulatory requirements and framework in which they operate.	Software systems need to be covered by processes covering amongst other things the storage and dissemination of personal data.

	Construction Project	Implementing a Software System
Environmental	The disposal of waste from a construction site is heavily regulated, partly to protect the surrounding environment. For example, a site such as a large brown field development would need a very high degree of cleansing and preparation prior to actual construction. Clearly necessary, but it will probably delay construction and affect the timing and schedules.	Power consumption for a software system was something not actively considered even a few years ago. Greater attention to these energy consumption issues now means that careful thought needs to be given to the installation of the machinery, the times it is available (and not available).

So we can see that two different types of project have different contextual issues to deal with.

Use of the **P-E-S-T-L-E** acronym is advocated by the APM as a means of helping to identify what they are. See if you can think of some areas from your own project back at work where these are evident.

There are other aspects of a project's context you may need to consider:

Area	Impact
Procurement processes	May need to plan a long time ahead if procurement is heavily directed by the organisation or elsewhere (e.g. European Union Procurement Regulations).
Regulatory requirements	Banks and insurance companies have to be aware of the regulation framework they operate in. This can place significant constraints over their projects.
Use of structured methods	In the UK, methods such as PRINCE2® or the Office for Government Commerce stage gate review process will be instrumental in how quickly or slowly progress can be made.
Appetite for risk	If the organisation does not have a large appetite for risk then this will have a big effect over the type and number of projects undertaken.
Strengths, Weaknesses, Opportunities and Threats (SWOT)	The organisation needs to be aware of what it is good at and not so good at. Analysing these factors will provide a significant insight into how a project ought to be managed. Organisations with a poor record of managing sub contractors may wish to run the project in-house for example.

WHIRLWIND BIKES

Give some thought to the case study in Section 16. What specific areas of project context can you observe?

Political Context

Economic Context

Sociological Context

Technical Context

Legal Context

Environmental Context

Use this space to make some notes

_____

_____

_____

_____

_____

_____

_____

_____

_____

_____

_____

_____

_____

Quick Quiz (Answers In Section 18)

	Question	Options	Your Answer
1	A project context is only concerned with external factors.	True or false?	
2	An example of a political context might be the impending election of a new mayor.	True or false?	
3	The APM sometimes calls a project's context the project environment.	True or false?	
4	Accommodating a more elderly passenger base on a transport network is an example of which of the PESTLE factors?	a) Political b) Sociological c) Legal d) Environmental	
5	The project will need to understand the context to help understand the need and wants of the stakeholders.	True or false?	

What Kind of Questions Might There Be in the Exam?

1)	Describe the term project context and explain four contextual factors affecting a project giving examples.

Assessment Criteria

3.8 Explain the importance of relevant legislation applicable to projects

The Legislative Context

The primary areas for consideration here are

- Health and Safety Regulations and Law

- Contract Regulations and Law

- Employment Regulations and Law

- Environmental Regulations and Law

Health and Safety Law and Regulations

The main enabling act of parliament was the Health and Safety at Work, etc. Act 1974. Its objectives were that of:

1) Securing the health, safety and welfare of persons at work and

2) Protecting persons, other than persons at work, against risks to health or safety arising out of or in connection with the activities of persons at work.

The Act introduced a new system based on less-prescriptive and more goal-based regulations, supported by guidance and codes of practice. For the first time, employers and employees were to be consulted and engaged in the process of designing a modern health and safety system.

The Health and Safety at Work, etc. Act 1974 also established the Health and Safety Commission (HSC) for the purpose of proposing new regulations, providing information and advice, and conducting research.

The HSC's operating arm, the Health and Safety Executive (HSE) was formed shortly after in order to enforce health and safety law, a duty shared with Local Authorities.

The importance of the Act is to enshrine in law the acceptable standards and mechanisms to achieve the objectives. The benefits of the Act are to provide:

- A healthy and safe environment for employees;

- A clear reporting and management structure to ensure that the processes are in place;

- Guidance on the interpretation of the law;

- Codes of conduct to be followed in specific industries.

Health and Safety - What Does a Project Manager Need To Be Aware Of?

In order to provide a proper working environment, the project manager (as part of the organisation's management structure) must consider the following:

- **Making sure that a Health, Safety and Environmental Management Plan is in place** — this document (possibly part of the PMP) will include the scope of the project, the roles and responsibilities associated with it, particular external standards that may need to be adopted, reporting mechanisms, specific project related procedures, training record keeping and other pertinent information. The plan will be developed in conjunction with stakeholders in the sponsoring organisation and approved by the relevant health, safety and environmental body in the organisation.

- **Making sure that risk assessments are carried out** — the project manager may not be able to carry these out themselves, but must make proper provision and funding available to ensure that they are done, properly recorded and any resultant actions completed. A typical example of a risk assessment is a specific one for the use of display screens in office environments.

- **That the project team is properly trained** — project staff may think that due to the temporary nature of the project they do not need to follow HSE regulations or are in some way immune. Accidents can happen everywhere and the project manager will need to instil in the employees a robust and serious attention these issues.

- **There is open and honest disclosure** — one of the main things that the project manager establishes is a safety culture in which staff are comfortable reporting dangerous situations and not be penalised for it. HSE is the responsibility for everyone. One of the areas required by law is the Reporting of Injuries, Disease and Dangerous Occurrences Regulations or (RIDDOR) to be adhered to where near misses are required to be reported.

- **That regular reviews are undertaken** — so that minor situations do not develop to become dangerous. Sometimes where a particular environment has been occupied for some time and familiarity becomes complacency there is a grave danger of accidents happening. Continual assessment and restating of the issues and procedures will make sure this doesn't happen.

- **That everyone is aware of stress as a potential HSE issue** — where a project has strict deadlines, difficult problems and resource shortages there can be a temptation to drive the team too hard and induce stress. The project manager should ensure that working hours are not unreasonable, that proper relaxation facilities are available and the project team are consulted as part of work allocation, which will help in this area. But as with all health and safety matters the project manager should seek support from their professional colleagues.

- **Proper safety equipment is provided** — personal protective equipment (PPE) should be made available to staff where the circumstances dictate. Codes of practice help to guide what is the minimum requirement, although many organisations seek to exceed this minimum. Fluorescent jackets, hard hats and rubber gloves are all examples of PPE. Machine tools guards, scaffolding, electrical equipment and working at height are all specific areas with stringent requirements for health and safety attention.

- **Environmental issues are addressed** — as well as the protection of employees and the public, the project manager will have to be aware of and conform to any relevant legislation relating to the environment. Rehabilitation of contaminated land, recycling of printer toner and disposal of waste are all issues that will need to be considered; once again the circumstances will vary depending on the project.

Please also note that it is advisable to obtain proper Health and Safety advice when the need arises.

Contract Law and Regulations

There is a lot of folklore about contracts but in essence they are simply an agreement between parties where one offers to sell (products or services) and the other offers to buy those products or services. Contracts do not necessarily need to be written and there is a need to ensure that they are not entered into inadvertently. Employees are normally insulated from some of the more arduous commercial consideration by virtue of operating within their organisations governance framework.

There are a number of things that have to be in place for a contract to be enforceable in English law - particularly:-

- Who are the parties and a description of the works or services, what are the relevant company names, registration details and are they actually legally entitled to enter into this agreement.

- The providers responsibilities with regard to design, approvals, subcontracting and assignment, this is particularly pertinent in construction projects. If the designers design something that is unsuitable then it is they that will need to rectify the problems.

- Timings, costs, milestones,when exactly will things be done, are there any damages for late payment or incentives for early payment.

- Quality and other standards to be followed, if there are standards to be followed who will assess those standards and where will project quality assurance and control be exercised.

- Payment and when payment is due etc, this will be very concerning to sub contractors where their cash flow may be sensitive and the need to have swift payment may be vital to their survival.

- What happens if things go wrong (compensation events); liquidated damages, penalty clauses, consequential loss are all phrases used in an around contracts.

- Who owns what during and after the contract particularly intellectual property rights (IPR) and copyright, the intellectual property vested in a project can be substantial and the ownership of it may be vital to understand. Some knowledge based suppliers will have a huge vested interest in the acquisition and reselling of IPR.

- Assignment and management of risk, who owns the responsibility for dealing with risk and can they in turn assign that responsibility to others.

- How disputes and arbitration will be carried out, in the UK most contracts are subject to the jurisdiction of the UK court system under UK law. Where multinational agreements are in place then this may not be the case.

There is more detail relating to the nature of contracts an procurement terms in general in section 14.3. Please also note that it is advisable to obtain proper legal advice when the need arises.

Employment Law and Regulations

Project managers are sometimes in a strange position effectively directing the activities of people who are actually line managed elsewhere. This concept will be discussed when considering Matrix Organisations. They therefore may (or may not be the persons legal employer). Nevertheless project managers will need to be aware of potential employment issues as they may have a direct influence over individuals covered by the legislation.

- Project managers must be aware that absence from work may be a sign of something more sinister. If an employee feels stressed at work they may be more inclined to stay away. Project managers must be aware that in a project environment there is a risk that people are put in stressful situations that are unreasonable and this must be avoided.

- The Public Interest Disclosure Act 1998 covers the case of whistle blowing. If staff feel that they are being directed to undertake activities they feel are in some way illegal or otherwise irregular they have protection should they inform others of the facts without fear of recrimination. The project manager must ensure that open and honest communication is encouraged and team concerns are taken seriously and dealt with.

- The Working Time Regulations 1998 prescribe rules regarding the amount of time an employee can work, have breaks and holidays. Employees have rights under this law and Project Managers must be aware that again there is a risk that in a pressured environment there may be the urge to work longer than is strictly allowed. Project managers must ensure that objectives and targets are fairly set and do not overburden the situation.

- It is illegal to discriminate on the basis of sex, gender, race, sexual orientation, age or disability. project managers like their line management colleagues need to be aware of the implications of contravening these regulations. Project managers must engender an environment of inclusion and fairness in all the project activities.

- The Data Protection Act 1998 lays down the rights of the individual with regard to the storage and retention of information. Project managers may inadvertently be storing personal data either of their team or of other individuals as part of the project they are running and be unaware that this may in fact represent a breach. Project managers must ensure that there is an appropriate information management plan that everyone can abide by.

Environmental Law and Regulations

These days project management is constrained in a number of ways by environmental considerations in a way that it never was before. There is literally hundreds of pieces of applicable legislation and the following are just a few considerations

Projects may need to consider undertaking an environmental impact assessment. This will take into account the wider range of environmental aspects that a project may affect or be affected by. It might include the discharge of water, traffic congestion, noise, smoke, etc. It would need to be done at an early stage usually as part of the planning stages and may be needed to support a planning application.

In construction projects the use of contaminated land to build on will result in the need to carry out proper surveys, along with the correct disposal of any waste from the site and recycling of any that can be re-used on the site.

ISO 14001:2004 sets out the criteria for an environmental management system and can be certified to. It does not state requirements for environmental performance, but maps out a framework that a company or organisation can follow to set up an effective environmental management system.

Energy consumption will be closely monitored for example on an IT project. Whilst there are still large rooms full of expensive and energy hungry computers there is a growing need and desire to throttle back the energy consumption of these installations, leading to a number of revisions to plans that only a few years ago would have seemed perfectly reasonable.

The "waste hierarchy" ranks waste management options according to what is best for the environment. It gives top priority to preventing waste in the first place. When waste is created, it gives priority to preparing it for re-use, then recycling, then recovery, and last of all disposal (e.g. landfill). The stages include (consider Figure 4)

- **Prevention** entails using less material in the first place. Designing in a longer product life cycle will help to keep the re-manufacture impact to a minimum. Computer design techniques have been a huge contributor to this avoiding 'over engineering'.

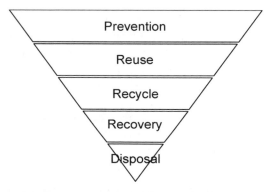

FIGURE 4 ENVIRONMENTAL CONSIDERATIONS

- **Reuse** involves taking the parts (machines, motors, etc.) and using them in similar applications after refurbishment. Car breakers yards are good examples of this.

- If materials cannot be reused then they can possibly be **Recycled** into a new product. Copper is extracted from old heating systems and melted down and used in electric motors perhaps.

- **Recovery** includes the use of the product to extract energy for use instead of fresh supplies. Examples of this might be anaerobic digestion to power heating plants.

- **Disposal,** landfill and incineration without energy recovery should be the last resort.

PLEASE NOTE - where consideration of employment or other legally orientated subject matter is proposed these notes should not be taken as comprehensive and are for the illustration of potential areas only and individuals should seek further guidance where appropriate.

Use this space to make some notes

WHIRLWIND BIKES

**Are there any potential Legal issues on Whirlwind Bikes?
What steps might you take to ensure that the road testing
trials are accident free?**

Quick Quiz (Answers in Section 18)

	Question	Options	Your Answer
1	Providing safety equipment is an employers responsibility under HSE legislation.	True or false?	
2	The Health and Safety Executive informs and enforces.	True or false?	

	Question	Options	Your Answer
3	Which of these can cause stress	a) Urgent time scales b) Working longer hours c) Working away from home d) All of the above	
4	RIDDOR is unique because it covers which of the following specific issues?	a) Nuclear contamination b) Food allergies c) Near misses d) Car crashes	
5	Which of these is concerned with Environmental management	a) ISO 14001 b) BS6079 c) BS5750 d) ISO 100001	
6	IPR stands for	a) Intellectual property rights b) Internal paper rights c) Inspection of personal records d) Implementation of paper receipts	
7	The layers of environmental considerations are Prevention, Reuse, Recycle Recovery Disposal	True or false?	
8	The Public Interest Disclosure Act covers	a) Stress at Work b) Near misses c) Whistle blowing d) Regular reporting	
9	The PM must ensure a health and safety plan in place on all projects	True or False	
10	Contracts require agreement	True or False	

What Kind of Questions Might There Be in the Exam?

1)	List and describe five ways in which the project manager would make sure HSE was dealt with correctly on the project.
2)	List and describe five key components of a procurement strategy.

SECTION 4
ORGANISATIONS AND PROJECT STRUCTURES

	Assessment Criteria
	4.1 Differentiate between types of organisation structures

Three Different Types of Organisation Structure

There are a number of potential ways in which a business chooses to organise itself and these ways are generally considered to fall into one of three main categories, namely a functional, project or matrix structure.

You should bear in mind that these organisational structures are theoretical, in that few organisations will comply with exclusively one or the other. They represent the ends (and middle) of a continuum. The principle is that as an organisation becomes more 'project based' so the project manager's authority increases as the authority of the line managers decrease.

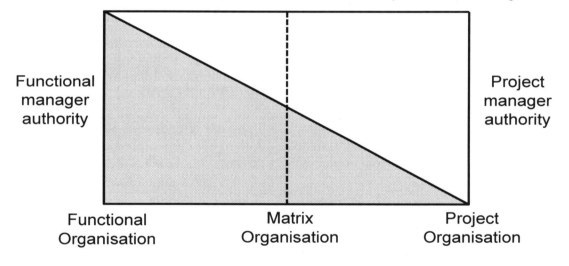

FIGURE 5 THE RELATIVE AUTHORITY OF THE PROJECT AND FUNCTIONAL MANAGERS

The Functional Organisation

At the left-hand end of this diagram we have the purely functional type of organisation, one which has very clear lines of reporting and accountability up and down through the organisation. Examples of this type of organisation are where key skills need to be developed and maintained, and there is a relatively low level of change going on. An example of this type of organisation structure appears in Figure 6.

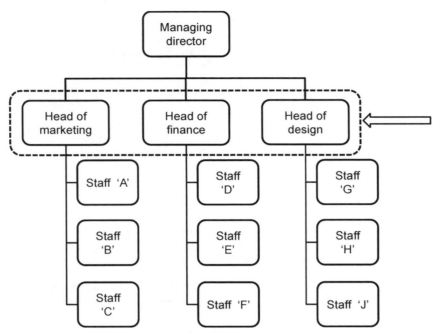

In a 'functional' type of organisation the staff work for their own line managers and report to them on a day to day basis. Any project work the organisation wishes to embark upon gets coordinated at the department level

FIGURE 6 THE FUNCTIONAL ORGANISATION

There are strengths and weaknesses associated with this type of organisation:

Strengths	Weaknesses
Maintains a cohort of very skilled staff, experts in their own chosen field. This can be very valuable where capability needs to be maintained (e.g. a fire service).	Inflexible, unable to adopt project working. The only way a project will happen is at the team manger level.
Allows for a lot of organisational learning due to its stable nature. The teams will be able to embed and utilise their specialist knowledge.	Does not provide variety for those that want it, thus affecting motivation. Staff will have no visibility of potential opportunities in other parts of the organisation.
Staff know who they report to and can easily determine priorities. This reduces conflict of priorities and associated stress.	Can lead to under-utilisation as there is an opportunity for under utilised staff in one part of the structure to not have access to potential opportunities in other parts.

The Project Organisation

At the other end of the continuum lies the project organisation. In this type, the project manager is king and the organisation only exists for the purpose of running its constituent projects. Once they have all finished then, in theory, the organisation ceases to exist. Some examples of this might be a construction consultancy or film production units where the holding company is only a skeleton and the project teams are brought together when needed and disbanded when not. Diagrammatically, it looks like this (see Figure 7):

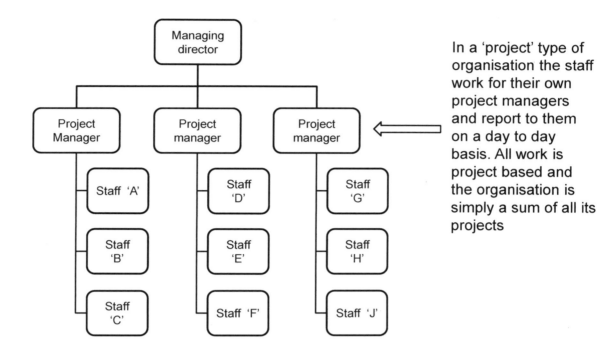

In a 'project' type of organisation the staff work for their own project managers and report to them on a day to day basis. All work is project based and the organisation is simply a sum of all its projects

FIGURE 7 THE PROJECT ORGANISATION

These too have strengths and weaknesses associated with them:

Strengths	Weaknesses
They have a very clear focus on the project objectives. They are not distracted by any line management responsibilities.	Little or no career progression and job security. Once the project is over so the team members are no longer required.
All the staff know who is in charge. The project manager is quite clearly in charge and the staff are able to identify and relate to this authority quite clearly.	Each project will recruit its own resources, which can cause duplication and under-utilisation. For example an under utilised team member on one project will not be utilised on another.
Easy to identify very clear roles and responsibilities without crossing organisation boundaries. There is no need for complicated and expensive systems to facilitate the location of staff when they are needed. The project managers have a strong project ethic and build their teams personally.	All experience leaves the organisation when the project finishes. The overall business does not have access to the experience of the team as it has been disbanded.

The Matrix Organisation

The third variation on this theme is a mix between the two main types as above. It is called the matrix type of organisation structure and has the potential (if implemented well) to deliver the strengths of the other two without too many downsides.

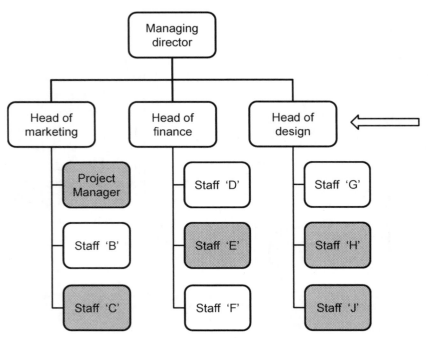

In a 'matrix' type of organisation the staff work for their own line managers and report to them on a day to day basis. All project work is carried out through the project manager utilising staff across the business (shaded) on an 'as needs' basis.

FIGURE 8 THE MATRIX ORGANISATION

In this type of framework, we see that we still have the staff reporting into a line manager, but now the project managers are able to draw on resources from across the business. In this way the project managers and the organisation get the best of both worlds. The main objective of the organisation is to deploy the right people to the right activities. This framework requires a sophisticated understanding of the organisation and the staff and roles within it, but offers the advantages of optimal resource utilisation whilst retaining organisational capability. In summary, these matrix organisations have the following:

Strengths	Weaknesses
There is visibility of resource skills and availability. The project managers can 'see' where their potential resources (teams may reside).	Needs quite a sophisticated resource management culture otherwise the potential teams are unknown and invisible to the project managers.
The project managers have an organisational authority over staff. The organisation recognises that project managers need to direct others and this concept is familiar.	Staff members can find their priorities conflict between project and line manager. If they have more than one person trying to direct their time they may be uncertain about which holds sway.
Specialist skills are maintained. When one project finishes staff move onto others. This can be balanced against the pastoral needs of the staff (holidays, training, etc.).	Project managers need to be good communicators and good at influencing others to get the job done. They cannot simply rely on an organisational authority in a line management sense.

Have a think about what type of organisation you work in.

Work based exercise
What type of organisation is yours — functional, matrix or project?
What inspires you to say that?
What complications does that cause your project managers?

 Quick Quiz (Answers In Section 18)

	Question	Options	Your Answer
1	A matrix organisation helps retain specialist skills when compared to a project organisation.	True or false?	
2	A functional organisation is most likely to retain specialist skills.	True or false?	
3	A project organisation is most likely to retain specialist skills.	True or false?	
4	In a matrix organisation, when the staff member has conflicting priorities between line and project manager, which might they naturally favour?	a) Line manager b) Project manager c) Neither d) Both	

	Question	Options	Your Answer
5	Which of these things is <u>not</u> needed in a true matrix organisation for it to work properly?	a) Good influencing skills by the project manager b) Sophisticated resource management systems c) Flexible and motivated staff d) Excessive paperwork	
6	In a functional organisation, who would coordinate any project if it took place at all?	a) The functional managers b) The project managers c) Nobody d) The staff themselves	
7	As the organisation becomes more project focused, the role of the functional manager increases.	True or false?	
8	A matrix organisation has the potential to reduce resource under-utilisation compared to a project or functional organisation.	True or false?	
9	A strength of a project organisation structure is that the teams have a clear focus.	True or false?	
10	Project managers need good influencing skills in a matrix organisation.	True or false?	

Use this space to make some notes

_____
_____
_____
_____
_____
_____
_____
_____
_____
_____
_____

	What Kind of Questions Might There Be in the Exam?
1)	Explain the concept of a matrix organisation and describe four advantages of such an approach.
2)	Explain five difficulties that a project manager may experience when working in a matrix environment and give examples of things they might do to alleviate them.

Assessment Criteria

4.2 Explain the way in which an organisational breakdown structure is used to create a responsibility assignment matrix

This Assessment Criteria is far better dealt with once you are familiar with Work Breakdown Structures. Please see "Organisation Breakdown Structure" on page 106

Assessment Criteria

4.3 Explain the role and key responsibilities of the project manager

4.4 Differentiate between the responsibilities of the project manager and project sponsor throughout the project life cycle

4.5 Describe other roles within project management

Project Roles

There is a fundamental issue at stake when we start to consider organisational roles as per Figure 10. The project manager reports to the sponsor for the purposes of the project. This relationship is separate and distinct from any line management or organisational relationship that may exist. The sponsor could be the project manager's line manager but may not be and certainly does not have to be.

The team is managed by the project manager and so are the suppliers. The latter of these though will have a contractual relationship with the project, and the project manager will therefore be managing them as a single entity as opposed to the team members, who the project manager will manage individually. The management methods and techniques for each of these is clearly very different. The sponsor has involvement throughout the project as indicated in Figure 5. This should not be taken too literally, as the sponsor will have varying levels of input at different times. The relationship between the sponsor and the project manager is vital to project success and a supportive but separate roles will need to be carefully defined and nurtured throughout.

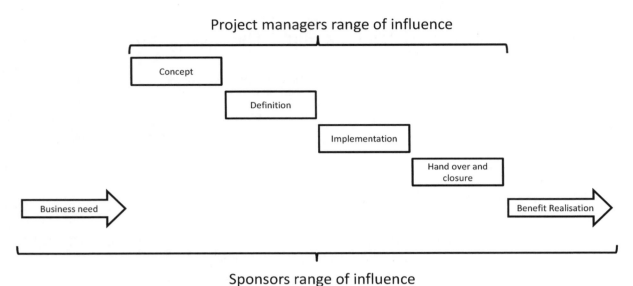

FIGURE 9 THE SPONSORS RANGE OF INFLUENCE

Organisational Roles

Consider the table below. The users operate the products and systems delivered and need to recognise the authority of the sponsor. They have a dotted line to the project manager because although the sponsor will have final say over any changes that may be required, it is impractical to expect the project manager to deliver a fully functional and beneficial set of products without becoming involved with and having a viable professional relationship with the users.

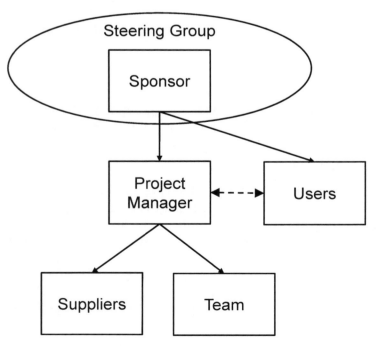

FIGURE 10 THE MAIN ROLES RELATING TO A PROJECT

The way in which a project sponsor is appointed is normally laid down in the organisation's governance framework.

In summary, the various roles have these characteristics and responsibilities:

Steering group	<ul><li>Nominates the sponsor. The steering group are the agent of the organisation in this respect.</li><li>Helps influence and manage key stakeholders. In some cases simply because of their seniority they will have much more contact with and ability to influence them.</li><li>Supports and advises the sponsor. The sponsor is a nominee of the steering group and as such will need proper an appropriate support at different times throughout the work in hand.</li><li>Authorises the business case. The sponsor alone cannot authorise the business case as they will have been closely involved in its preparation and it will need to be challenged rather than simply accepting it as correct and complete.</li></ul>
Team	<ul><li>Deliver the products to time, cost and quality parameters. The will produce the technical products associated with the project under the direction of the project manager.</li><li>Help identify changes, risks and issues. They will be very close to the actual work and as such be the first ones to notice a lot of the detail that may trigger the project processes such as change control.</li><li>Supports the project manager. The team need to be motivated by the project manager but must reciprocate with adequate levels of support and help and advice to the PM when it is needed.</li></ul>
Project manager	<ul><li>Manages the project. Is so doing they implement the plans and processes incorporated within the PMP. The manage the team, report progress and seek support from the sponsor and will be ultimately accountable for the effective delivery of the project deliverables.</li><li>Owns the project management plan. The PM will keep this document firmly in step with the business case at all times. It must reflect the plans and processes for the future and it is incumbent upon the PM to ensure that it remains relevant and appropriate for the job in hand.</li><li>Manages stakeholders. The sponsor will manage some of the more major or key stakeholders, but he day to day activities of the PM is directly with the project stakeholders on a day to day basis.</li><li>Liaises with end users. The PM will need to ensure that the deliverables are on track and that they will ultimately deliver what they want / need.</li><li>The PM manages suppliers usually by virtue of some form of contractual arrangement, in this they may sometimes be acting as a 'contract manager'.</li></ul>

Sponsor	<ul><li>They own the business case and the realisation of benefits. The PM delivers the project and delivers the products but the use to which they are put and the effectiveness of that use has to be overseen by the sponsor.</li><li>Helps the project manager manage key stakeholders. They may manage stakeholders directly and may need to do so personally and directly.</li><li>Usually a peer of the steering group members. They will be selected from a cohort of senior business managers and directors and as such have a collective responsibility for the effective implementation of the project and the embedding of its deliverables.</li><li>The PM will look to the project sponsor to help resolve those really tricky issues that they cannot deal with. The sponsor in this respect may need to exert their political influence and wider range of network to open doors and remove blockers.</li><li>Helps identify key strategic and business risks along with others and in this way pass down information that helps the PM deliver the project rather than simply dealing with risks and issues on the way up from the PM.</li><li>Helps the project manager deal with contingencies because the PM does not own the contingent funds. If they are needed then the sponsor will need to release them when required thus altering the project budget.</li><li>They approve changes as the PM cannot necessarily agree alterations to the scope of the project in case it in some way affect the potential for the delivery of the benefits in the business case.</li><li>Arbitrates between different user and stakeholder requirements</li></ul>
Users	<ul><li>The users need to define what is required to be achieved from the products once delivered. They may need to describe in formal terms the requirements of the finished products.</li><li>They advise the sponsor on the suitability of the delivered products as being conformant to the specifications and requirements. In practice the sponsor will not be able to do this alone although they (the sponsor) will actually sign for them</li><li>They will operate the products, acting as the owner of the finished products they will put it to use and need to make sure that it is operated in a way in which the benefits can be derived.</li><li>They will liaise with the project manager with regard to changes so that the plans and the registers of deliverables are up to date and that any issues relating to the appropriateness of the deliverables can be assured.</li><li>They users need to accept the authority of the sponsor, it is the sponsor that owns the accountability for the suitability of the final solution and as such it is the sponsor that will have final say over which user requirement has priority over which. In this way any disputes amongst users will be resolved by the sponsor and not the project manager, releasing the PM to deliver the project.</li></ul>

Suppliers	<ul><li>Suppliers can help identify key technical solutions. As the experts they will be able to suggest specific solutions, provide proposals, in turn manage other suppliers (as a prime contractor) and actually deliver the subject of these proposals to the PM and hence the users.</li><li>Suppliers are distinct from the team as they will be engaged via a contract and as such required to perform the terms of the contract accordingly.</li><li>They have a responsibility to report progress. This may seem obvious but as they are managed by the PM it is necessary to instil in any supplier the need to do this and in a consistent and meaningful way.</li><li>It is incumbent upon the supplier to ensure that any issues and risks are properly aired, communicated and if necessary resolved.</li></ul>

Who does what on your project?
Work based exercise
Who is the sponsor?
Who are the users?
Who are the team?

Quick Quiz (Answers In Section 18)

	Question	Options	Your Answer
1	The project sponsor is the project manager's line manager.	True, false or maybe?	

	Question	Options	Your Answer
2	The suppliers are managed by the project manager, usually through a...?	a) Gentleman's agreement b) Contract c) PMP d) Goodwill	
3	Who owns the business case?	a) Project manager b) Sponsor c) Users d) Internal audit	
4	Who owns the project management plan?	a) Project manager b) Sponsor c) Users d) Internal audit	
5	Which of these do the users NOT do?	a) Operate the deliverables b) Specify requirements c) Agree acceptance criteria d) Deliver work packages	
6	The sponsor is a peer of the other members of the steering group.	a) Yes b) No c) Possibly d) Must not be	
7	How many sponsors can a project have?	a) One b) Two c) Three d) Four	
8	Who selects and appoints the sponsor?	a) The steering group b) The organisation's governance framework c) They are self elected d) The project manager	
9	Changes to the project scope are approved by?	a) The sponsor b) The project manager c) The users d) The suppliers	
10	The organisation's governance structure has a major influence over the appointment of the sponsor.	True or false?	

Use this space to make some notes

 What Kind of Questions Might There Be in the Exam?

1)	List and describe five roles associated with a project and explain their main responsibilities.
2)	Explain how the relationship between sponsor, project manager and users operates through the life cycle of the project; make five points in your answer.

 Assessment Criteria

4.6 Describe the functions and benefits of different types of project office

The Basic Project Roles

The basic roles of a project office are described in the following diagram:

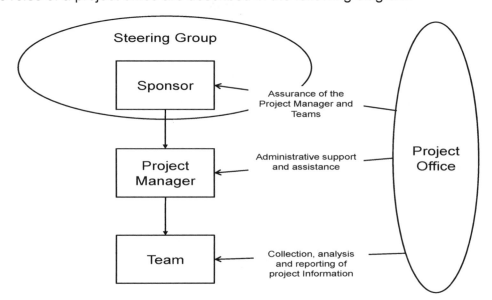

FIGURE 11 THE ROLE OF THE PROJECT OFFICE AND THE MAIN RESPONSIBILITIES

There are as many interpretations of these basic roles as there are project offices. A common manifestation of a project office is that of simple administrative support to the project manager. They are very often tasked with filing, administration, organising meetings and deputising for the project manager. Whilst valuable, these are potentially only part of the role. In a larger organisation, and especially one which has a mature project management approach, the project office can be 'virtual'. That is to say that the different services are provided by distinct different parts of the existing organisation. Most large construction companies have a planning department where the project manager can go for this type of specialist advice. This is therefore a form of this 'virtual' project office team.

Key roles	What the project office may do	Describe briefly areas in your organisation where you witness these roles
Administrative support and guidance	■ Be responsible for configuration management activities ■ Have experts in given fields such as risk, planning or estimating. ■ Be able to offer some degree of support to the project manager during absences. ■ Be heavily involved in the meetings cycle, issuing agendas and minutes and chasing actions.	
Collection, analysis and reporting of project information	■ Collate and tabulate the time sheets and other accounting information from the team and provide such reports as the project manager and sponsor may require. ■ Maintain a schedule according to which reports are produced. ■ Sit in on specialist workshops to help gather information on risks and other detailed information.	
Where the project office has expert resources in project management fields	■ Provide coaching and mentoring to the project managers in the application of tools and various techniques.	
Centre of Excellence	■ Act as the repository for the strategic implementation of not only the individual projects but the portfolio as well. This is sometimes referred to as the enterprise project management office or EPMO.	

Key roles	What the project office may do	Describe briefly areas in your organisation where you witness these roles
Continuous improvement	▪ Be instrumental in ensuring the lessons from the project are properly documented and embedded across the organisation.	

Project office is a generic term and you may hear it referred to as project support office, project management office, project and programme support office, portfolio support office, enterprise project management office.

Work based exercise
Does your organisation have a project office? What do they do? Are they centralised or virtual?

 ## Quick Quiz (Answers In Section 18)

	Question	Options	Your Answer
1	A project office has to be a single autonomous unit.	True or false?	
2	A project office manager reports directly to the project manager in all cases.	True or false?	

	Question	Options	Your Answer
3	Which of these activities is fulfilled by the project office?	a) Approving changes b) Administering the change control procedure c) Estimating the costs of changes	
4	The project office can deputise for the project manager only if.....?	a) They do not provide an assurance role for the sponsor b) They are competent c) The team agree	
5	EPMO means?	a) Exclusive project management office b) Enterprise project management office c) Everyone's project management office	
6	The team may provide information to the project office for reporting purposes.	True or false?	
7	The team have to follow the direction of the project office.	a) True b) False c) On occasions	
8	The project office may be responsible for standards and procedures, and provide advice across multiple projects.	True or false?	
9	The project office costs come out of the project budget.	a) True b) False c) Maybe	
10	The minimum number of people in the project office is __ and the maximum is __?	a) 1 / 4 b) Any number / any number c) 1 / any number	

 Use this space to make some notes

_____

_____

_____

_____

	What Kind of Questions Might There Be in the Exam?
1)	List and describe five key activities that a project office may undertake.
2)	Explain five distinct benefits of a project office.

SECTION 5
PROJECT LIFE CYCLES

 Assessment Criteria

5.1   Define a project life cycle and project life cycle phases

5.2   Explain why projects are structured as phases

5.3   Explain the differences between a project life cycle and an extended life cycle

5.4   Outline the processes for sharing knowledge and lessons learned throughout projects

5.5   Explain the benefits of conducting reviews throughout the life cycle

The Project Life Cycle

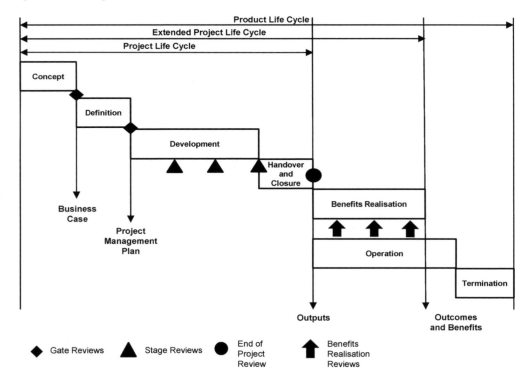

FIGURE 12 PROJECT LIFE CYCLE

(APM Body of Knowledge 6th edition)

The project life cycle (above) allows us to consider a managed and evolutionary progression through the stages of a project. The length of each of these phases can vary considerably between different projects and the naming of the various phases whilst important for the exam and consistency are not necessarily those adopted by organisations in real life.

The Concept phase encompasses everything up to and including the production of the business case. It includes the feasibility and 'optioneering' to arrive at the chosen single solution for development into the project. It is overseen by the sponsor, and a project manager may well be appointed to develop the business case.

The Definition phase includes the production of the project management plan and all the subsidiary plans such as the risk management plan and quality plan. It culminates in approval to proceed to development. The primary output is the project management plan (PMP). This documents the entirety of the project and what it will produce.

The Development phase covers the construction of the various components that comprise the end product of the project according to the plans constructed in the definition phase. During the development phase there may be many sub phases (each separated by a Stage Review) to allow for a proper evaluation of progress. The primary outputs are the products of the project.

Handover is the process of commissioning the products and the migration of them to practical use, and **Closure** is the administrative closure of the project and disbanding the team. Acceptance is the key output as this will signify the users' acceptance of the products into operational service.

The Extended Project life cycle

The extended project life cycle casts the net a little wider and allows the consideration of the wider project life cycle, including operation and termination. The extended life cycle along with the consideration of the product life cycle means we have a focus on whole life costing (i.e. the recognition that the cost of producing the asset must be considered alongside the cost of operating it).

Benefits Realisation phase this allows us to consider the beneficial outcomes of the project. We don't generally do projects just because we are able to. Most investment is undertaken in order that some longer term benefit can be derived. We build a railway so people can travel more easily from place to place for example. This is covered in more detail in section 10.3

Operations is the component that gives us the framework within which to consider the operational costs. As mentioned through life costing necessarily demands that the benefits of having and using the products are valued but this needs to be mitigated by the costs of doing so. Our railway will consume electricity, staff costs, maintenance, ticket sales etc. We cannot simply count the income from ticket sales.

When considering the life cycles there are some things to note

- At the end of both **Concept and Definition** a Gate Review will take place. The purpose of this is to review the project against the Business Case **(Concept)** and Project Management Plan **(Definition)** and decide if the project should proceed to the next phase.

- Stage Reviews take place throughout the **Development** phase. These reviews evaluate the progress of the project against the agreed plans with the aim of identifying variance and corrective actions.

- A Post Project Review is carried out at the end of the **Handover and Closure** phase to ensure complete handover of the project to the customer and learn lessons for future projects.

- Benefits realisation will happen during after **Handover and Closure**.

- Very often the **Development** phase is split into more than one 'stage' with Stage Reviews in-between. These stages will offer the opportunity to review the evolution of the project and the resultant products and make sure that things are on track in a formal manner.

The Product Life Cycle

The final component of the life cycle model includes the **Termination** phase. This is intended to draw our attention to (and thus encourage us to consider) how much it will cost to dispose of the product at the end of its useful life. The example often quoted is that of nuclear power stations and would they have been justified had the cost of decommissioning (environmental as well as economic) them at the end of their useful life been considered.

Many organisations and indeed whole industries have a well understood project life cycle and there are also a number produced and recommended by other professional bodies, such as the Royal Institute of Chartered Surveyors and Royal Institute of British Architecture in the UK.

The Benefits of Having a Life Cycle?

- It is an easily communicable way of demonstrating the logical progression though the time frame of a project, with clearly defined activities and outputs for each phase.

- It's an obvious point at which to stop the project (i.e. between phases, at the end of one and the start of the next), where the business case, plans and risks are considered and detailed plans for the next phase agreed.

- When combined with the principle of processes they help us understand in greater detail the evolution of a project, being able to identify areas that need greater attention at different times such as risk management in the early stages.

- They give us an understanding of which resources may be required (both in number and nature) and when. This helps the organisation to plan its necessary levels of resource requirements.

- They provide the high level initial breakdown so that detailed planning can be carried out (within each phase).

- They provide an indication of when key project reviews can take place, ensuring the relevant authorities are in place and coordinated to proceed.

- They make sure that proper attention is given to the early stages by demanding that the project goes through a number of phase gates.

- They are important as we can link progress directly to them and recognise the completion of a phase which will provide increased confidence on the part of stakeholders.

The Different Types of Review

Type of review	Scope of review and outcomes
Gate reviews	This is a formal review, usually commissioned by the sponsoring organisation as part of its governance structure. It will have a formal agenda, usually supported with a checklist of products and criteria. They will happen as a minimum at the end of the Concept and Definition Phases. Very often a stage gate review will be a formal funding gate, granting permission for the project to proceed. There are usually three outcomes to a gate review — pass, pass with reservation and fail. **The benefits of undertaking a Gate Reviews are:** • That they encourage a regular and structured control framework on a regular basis to ensure that progress is as it should be; • They encourage the development of a relationship between the project manager and their sponsor thus developing trust; • They represent a documented statement of progress to demonstrate to the organisation that a requisite level of control is being undertaken.
Post project review	Carried out soon after the project has finished these reviews will provide a clear forum for the production of lessons learned (see below). Similar to a stage review, they will consider not only the project's satisfaction of its success criteria but will also be a thorough analysis of the effectiveness of the project management methods, tools and practices and team performance. The organisation will receive the assurance that the project has been successful (and if not, why not) such that it can make adjustments to its working practices and systems. It will also demonstrate that the project has actually finished and all materials and information have been recorded appropriately. **The benefits of undertaking a Post Project Review are that:** • They are a key component of 'Lessons Learned; thus aiding knowledge management ambitions; • They record formally the out-turn, this will practically help estimating and risk management for future projects; • Help identify excellent behaviours and results and provide an excellent opportunity to recognise and reward individuals and teams.

Type of review	Scope of review and outcomes
Benefits Realisation	Only after the products have been completed and handover has been carried out can a proper evaluation of the benefits be achieved. Managed and chaired by the sponsor, these reviews will involve the thorough analysis by the business of the relevant achievement of the stated benefits as defined in the business case. The project manager will not be available (the project has finished after all) and therefore the sponsor's role in achieving these is paramount. The outcomes will be for the business to understand whether the project was a success and delivered the necessary products that achieve the benefit. **The benefits of undertaking a Benefits Review are that:** - The project can be recognised for having 'made a difference'; - The organisation can review the real benefits obtained and reconcile them with the ambitions stated in the business case; - Draw out areas where benefits may not be as expected and lay plans to modify the situation and rectify this.
Stage Reviews	These are carried out during the project using KPIs established for the purpose, to ensure that activities are progressing as planned. Usually convened by the project manager, supported by the team and chaired by the sponsor and users, they are internal (that is to say they are for the project's use to ratify progress against plans). They review not only the project indicators but also provide an analysis of the effectiveness of the project management tools and processes. Minutes will record progress against time, benefits, and risk, cost and quality parameters. Any decisions and corrective action will be identified to ensure that the project remains on track. Where significant risks are observed as likely, then measures will be put in place to mitigate them. The number of stage reviews throughout the project will be dependent upon a number of factors including the length of the project, the risk presented if the project is not reviewed often enough and as a result of the organisation's governance framework. **The benefits of undertaking a stage review are:** - The progress of project will be measured objectively against its KPI's; - Corrective actions will be identified and actioned; - The sponsor has an formal opportunity to intervene in a project in an organised and predictable manner; - Risks and issues can be formally an properly addressed and the various logs updated.

Lessons Learned Generally

It is too late to learn lessons after the end of a project. If the organisation merely carries out one review at the end then the opportunities to capitalise on the knowledge gained will be lost. A continual review of project documentation, KPIs, metrics and team performance all provide clues as to where things could be improved. It must be clear that the analysis is only a part of the picture. The organisation should be prepared to take the information available and actually circulate it around the business to make sure that other projects can make use of it. A lessons learned report is not just another piece of bureaucracy to be filed away. Breakfast team meetings, published journals, updated estimate tables, metrics and risk checklists are all examples of where lessons learned can be made available and used productively.

Audit

One formal activity most organisations undertake is that of audit. These are external to the project (but may be internal to the sponsoring organisation). they will be more procedural in nature and seek to assure the organisation that the project is conforming to its stated principles and procedures and has a good chance of succeeding. They take many forms, usually financial or procedural but may include health and safety, procurement, etc. They will normally be of use to the organisation and in some instance to a much wider audience (e.g. The National Audit Office in the UK) hopefully providing information relating to good (and poor) practice.

Work based exercise
Do your projects have a life cycle? What is it? What document do you have that serves as a business case?

 ## Quick Quiz (Answers In Section 18)

	Question	Options	Your Answer
1	There is only one possible life cycle for all projects.	True or false?	

		Question	Options	Your Answer
	2	When thinking about an extended project life cycle it allows us to consider the termination costs of a project.	True or false?	
	3	A project manager would need to understand the nature of the project and the industry it is in to make sure the life cycle is appropriate.	True or false?	
	4	Which review takes place during the operations phase?	a) Benefits realisation review b) Phase gate c) Project evaluation review d) Design review	
	5	Project audits are normally internal to the project.	True or false?	
	6	Benefits realisation reviews happen during which project life cycle phase?	a) Operations b) Termination c) Concept d) Definition	
	7	Lessons learned should be recorded all the way through a project.	True or false?	
	8	Only a sponsor sees the output from a project audit.	True or false?	
	9	The project management plan is not started until the beginning of definition.	True or false?	
	10	The life cycle model mentioned is the only one that you can use	True or false?	

Use this space to make some notes

_____

_____

_____

_____

_____

What Kind of Questions Might There Be in the Exam?

1)	Explain five distinct benefits of using a structured life cycle approach
2)	List and describe five key phases of a life cycle, the activities undertaken during and the outputs of each.

SECTION 6
ORGANISATION AND GOVERNANCE

 Assessment Criteria

6.1 Describe the principles of governance of project management

What is the Governance of Project Management?

Governance of project management fills the void between the project environment and that of the board of the organisation. Just about everything in the syllabus contributes towards project governance, but the concept that an organisation will want to govern its projects and programmes in a certain controlled way gives a clue to the fact that this governance overlaps quite heavily with that of portfolio management. Effective governance will ensure that their projects operate in a predetermined and controlled manner. The actual things that are witnessed on the ground, so to speak, are evidence that governance is being carried out. When talking about governance as a principle, it is necessary to elevate the discussion from that of the single project and begin to consider project<u>s</u> in the plural.

The absence of project governance may have a significant bearing on the success or failure of a organisation and / or the project.

The governance of project management is intended to compliment an organisation's governance and to link it and the projects governance together to provide a productive framework in which they can operate in a managed and controlled way providing effective oversight.

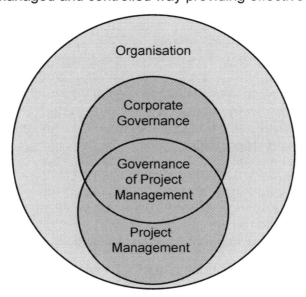

FIGURE 13 THE NATURE OF GOVERNANCE OF PROJECT MANAGEMENT

Work undertaken by the APM structured the question of Project Governance into a number of key areas. You may be required to recognise these areas and they are simply included here as headings. The descriptions of the terms in most cases are self explanatory but a few notes are included here to help.

Portfolio Direction is associated with the way in which the organisation organises its project and programmes, groups them, sifts and filters them and ultimately includes or terminates them according to their specific needs and appropriateness.

Disclosure and Reporting is concerned with the need to be open and honest with regard to how the projects and programmes are progressing and to be in full possession of all the relevant facts and details in order to govern the portfolio adequately.

Project Sponsorship is concerned with the overall organisational commitment to a project or programme and the extent to which it is exerted over the portfolio.

Project Management Capability principle is concerned with the advancement and control of the project management resources and teams and how they are best able to perform their duties commensurate with the needs of the governance structure.

Just some of the questions that effective governance will resolve for an organisation are:

These various principles fit broadly into a number of more generic categories and these categories are sometimes helpful to delegates to help relate them to their own work. The possible headings are annotated at the end of each description.

1)   How do we know our projects are on track? All projects have an approved plan containing authorisation points at which the business case is reviewed and approved. Decisions made at these authorisation points are recorded and communicated. This could be an example of **Portfolio Direction.**

2)   Where does the responsibility for governance of projects and programmes lie. The board of directors has overall responsibility for the governance of project management. This means they have to set policy and define the governance framework to be used. This could be an example of **Portfolio Direction.**

3)   How do we know the information we are getting to make decisions is correct? The organisation fosters a culture of improvement and of frank disclosure of project information. This implies that project managers and staff should feel able to discuss the true state of projects with senior managers. The roles, responsibilities and performance criteria for the governance of project management are clearly defined. This would be reflected in the organization's governance documentation. This could be an example of **Disclosure and Reporting.**

4)   What are the governance arrangements - have they been agreed and documented? Disciplined governance arrangements, supported by the appropriate methods and controls and ensuring they are applied through the project life cycle. This implies an agreed and implemented reporting system that has some consistency across projects. This could be an example of **Portfolio Direction.**

5)   How do we know we are doing the right things? A coherent and supportive relationship is demonstrated between the overall business strategy and the project portfolio, i.e. the

projects are aligned to support the organisation's goals and objectives. This could be an example of **Portfolio Direction.**

6) How does the organisation know when things are going well (or not so well)? The board, or its delegated agents, decide when independent scrutiny of projects and project management systems is required, and implement such scrutiny accordingly. For example, they should make the time to attend gate reviews. This could be an example of **Disclosure and Reporting.**

7) Are risks being dealt with appropriately? There are clearly defined criteria for reporting project status and for the escalation of risks and issues to the levels required by the organisation. Again, this implies a standardised reporting process. This could be an example of **Disclosure and Reporting** and possibly **Project Sponsorship.**

8) How do we know the organisation is doing the right things? The business case is supported by relevant and realistic information that provides a reliable basis for making authorisation decisions. The word 'realistic' is key; the organisation should not allow itself to follow an unrealistic plan. This could be an example of **Project Sponsorship.**

9) Are all of our stakeholders on side with what we are doing? Project stakeholders are engaged at a level that is commensurate with their importance to the organisation and in a manner that fosters trust. For example, the stakeholders should make time available to understand the challenges the project faces. This could be an example of **Project Management Capability.**

10) Are we actually competent to govern ourselves? Members of delegated authorisation bodies have sufficient representation, competence, authority and resources to enable them to make appropriate decisions and, for example, the people appointed to make decisions must have delegated authority and be able to exercise that authority in a competent way. This could be an example of **Project Management Capability.**

These are fine and noble principles but to bring them to life, think about your own organisation. For the purposes of the exam, if you can relate some of the principles of governance to your own organisation you will be more likely to be able to remember them. Have a think about what type of organisation you work in.

Work based exercise
What components of Governance do you witness in your organisation?
How does your organisation govern its portfolio (decide what is in and what is not in it)

Work based exercise
What components of Governance do you witness in your organisation?
How does your organisation sponsor its projects (does it have nominated sponsors?)
What arrangements are there for governing the projects (are there set methods to use for example)
What do project managers do by way of periodical reporting and how does the organisation respond to this?

 ## Quick Quiz - you will need to mark these yourself

These are questions derived directly from Directing Change — A Guide to the Governance of Project Management an APM publication. Again think about your own organisation and use these questions to prompt in your own mind what your organisation does well and what it does not so well. Combine it with your observations from above. Give each a score of 1 (poor) to 10 (excellent).

	Question	Provide a score 1-10
1	Do all projects have clear critical success criteria and are they used to inform decision-making?	

	Question	Provide a score 1-10
2	Is the board assured that the organisation's project management processes and project management tools are appropriate for the projects that it sponsors?	
3	Is the board assured that the people responsible for project delivery, especially the project managers, are clearly mandated, sufficiently competent, and have the capacity to achieve satisfactory project outcomes?	
4	Are project managers encouraged to develop opportunities for improving project outcomes?	
5	Are key governance of project management roles and responsibilities clear and in place?	
6	Are service departments and suppliers able and willing to provide key resources tailored to the varying needs of different projects and to provide an efficient and responsive service?	
7	Are appropriate issue, change and risk management practices implemented in line with adopted policies?	
8	Is authority delegated to the right levels, balancing efficiency and control?	
9	Are project contingencies estimated and controlled in accordance with delegated powers?	

 Use this space to make some notes

_____
_____
_____
_____
_____
_____
_____

What Kind of Questions Might There Be in the Exam?

1)	Describe the term project governance and explain four of the principles of the Project Governance and what effects there might be on the organisation's projects if they are not practiced.

	Assessment Criteria

6.2 Explain how project management methodologies can be used to support the governance structure

6.3 Explain the advantages of using standard project management methodologies across an organisation

What Does a Project Management Method Contain?

A project management method contains the framework within which the project can operate.

There are two types of project management method: the public ones, such as PRINCE2®, and the proprietary methods within a specific given organisation. Many organisations write their own so that they can integrate it with their own systems and procedures, such that the project management teams witness a seamless environment in which to work in a coordinated manner across the business.

Generally speaking, a project management method has a number of key elements:

PEOPLE

A method will have a standard way of describing the individual roles and effectively who does what. Some common terms to be adopted are those of the sponsor, project manager, project office and so on. In this guide we have used terms such as these consistently, although some methods such as PRINCE2® have other specific roles such as a project board which consists of representative from the user, supplier and business.

PRODUCTS

The term product is used to describe all of those things that will be produced by the project. They can fall into one of two different categories:

- Products that help run the project, which includes all of those things that are produced in order to manage the project correctly, such as a project management plan, schedule, risk log and so on; and

- Products which are those that are directly related to the end product of the project; the things that are output from the project and form part of the deliverables to the client, such as a bridge, software system, etc.

They are differentiated because a) they have a different target audience; b) managerial products are there to assist in the running of the project whilst the technical products are delivered to the users and accepted by them; and c) by drawing attention to them it makes sure that they are considered when it comes to the scope planning of the project. Methods normally describe which products are produced when.

PROCESSES

The processes are those things that need to be followed in the running of the project, the framework in which the project will be managed. An example might be the way in which risks are identified, assessed, planned and managed through the life cycle. The APM would advocate the use of the principles in the Project Risk and Management Guide but other organisations may well have their own, adapted to their own specific needs. A lot of these processes will be documented or referenced by the Project Management Plan (PMP).

TEMPLATES

Methods will normally prescribe the form in which some of the managerial products will be produced. Typically the business case, PMP, risk log and product specifications will all have predetermined formats and they are quite often already populated with text and helpful hints that have been incorporated as a result of experience in earlier projects.

TOOLS

Some methods include specific tools that can be deployed. In others, references to specific tools mean that the project teams can be directed to practical solutions to assist them in their day to day activities. These might include planning software, document management systems and flowcharting techniques and so on.

Advantages of a Standard Project Method

A method provides a link to organisational governance — it requires us to think hard about how the project interacts with the organisation. Part of the governance framework will impose an authorisation gate where funding is approved for example, how sponsors are appointed, what delegated authority applies. These are all areas where a project method provides the clear manifestation of an organisation's governance framework. It will provide a framework to help achieve coordination across the business of various projects and the adoption of a single method will mean they are all executed in the same manner, thus providing:

- **Consistency** — of approach so everyone does the same things in the same way producing the same recognisable products at the same time in the life cycle..

- **Continuity** — Because the processes and templates are properly documented and recorded it is possible to swap key staff in and out of the project as needs arise.

- **Communication** — A method has a very clear layout, is easily described and forms a basis for a common language across different projects. It also provides for integration between multiple projects to enable teams to be interchangeable.

- **Clarity** — Everyone knows what is going on. There is no ambiguity about roles, the purpose of the product or its route through the system from creation, through testing to approval.

- **Capability** — A method encourages the retention of documentation that can be used for future analysis of success and failure, better informing those that projects that come after thus enhancing the organisations capability.

Project methods are not used instead of a project life cycle, but compliment it. Quite often a project life cycle is documented within a method and is consistent across the organisation.

Quick Quiz - Quick Quiz (Answers In Section 18)

	Question	Options	Your Answer
1	Project methods _____ guarantee the success of a project	a) Always b) Never c) Help contribute to d) Get in the way of	
2	A method replaces a project life cycle.	True or false?	
3	Properly documented methods overlap with some areas of project governance.	True or false?	
4	The main areas that a project method is NOT intended to help with are what?	a) Consistency b) Clarity c) Communication d) Bureaucracy	
5	The project manager can work to one project method whilst the team can work to another.	True or false?	

Use this space to make some notes

_____
_____
_____
_____
_____
_____
_____
_____
_____
_____

What Kind of Questions Might There Be in the Exam?

1)	Describe the main components of a project management method; make five points in your answer.

SECTION 7
COMMUNICATIONS

 Assessment Criteria

7.1 Describe the key contents of a project communication plan

7.2 Explain the benefits of a project communication plan

7.3 Explain the importance of effective communication in managing different stakeholders

7.4 Identify factors affecting communication

The Role of the Communication Plan

The communication plan is a section of the main PMP (therefore owned by the project manager) and includes a number of key areas. You should note that there is a large degree of overlap between the topic of communication and that of information management, reporting and stakeholder engagement. Typical contents of the communication plan might include the following:

- **The target for the communication** — the work done on stakeholder analysis in the start-up phases will be vital in identifying who the project needs to communicate with. The list of stakeholders is very helpful in understanding which individuals and groups need to be influenced for the project to be successful. The stakeholder analysis helps to prioritise our communication efforts and should be updated as the project progresses, so that the changes in the attitude of stakeholders to the project can be mapped. This enables us to demonstrate the effectiveness of the communication strategy.

- **What communication will be undertaken** — the plan will describe the information that needs to be communicated into and out of the project. This may include reports and other formal documents on a regular basis and also describe what informal information needs to be disseminated and when.

- **How** — The plan must have a clear strategy for the various communication channels available. These fall into the following main categories of communication:

  Formal verbal — includes such things as meetings, interviews, presentations, briefings, etc. They may be formal phase gate reviews, team meetings, stakeholder briefings, etc. They are recorded in minutes or other means so they can be referenced if required.

  Informal verbal — which includes water cooler conversations, unrecorded telephone conversations, etc. It is exceptionally difficult to script these types of communication, but some organisations will give their staff a large amount of training to deal with the press interviews, for example, so it is possible. Good practice dictates that any verbal communication be followed up with a written record.

Formal written — includes reports, presentations, minutes, specifications, designs, etc. They are anything planned to be produced and which is a fundamental component of the project. Their production is planned and intended to be formal.

Informal written — includes things like 'post it notes', email (although very often considered formal), blogs, forums, etc. If an individual takes action based upon informal information it can be a good indicator as to whether it is in fact informal or not. Leave a note on someone's desk to meet you for a meeting at two o'clock, they will probably go. Is this formal or informal?

Non verbal — this type of communication relates to how individuals convey messages directly one to one or one too many. They are related to our own personal mannerisms and our way of deporting ourselves, which is usually referred to as body language. The main principle is that our body language cannot be denied and will often convey more of the message than the words spoken or written. It also includes the tone and pitch of our voice, which can have a big impact on how the message is conveyed and received.

In all cases we anticipate that the recipient will take some action based upon the communication, and a measure of its effectiveness will be whether they understand and their attitudes, behaviours or actions of the recipient do actually change as a result. Informal communication is more difficult to manage and dependent upon the culture and networks existing in the organisation and, being unplanned, it can happen anytime. Care is needed when considering informal communications as a channel as there is usually an onus of proof required, an area of particular interest where contracts are concerned.

- **Use of various media** — the project has a number of channels available to it in order to disseminate and receive any information. The most common channels are the traditional written word (or, more usually, typed on computer and emailed). There are now a huge and growing number of options available to most organisations in the way they disseminate information. Obviously these include all of those mechanisms above, but also social networking sites, workspace and SharePoint services, websites, podcasts and other more innovative ways of getting a message across.

- **Understanding the audience** — the communication plan must consider the nature of the audience and how they may wish to receive information, not only the mechanics of it, but their own personal preferences. The plan should take into account the options for delivering messages in a different format to different individuals, while balancing that with the costs involved.

- **Costs** — communication costs money. The type and volume of communication is largely dependent upon the resources required to deliver it. Face to face meetings are valuable but can be terribly expensive especially if long distance travel is involved. Each of the activities associated with communication on the project will need to be included in the scope and therefore costed into the budgets.

- **Feedback** — know how feedback will be collected and what will be done as a result. Communication is a two-way process and if you are continually in 'send mode' you will not be able to adapt the message to accommodate changes or pick up on the impact of barriers.

Barriers to Communication

The project manager must be aware of the potential barriers to communication and make allowances for them. We typically think of physical barriers, but there are also cultural and psychological ones.

Think about your own environment and how these barriers have got in the away of your own communications and what you did (or could have done) about them.

Barrier	What can be done to overcome	If you witnessed it, what did you do?
Perception on the part of the receiver	Make the message clear and unambiguous so that the message is not open to mis-interpretation. Use plain language without too much jargon or technical language, if it can be avoided.	
The environment, noise, fumes, heat, etc.	Try and make sure that the environment is fit for purpose for the message you are trying to convey. If you are having a personal conversation, do not do it in an open office.	
People's own attitudes and emotional state	Try and understand the person who will receive the information and be sympathetic to their needs. A logical argument in an emotional situation may not have the desired effect.	
Selective listening (pretending not to have heard)	Try active listening, where you become involved in the message, replay it to the sender and recipient and check understanding.	
Time zones and geography	These days it is more common that the project manager will be dealing with people dispersed across the globe. This introduces delays, unreasonable meeting times, etc. Try and get a regime that everyone can be comfortable with.	
Indirect communication	Individuals will be talking to each other frequently and the project manager will have little or no influence over this. Project managers need to be part of the informal networks, but at the same time they must not 'go native' in such a way that they lose authority.	
Distractions and other priorities	Sometime you will not appear as high up someone's list as you might like. Make life easy for them; suggest options and offer to go to them, keep meetings short and frequent.	

Some Examples of What Happens When Project Communications Go Wrong?

- Different groups or individuals get differing messages, which causes doubt, concern, confusion and rework. Just think back to a meeting where not everybody got the same invitation!

- The costs are not automatically included in the budget. We need to hold a team meeting to discuss a topic and call people from around the world but nobody has a budget for it.

- We fail to understand the needs of the stakeholders, the risks, benefits and costs are not fully appreciated and different stakeholders believe they are getting one thing when in fact the plan is for them to get something else.

- Stakeholders do not know where to go for data, causing the wrong information being used and incorrect decisions being taken.

These are just some of the things that might cause problems. Refer to your own experience to see what problems you have had where communication has broken down or been ineffective.

 Quick Quiz (Answers In Section 18)

	Question	Options	Your Answer
1	Who owns the communication plan?	a) The project sponsor b) The project manager c) The team d) The users	
2	The stakeholder management activities are included in the plan.	True or false?	
3	The project manager can control indirect communication.	True or false?	
4	When is the communication plan first considered?	a) At the start of the project b) Once the stakeholder analysis has been completed c) At the start of definition d) As the PMP is finalised	
5	How do you know if communication has been successful?	a) Someone tells us b) There is a feedback mechanism c) Whether people like us or not d) If the project wins an award	

	Question	Options	Your Answer
6	Which of these is NOT an example of a barrier to communication?	a) Noise b) The office environment c) Body language d) Risk Management	
7	The tone or pitch of your voice would be an attribute of which of these?	a) Body language b) Verbal communication c) Written communication d) Formal communication	
8	The topic of communication overlaps with which other APM syllabus area?	a) Configuration management b) Change control c) Information management d) Business case	
9	Personal preferences on the part of the recipient can be a barrier to communication.	True or false?	
10	The cost of communications is a project cost.	True of false?	

Use this space to make some notes

_____
_____
_____
_____
_____
_____
_____
_____

What Kind of Questions Might There Be in the Exam?

1)	Describe five main components of a project communication plan.
2)	Explain what might go wrong if project communications are not dealt with appropriately; make five points in your answer.

	Assessment Criteria

7.5 Identify sources of conflict within the project life cycle

7.6 Explain how to plan and conduct different negotiations

Positive and Negative Conflict

These two types of conflict can be prevalent on any undertaking. Because a project by its nature is seeking to introduce change, there is a large opportunity for conflict to occur. People sometimes baulk at the idea of changing the way they work, where they work etc., and the project manager must be able to deal with it all in a proactive and constructive manner.

We often think of conflict as a bad thing. It is very cogently argued however, that conflict if handled correctly will provide a huge resource and act as an agent for change. The project manager must be able to recognise this and allow it to take place without it becoming distracting or problematic.

Some significant areas where conflict may arise are:

- Disagreements about timings and dates.

- Conflict over money and budgets.

- Differing requirements from different users.

- Conflict between time devoted to the project and time on other work.

- Conflict between individuals.

- Not able to obtain acceptance of the project deliverables.

- Stakeholders views needing to be taken into consideration.

- Balancing between the various project objectives.

Project managers need to be adept at understanding the nature of the environment they are in and work towards building a network and infrastructure that allows for the resolution of conflict in a procedural and systematic way. This will not be possible in all cases though and the use of their interpersonal communication and influencing techniques will be crucial to a successful outcome.

Dealing with Conflict: the Thomas–Kilmann Model

In 1974, Kenneth W.Thomas and Ralph H. Kilmann introduced their Thomas–Kilmann Conflict Mode Instrument (Tuxedo NY: Xicom, 1974). The model popularised conflict styles according to an individual's ranking on the cooperativeness and assertiveness scales. Through the use of a self assessment questionnaire, the candidates are able to determine which style of conflict resolution they would choose in a given situation with relation to the two axes of a hypothetical grid.

According to the analysis of a given situation, it is possible to conceive a series of situations where 'opposing' parties, who appear to be in some form of conflict, will adopt a greater or lesser degree of cooperativeness and similarly with assertiveness.

Avoiding

If an individual is demonstrating low cooperativeness and low assertiveness they are said to be 'avoiding' the situation. They will not wish to become engaged in the discussions at all and simply avoid the issue. This is not a very good state of affairs as usually the problem will simply re-emerge at a later date.

Accommodating

A highly cooperative person exerting little or no assertiveness is said to be 'accommodating'. In this situation, they will merely 'go with the flow' and not seek to rock the boat. They will tend to simply go along with the proposals. This is not good, as without a reasonable level of challenge there is always the chance that the wrong ideas get developed.

Competing

A highly assertive but uncooperative person will compete and try and get their way. Clearly this is not ideal, as they may end up winning the battle and losing the war. When faced with this type of individual it might be best to adopt a manner that seeks to increase their level of cooperativeness.

Collaborating

In this space a highly assertive and highly cooperative person will work with you to solve the problem. This is the ideal solution, although in itself may not yield a result, with a further move down both scales to arrive at a compromise.

Compromising

This is where the individual is prepared to sacrifice some of what they have been striving for in order to make the deal. In essence, however, it does mean that if both parties agree to compromise then neither gets all of what they want. In a real world situation, however, this might just have to be the price that is paid to move things forward.

The Negotiation Process

Negotiation is a process/arena for reaching agreement and where conflict may occur. In principle, each party in the negotiation requires the other to agree. In quite a few instances, negotiations are helped and facilitated by a third party. In this case, a disinterested party can be instrumental in removing the emotional context from the issues at stake.

Much of the time negotiations just happen; we negotiate when we need a team member to book a meeting room, or when we want to organise a business trip or need to get a lot of diaries in line. This is not entirely the sense in which the APM use the term negotiation. If we need a process to adopt, then it will be applicable in all cases, but the nature of the more difficult and contentious negotiations will demand a much higher degree of attention to the process than might otherwise be the case.

A project manager will need to be absolutely clear on which role he or she is playing in a particular situation. They may be the broker of a potential deal or someone who wants something out of it. Inevitably, a negotiation goes through a number of stages and if we take the example of a face to face meeting in an organised and formal situation, then indeed it may take place over a number of days or even weeks.

Negotiation may be needed under varying circumstances:-

Formal - here, an organisation wishes to negotiate on a formal basis with another organisation or and individual. Examples of this might be where a redundancy package is being discussed or it may be during a corporate takeover. There may be personal or strategic issues at stake. In a formal negotiation however one party will need to document the outcome of a pre-agreed and measured process.

Informal - these sorts of negotiations may be more relaxed in style and may not need all of the process and procedure that may surround a formal negotiation. One party may approach the other to undertake a task for them, perhaps cover a days absence or help review a document. These sorts of negotiation will not require the panoply of bureaucracy that might be needed under other conditions.

A **Competitive** negotiation is where a very structured approach may be necessary. For example where goods or services are being procured and the relationship between the buyer and potential sellers may become very competitive in nature (between the suppliers). In other arena where there is seeking to gain an advantage at all costs over the other. Referring to the Thomas Kilmann model (on page 84)is where both parties are very Assertive and not very Co-operative.

Collaborative negotiation is the optimum state, both parties (again with reference to Thomas Kilmann this is where both parties are very Assertive and also very Collaborative. In this state there is an opportunity for both parties to get more than either of them could achieve alone.

Steps in a typical negotiation process

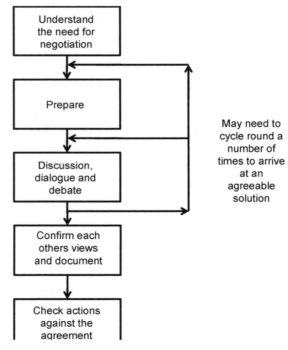

FIGURE 14 A SIMPLE NEGOTIATION PROCESS

Step One — Recognise That a Negotiation is Necessary. The need to negotiate develops over time and in certain circumstances. It might be overt as in the case of arms reduction treaties, or creep up quietly like a contract that needs to be signed in order to proceed. It is important that the parties recognise this and develop a strategy to deal with it in a proper and equitable fashion. Both parties have to agree that this negotiation will be the one and only forum for discussions and will firm up the solution.

Step Two — Thorough Preparation and the development of an understanding of the other side's position. You may also:

- Brief your team to make sure you are all 'on the same page and there will be no different views expressed from your team that may undermine a position.

- Look out for their WIFT or 'what's in it for them'. If you can put yourself in the shoes of the people on the other side of the table and begin to understand what it is they want from the arrangements, you will be well-placed to arrive at a mutually agreeable arrangement.

- You will need to explore your own BATNA or 'best alternative to a negotiated agreement'. What happens if you cannot agree? Where do you go, if you walk out and then walk back in, it will not be on the same terms as you had previously.

- Think about the territory of where the negotiation will take place (ours, theirs or neutral offices for example).

- Who has the power to make decisions.

- What is the absolute bottom line that we are prepared to accept.

- Do your research, find out when their year end is, what markets do they operate in, what are the company circumstances, do they need the business, etc.

Seek agreement to all of the above before commencing and discussions or debate.

Step Three — Observe Protocol and Pleasantries, build and exchange ideas and offer and accept offers in order to try and build a bridge between the two positions. Watch out for devious tricks to unsettle you like substituting new negotiators, referring for authority, and so on. Be aware of cultural issues, in some environments a nod of the head indicates 'yes I understand', not 'yes I agree'. Understanding this will all have been part of your preparation. As the negotiation progresses, do not get dragged into saying things because you want to be liked. Separate the issue from the emotion. If necessary, you may call on the services of a third party arbitrator to chair and help mediate.

Step Four — Document the settlement arrived at, make sure it is documented and unambiguous. A contract is simply an agreement, if it has been signed then there can be no argument (as long as it is clear).

Step Five — Follow Up and make sure that the agreement is being enacted as agreed.

At any stage be prepared to revert back to an earlier stage; there are inevitably a number of rounds to go through, each time the two sides growing closer together and sometimes perhaps for a short period further apart.

Quick Quiz (Answers In Section 18)

	Question	Options	Your Answer
1	Which of these is not a step in negotiation?	a) Preparation b) Discussion c) Bargaining d) Documenting	
2	Referring for authority might be a tactic used in negotiation.	True or false?	
3	Negotiation can happen at any time during the project life cycle.	True or false?	
4	WIFT stands for What's In it For Them	True or False?	
5	The Thomas Kilmann conflict model contains the steps Avoiding, Competing, Collaborating, Compromising and _____	a) Accepting b) Altering c) Accommodating d) Actuarial	

Use this space to make some notes

_____
_____
_____
_____
_____

What Kind of Questions Might There Be in the Exam?

1)	List and describe five main components of a project communication plan.
2)	Explain five consequences if project communications are not dealt with appropriately.
3)	List and describe five things a project manager might do to prepare for a negotiation.

SECTION 8
LEADERSHIP AND TEAMWORK

 Assessment Criteria

8.1 Describe typical leadership qualities

8.2 Explain the principles and importance of motivation

8.3 Explain the impact of leadership on team performance and motivation

What Makes a Good Leader?

> *"Leadership is the ability to establish vision and direction, to influence and align others towards a common purpose and to empower and inspire people to achieve success." (APM Body of Knowledge 6th edition)*

So much has been written and discussed on the nature and role of leadership, both in the commercial world but also in the world of politics and religion. There are a huge number of varying views and opinions, and it would be impossible to try and encapsulate them all here.

The APM have three specific requirements of candidates of the APMP and these are summarised in the learning outcomes above. Leadership should take place at all levels in the organisation, with the entire project team taking some form of leadership role, not necessarily a hierarchical or authority leadership, but often peer to peer.

We need to be able to describe typical leadership qualities. The Body of Knowledge describes a leader's attributes as follows:

- Help maintain and promote the project's vision amongst both the project team and elsewhere.

- Have energy, drive and commitment, leading by doing and motivating the team throughout project difficulties.

- Reinforce positive relationships, for example, providing clear feedback on performance.

- Build a productive project and working environment in which a focus is maintained on getting work done and moving the project forward.

- Work to raise morale by setting clear achievable goals.

- Empower and inspire the individuals by delegating responsibility.

- Help ensure that exceptional events are resolved, and spotting opportunities as well as threats helps provide motivation.

- Ensure that productive and constructive feedback is provided to enable individual and organisational improvement.

- Protect the project from unwarranted external criticism.

- Lead with a different focus at different times, according to the situational demands at the time.

Principles and importance of motivation

Motivation is a vital element in the project world. It is necessary for a project manager to ensure that the staff who report to them are fully motivated so that the problems associated with poor or lack of motivation can be avoided. These are many, but as an indication, poor motivation will lead to:

- Interpersonal conflict; poor motivation can lead to individuals misunderstanding their roles and that of others. They may stay insular and apart from people that they do not know or understand, if their respective roles are not made clear and open.

- High staff attrition rates; Working in a down beat organisation can lead to people leaving after only a short period. Widely in the news there are examples of 'poor motivation' in some sectors (health service is sometimes cited) and this causes staff to seek employment elsewhere.

- Difficulty in recruiting; if a project has a reputation for poor morale it will be more difficult to recruit staff into the project roles. This may mean needing to offer higher rates of pay or maybe other incentives.

- Absence and Sickness; this is sometimes prevalent where team motivation is not attend to adequately. People will be more inclined to stay home rather than go into an environment that does not offer opportunity and advancement.

- Poor quality of work nearly always accompanies poor motivation. If people are not motivated in the right way then they can become a bit slp-dash in their approach and not really care about the quality of what they are doing and just end up with 'its good enough'

Two of the theories pertaining to motivation that are quite widely recognised are those of Frederick Herzberg and Abraham Maslow.

Maslow's Hierarchy of Needs

Abraham Maslow developed the Hierarchy of Needs model (Maslow, A.H. (1943). A theory of human motivation. Psychological Review, 50(4), 370–96). In it he proposed that in order to be motivated in any walk or sphere of life, then there has to be something in the tier above which you currently sit in order to motivate you. Thus, you always aspire to the next tier up.

These tiers are from least motivating to most motivating

Physiological - Heat, light, food, water

Safety - Protection , laws, security

Belongingness and Love - Families, work colleagues, societies

Esteem - Reputation, status and achievement

Self actualisation - Personal growth and fulfilment

The principle here is that as one level of 'need' has been satisfied, then the motivating force for an individual will be that of striving for the next level up. The other overriding principle of the theory is that if any of the lower levels are removed or become unavailable, then a person's motivation will revert to the level below and the lost level will be the motivator, despite what has gone before.

Herzberg's Two Factor Theory

Frederick Herzberg developed "The Motivation-Hygiene Concept and Problems of Manpower" in 1959 which has become a well cited theory of motivation. In it he hypothesised that job satisfaction and job dissatisfaction were independent of each other and that there are certain factors in the workplace that cause job satisfaction, while a different set of factors cause dissatisfaction. The term 'hygiene' was coined by Herzberg to represent the fact that if you wash your hands once they will become clean, wash them again and they will become a bit cleaner, and so on. Ultimately though, there can be no point in washing your hands any further as there will be very little benefit. Hence the topics that reside in the hygiene factors of the table below. Ever increasing attention to the provision of more or greater levels of hygiene factors, will not motivate beyond a certain point. The true motivators are ones that we need to be present in order to be truly motivated. The following table presents arguably the top factors causing dissatisfaction and satisfaction for individuals, when considering their workplace, conditions and so on. They are listed in the order of higher to lower importance, and relative significance in motivating those individuals to do a good job.

True motivators (leading to satisfaction) These are psychological needs to achieve and to grow	Hygiene factors (leading ultimately to dissatisfaction, particularly if they are withdrawn) These are physiological needs; we need money to buy food and shelter
Achievement — being given the opportunity to achieve at one's job, having short definite achievable targets and being clear what is expected.	**Company policy** — a typical example would be whether you qualify for a company car. If you have had one for years and then it is withdrawn, this will definitely lead to dissatisfaction as will not getting the exact model you want.
Recognition — being recognised as the expert in one's field, having people seek your opinion.	**Supervision** — being closely supervised, whilst giving the company the control it desires, this will have a detrimental effect on motivation over the long-term.
Work itself — actually enjoying what you do, being able to look forward to the day's activity rather than dreading it.	**Work conditions** — we expect a certain level of health and hygiene to be prevalent in our workplaces. Again though, continually enhancing the facilities and amenities will not motivate, and the removal of them will have the opposite effect.
Responsibility — giving people more responsibility for their work, and making them accountable for it, has a huge motivating influence.	**Salary** — it is not possible to continually pay individuals more and more salary. There comes a point where this no longer motivates and just becomes 'the norm'.

True motivators (leading to satisfaction) These are psychological needs to achieve and to grow	Hygiene factors (leading ultimately to dissatisfaction, particularly if they are withdrawn) These are physiological needs; we need money to buy food and shelter
Advancement — as individuals grow, so they need new challenges to take them to the next step on their career for nonmonetary rewarded.	**Relationship with peers** — we expect a certain civility and professionalism. Once this has been achieved though there is little else to be gained from further enhancing the environment.
Growth — we all seek to grow in one way or another, whether to learn new skills, make new networks or simply let our organisational ambition take us on.	

Work based exercise
Take a bit of time to think about times when you have been de motivated. What particularly about those circumstances was it that inspired that reaction and which side of the Herzberg model did it stem from?
See if you can draw any conclusions from your reflection and the basis of the theory.

Hygiene factors (i.e. was your reaction based around the company policy, pay, etc.)	True motivators (e.g. being given the chance to advance)
Hygiene factors (i.e. was your reaction based around the company policy, pay, etc.)	True motivators (e.g. being given the chance to advance)

Quick Quiz (Answers In Section 18)

	Question	Options	Your Answer
1	Which of these is NOT a hygiene factor?	a) Salary b) Advancement c) Work conditions d) Company policy	
2	Maslow's theory of motivation includes selling, telling, delegating, participating.	True or false?	
3	Which of these is NOT a motivator?	a) The work itself b) Growth c) Salary d) Responsibility	
4	A project manager does not have a role to play in the motivation of project staff.	True or false?	
5	Which of these may occur if the motivation of a team is not good enough?	a) Sickness b) Poor Quality c) Absenteeism d) All of the above	

Use this space to make some notes

What Kind of Questions Might There Be in the Exam?

1)	List and describe five ways in which a project manager might seek to motivate their team

Assessment Criteria

8.4 Explain the benefits of adopting a situational leadership approach within project management

Situational Leadership

The term was popularised by Hersey and Blanchard, (Hersey, P. and Blanchard, K. H. (1977). Management of Organizational Behavior: Utilizing Human Resources (3rd ed.) New Jersey/ Prentice Hall) who postulated that leadership styles can be categorised as being of one of four styles. Each of these can be categorised by virtue of their relative levels of Support or Direction that is provided to the follower. The leader will need to adapt their approach to various types of follower depending upon their willingness (or maturity of being led).

- **Telling** — where the leader provides one-way communication, defines the role and spends a lot of time explaining and 'telling' what to do and how to do it.

- **Selling** — the leader is still providing direction, but they are now seeking to explain more about the 'why' of the job so the individual is more inclined to subscribe to the purpose and become more involved in the solution.

- **Participating** — the leader and follower start to make decisions together about how the task can be accomplished better/faster/cheaper and the leader stays in touch, but provides less direction and supports the follower in their choices rather than the other way around.

- **Delegating** — the leader still remains involved to monitor what is going on, but full responsibility for the task, the method of achieving it and the processes involved now lie with the follower.

No one style is considered to be the best in all situations at all times (hence the title of the research); to be effective, leaders need to be flexible and adaptable. In order to be fully understood, the nature of the follower's needs to be considered.

- They may lack the specific skills to do the job and are unable and unwilling to do or to take responsibility for its completion.

- They may be unable to take on responsibility for the task being done, but they will be more willing to try and work at it.

- They are experienced and able to do the task, but lack the confidence to take on responsibility.

- They are experienced at the task and comfortable with their own ability to do it well. They now are comfortable to take on both the responsibility for doing the task but also the accountability for doing it well.

Maturity levels are also task specific. A person might be generally skilled, confident and motivated in their job, but would still have a lower maturity level when asked to perform a task requiring skills they don't possess.

Use this space to make some notes

Quick Quiz (Answers In Section 18)

	Question	Options	Your Answer
1	The two axes on Hersey and Blanchards' situational leadership model are?	a) Supporting and directing b) Supporting and following c) Following and directing d) Changing and building	
2	The sequence of leadership styles through the Hersey and Blanchard model is selling, telling, delegating, participating.	True or false?	
3	The maturity of followers is about how old they are.	True or false?	
4	A leader might need to adopt a different style in different circumstances.	True or false?	
5	Which of these is not an attribute of a leader?	a) Visionary b) Energy c) Systems-focused d) Commitment	

What Kind of Questions Might There Be in the Exam?

1)	Describe the term Situational Leadership and four approaches they may adopt to respond to the need to adjust their style of leadership.

	Assessment Criteria
8.5 Describe the characteristics and benefits of effective teams and teamwork	

Team Development

"Teamwork is a group of people working in collaboration or by cooperation towards a common goal (APM Body of Knowledge 6th Edition)

This is vital in any project. At a very early stage in their career, a project manager has to come to terms with the fact that they cannot do everything themselves. They therefore need to be able to motivate others to want to do the work required. Individuals will rarely have the ability to do all of the diverse tasks on a project and therefore we need more than one. This in turn leads us down the road of having teams of multi-disciplinary individuals, all working towards a common goal — the essence of a team.

We will consider here two distinct theories to help understand what is important both:

- **Before** the team has formed and how we might select that team. The APM would advocate the use of a social roles model, the most common of which was developed by Meredith Belbin and is often used to explain the nature of team members and their preferred 'style'.

- **After** the team has formed helping to understand the team's evolution. The one the APM has adopted is the Tuckman model of group development, first proposed by Bruce Tuckman.

The Belbin 'Social Roles Model'

Meredith Belbin studied at Cambridge in the UK and with associates he developed the concept of social team roles. It has become one of the most recognisable and well-used tools to help analyse the nature of individuals and their preferred style within a team environment. One of his main conclusions was that an effective team needs to have members that between them cover eight major roles within the team.

These roles were:

1) **Plant** — creative, imaginative, and unorthodox, solves difficult problems. Sometimes distant from the remainder of the team, they have the brilliant ground breaking or problem solving ideas.

2) **Resource Investigator** — this is the networker. Always on the phone — they don't know how, but they know someone that does. They are adept at rallying support from external stakeholders and disparate partners; they are well connected. They can sometimes appear detached and not worried about the important things.

3) **Coordinator** — makes sure that all the team members have a voice and contribute. They will ensure fairness and equality, and will go to great pains to make sure the decision is the right one. To more laterally thinking members of the team, they can seem slow to act and frustrating through their insistence to consult everyone.

4) **Shaper** — this team member is dynamic, relishes pressure and thrives on challenges. They possess the drive and enthusiasm to overcome obstacles.

5) **Monitor Evaluator** — they try to see all the angles, weigh up all the pros and cons to fully understand the risks of a course of action. They are very capable to carry out detailed analysis and provide a balanced view.

6) **Team Worker** — has to make sure that all the other team members are comfortable and happy. The team worker can seem to spend too much time on the people issues by those who want quick progress, but the team worker will win 'hearts and minds' to make sure the job is done with consensus.

7) **Implementer** — is the hands-on person, comfortable with working the system and process to get the job done. They are full of common sense and have an eye for the practical, making sure that the ideas can be fulfilled. They are not particularly visionary but can in most circumstances be relied upon to deliver the goods.

8) **Completer Finisher** — this is the 'i' dotting and 't' crossing person. The person happy with the detail, knowing exactly where the team is on schedule and cost. They are meticulous and their attention to detail ensures a quality approach and a satisfactory finished product.

9) **Specialist** —The specialist was identified and incorporated into the model sometime after the original search. They are those individuals who (un-surprisingly) bring specialist knowledge and skills to the project and are a source of expertise to draw on. They are happiest when engaged in the minutiae of the products and embedded in the detail.

Belbin was not at all judgemental about which was best or worst, he merely stated that there needs to be an element of all of them in all teams to deliver a quality product in a harmonious and low conflict way, be it a project or an operational environment.

The Tuckman Model of Team Development

In 1965 Bruce Tuckman identified four key stages in team development Tuckman, Bruce W. (1965) 'Developmental sequence in small groups', Psychological Bulletin, 63, 384-399.

The stages thus described include

Forming

Tuckman observed that the team on first coming together can be said to be in a forming stage. They are brought together in the first instance of a project. They may not know each other and may be distrustful of their managers and their co-workers. They begin to understand the task in front of them and will behave independently of each other so they can each understand their role in the endeavour. They are largely uninformed about the team goals and may make incorrect assumptions about what is coming up.

Storming

In this stage the team begins to gel, but struggles to understand how they will inter-operate with the others in the team. There will be competition and confrontation between team members, who each have a view of how things should work, and conflict resolution is a key project management skill during this stage. To help them through this stage, they will begin to be a little more open with their co-workers and between them agree what control structures and leadership influences they are prepared to accept. Some members of the team may be able (through their experience and individual maturity) to coax, coach and coerce others to grow out of the storming stage and into the vastly more productive norming stage.

Norming

Team members are now more accepting of their fellow workers and begin to deliver. They will begin to operate as a unit and support each other in the job in hand. They understand their objectives and will continue to deliver the products in an acceptable manner. The danger is that they fall into a complacent and protective arrangement, whereby they begin to believe that the team is more important than the job in hand. This is called groupthink and must be avoided. The team appears coherent and fluid, adapting to changes well but there is always the danger that they are merely in their 'comfort zone' and not being creative or maximising their potential.

Performing

This is the optimum state for the team to achieve. They function as a cohesive unit and demonstrate the ability to get the job done with little or no supervision. They are creative and open to new ideas and actively develop their working practices and methods to achieve optimization. They are fully motivated and knowledgeable about the job in hand and will be able to solve their own problems. Creative conflict abounds, but the team are more than able to deal with it.

It is possible to witness a team reverting back to one of the earlier stages in the model. This is usually caused by some form of change in the environment, such as people leaving or joining, new supervision, new buildings, etc. Also a team may simply achieve its current objectives and then search for a new challenge. If an acceptable one is not forthcoming, the team may simply dissolve. Tuckman termed this as adjourning and this term was added to the model some years later.

What Can Go Wrong When Teamwork is not Effective?

If there is insufficient attention placed on team development the project will not be in the best possible position. Lack of attention can lead to a number of negative circumstances that will impede progress. They are all interdependent and cannot be said to be cause and effect, but collectively or in isolation, they will need to be dealt with by the project management teams. Some obvious areas are:

- **Lack of motivation** — leads to high team attrition, conflict and difficulties in recruitment.

- **Poor attention to detail** — leads to rework and potential customer dissatisfaction and a lot of claims.

- **Interpersonal conflict** — leads to distress, arguments and a a great deal of managerial time being consumed.

- **Lack of focus** — means idle time and increased sickness levels, time wasted on debating inconsequential issues or continual criticism.

- **Poor external perception** — means the team becomes 'not the place to work' and gains a poor reputation.

Use this space to make some notes

_____
_____
_____
_____
_____
_____
_____
_____

Work based exercise
Are you part of a team at the moment? Can you observe where in the development cycle it is? Do you observe any of the individual Belbin styles?

Quick Quiz (Answers In Section 18)

	Question	Options	Your Answer
1	Forming is a Tuckman phase of team development.	True or false?	
2	Which of these is not a Belbin role?	a) Implementer b) Completer finisher c) Plant d) Operator	
3	Changes to a team's environment can cause a regression back to earlier team development stages.	True or false?	
4	Fill in the gap forming, storming, _____, performing?	a) Working b) Adjourning c) Failing d) Norming	
5	What does a team NOT demonstrate during the storming phase?	a) Competition b) Conflict c) Hopefulness d) Confrontation	
6	How many Belbin roles are there?	a) 8 b) 2 c) 5 d) 9	
7	Which Belbin role is suited to detailed meticulous work?	a) Shaper b) Completer finisher c) Plant d) Implementer	
8	If team work is not treated seriously and developed there may be a lack of motivation amongst the team members.	True or false?	
9	A 'norming' team are considered as high performing.	True or false?	
10	Plants are the 'ideas' people.	True or false?	

	What Kind of Questions Might There Be in the Exam?
1)	Describe the term 'teamwork' and describe four stages through which a team might develop

SECTION 9
SCOPE MANAGEMENT

	Assessment Criteria

9.1 Define scope in terms of outputs, outcomes and benefits

(NB includes 4.2 Explain the way in which an organisational breakdown structure is used to create a responsibility assignment matrix)

What is the 'Scope' of a Project?

Planning how the project will be managed during the definition stage culminates in the preparation of the project management plan (or PMP). The contents, ownership and authorship are covered in section 10.7 and section 10.8 of this guide. One of the key components of the PMP is that of a definition of the scope of the project. Scope is a term much used but usually poorly understood.

In essence the SCOPE of a project is all the products and all of the work undertaken to produce them. In essence (and we will see more later) they are the combination of the Work Breakdown Structure and the Product Breakdown Structure.

Scope management is the first key component of constructing a project schedule (section 11.1). The production of the Work Breakdown Structure will culminate in the generation of Work Packages and these will have associated Products. Scope develops over time as the project becomes known and the nature of the scope changes through the requirements capture and analysis and business case definition activities. Through the preparation of the PMP the scope finally becomes nailed down in the WBS. Throughout the process various 'Freezes' of design are made so that some form of stability can be exerted on the design so uncontrolled change does not cause too much uncertainty and error.

During the Development phase the scope is further redefined but on an ever increasing level of detail as more and more becomes known about the products and Work until eventually the appropriate level of detail is understood such that the products can be created.

Consider the diagram below

Projects - these are the undertakings that produce Outputs.

Outputs - These are the products associated with the project. A nuclear submarine is a product as is the switch that turns on the light in the captains cabin of that submarine. Sometimes we wish to manage at one level of detail and sometimes at others.

Outcomes - an outcome is the changed circumstance or behaviours resulting from the putting to use of the products. A reduced hospital waiting list time is not a product. The new computer system, more doctors and more wards that make it happen are the products. Collectively they enable an outcome.

Benefits - Stakeholders observe the outcome and choose to put a value on their perspective of it. A reduced waiting time for an operation clearly has a benefit if you are waiting for that operation, if you are not waiting then it will have relatively little value. Benefits are discussed more in later sections.

Consider the diagram below

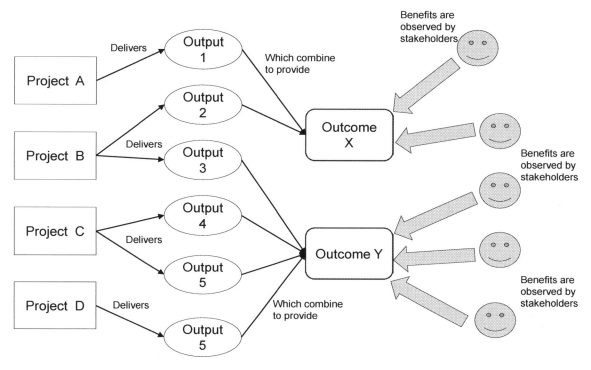

FIGURE 15 PROJECTS - OUTPUTS - OUTCOMES - BENEFITS

When the scope of the project is considered early on in the project very generic terms might be used for example:

- The project will build three new buildings.

- The project will only test the products in Thailand and Indonesia.

- The scope includes the design build and test stages but not roll-out.

These high level conceptual statements are fine but they leave quite a bit to the imagination. They are very often found within the business case when the intention is to set the scene and to literally conceptualise the project. As discussed as the project definition progresses, the PMP requires ever more detailed refinement of the scope so that the exact nature of the precise deliverables is evidenced.

It is important to keep the business case in mind so that the PMP does not diverge from it and to make sure that the resultant project does in fact adhere to the principles and materiality of the requirements in it.

The two key components (products and work) that help us to develop the eventual plans and schedules ensure that we are be able to manage properly. It can be helpful to think of the project work breakdown structure and product breakdown structure as two sides of the same coin. One describes the work required (to produce the products) and the other describes what will be produced (as a result of the work). Very simplistically, the WBS is a hierarchical structure that is normally conveyed as a diagram, as in Figure 16.

Work Breakdown Structures

The WBS is a tool for defining the hierarchical breakdown of work required to deliver the products of a project. Major categories are broken down into smaller components. These are sub-divided until the lowest required level of detail is established. The lowest units of the WBS become the work packages in a project. The WBS defines the total work to be undertaken on the project and provides a structure for all project control systems such as Earned Value.

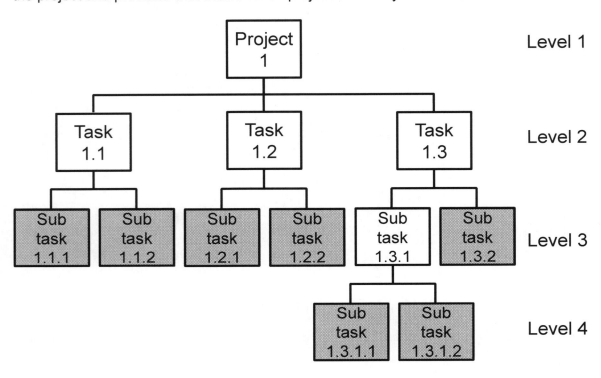

FIGURE 16 A WORK BREAKDOWN STRUCTURE

There are a few key components to recognise in a WBS:

- In the diagram above all of the shaded boxes represent work packages.

- Each level is clearly identified (through the numbering structure) as being a breakdown of the level above (1.1.n. etc.).

- The levels start at one and develop as the granularity and precision of definition increases.

- At the the lowest level of the structure there are work packages.

- Each work package can be comprised of a number of activities where it is required to plan at this level of detail. It is these activities that would find their way into the precedence diagram alongside any work packages that have not been so decomposed.

- There are no predetermined numbers of levels, it is a judgment that must be made for each set of circumstances.

- The activities must include project management as this is a component of the project work and must therefore appear in the WBS.

- The WBS includes everything that is in (and therefore by definition, everything that is outside) of scope.

Work Packages

- Work packages are the level of definition or unit of work for which a budget is estimated and reported. There can be different levels (as above) and each is a decomposition of the one above.

- They should be able to have a discrete estimate associated with them so that proper recording can be maintained for lessons leaned purposes.

- They have a discrete budget allocated to them, so an accurate cost can be compared to them.

- They should be allocated to a single accountable person, to avoid confusion.

- They should not overlap, each containing a discrete self-contained package of work.

- They should have some form of consistent numbering to identify them.

- Each work package either has a relatively short duration, or can be divided into a series of activities whose status can be objectively measured.

- They can be further decomposed if that detail is required.

Product Breakdown Structures

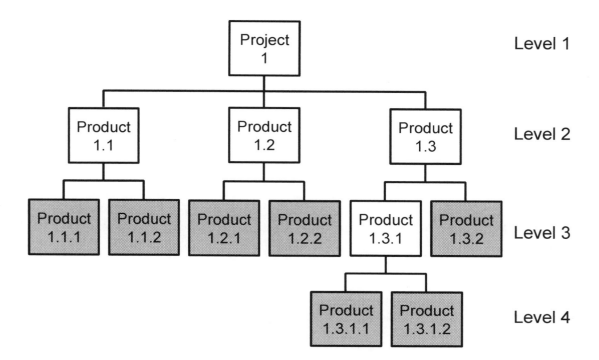

FIGURE 17 A PRODUCT BREAKDOWN STRUCTURE

Those eagle-eyed amongst you will notice very little difference in practice between a PBS and WBS. The main points to note are that the WBS talks about work and will use verbs whilst the PBS talks about products and will therefore use nouns. You can use either as the primary breakdown and may want to do both. Quite often your organisation will have a stated preference and will dictate how these breakdowns are constructed and indeed which type to use. The key advantage of the PBS is that it gives you a definitive list of interrelated products that will prove invaluable when you come to do configuration management as it will form the backbone of the configuration library.

Organisation Breakdown Structure

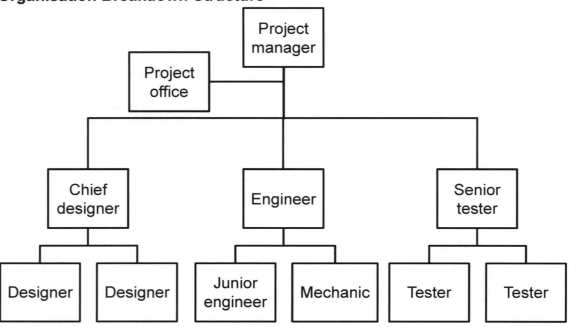

FIGURE 18 AN ORGANISATION BREAKDOWN STRUCTURE (OBS)

There are a few key components to recognise in an organisation breakdown structure (OBS):

- Each person who has a role in the project should be identified in the OBS.

- It is not merely a cut and paste from the company's organisation chart, careful thought will be needed.

- Anyone who has a role must appear, even if it is just a small involvement

- The OBS demonstrates a reporting hierarchy for the project; it does not necessarily represent line management roles.

- Each role ought to have either a role description, terms of reference, statement of work, or some other mechanism to clearly identify what is required of the individual.

The primary use of the organisational breakdown structure is to be able to communicate to stakeholders the relevant individuals associated with the project. However, the real power of the OBS comes when it is combined with the WBS to provide a matrix of roles called a responsibility assignment matrix.

The Responsibility Assignment (RACI) Matrix

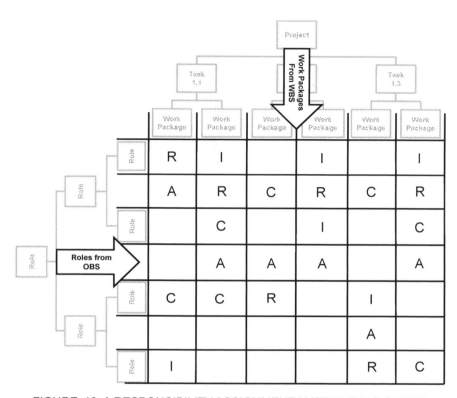

FIGURE 19 A RESPONSIBILITY ASSIGNMENT MATRIX (RAM) CHART

As can be seen, the roles described in the OBS are mapped across to the tasks from the WBS to provide (at the intersection) an opportunity to classify an involvement on the part of the role described. At these intersections it is possible to annotate:

R — Responsible. This is the person who is responsible for carrying out the task, the person who will do it. (Only one person should be responsible for the task).

A — Accountable. This is the individual or organisation that is accountable for getting the job done. They may choose to make an individual or organisation responsible (to them).

C — Consulted. These are the individuals who are consulted in the execution of the task.

I — Informed. These are the individuals or organisations that are informed about the activity and provided with the output.

These RAM charts are sometimes referred to as RACI charts.

The real benefit of them is that, at a glance, it is possible to identify who is doing what. There should be no missing responsibilities and likewise there should not be more than one. It is a very powerful tool for the project manager and is a key component of the PMP.

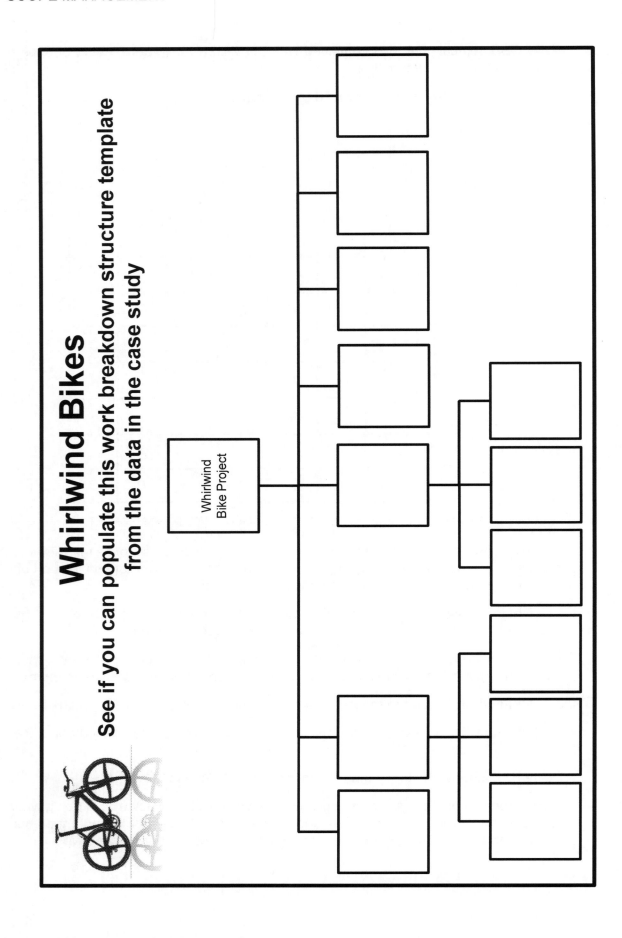

Use this space to make some notes

_____
_____
_____
_____
_____
_____
_____

Quick Quiz (Answers In Section 18)

	Question	Options	Your Answer
1	OBS means?	a) Organisation breakdown structure b) Outline breakdown structure c) Organisation benefits Structure d) Organisational benefits system	
2	WBS means?	a) Work benefit system b) Work baseline system c) Work bottom system d) Work breakdown structure	
3	Each level of the WBS will be easily identifiable as a sub level of the level above.	True or false?	
4	An example of a component of a scope statement might be what?	a) Which sites are included b) When the project will take place c) Who will manage the project d) Why the project is taking place	
5	The project manager is responsible for producing the scope breakdown.	True or false?	

	Question	Options	Your Answer
6	A RAM chart shows what?	a) The task and the when it will take place b) The task and the person involved in it c) The person involved and when it will take place d) The risks associated with the task	
7	The scope statement is a key component of the project management plan.	True or false?	
8	A WBS shows the decomposition of tasks.	True or false?	
9	The lowest level of a WBS is called a...?	a) Work package b) Task c) Activity d) Change module	
10	Stakeholders will place a value on the benefits of a project.	e) True or False	

	What Kind of Questions Might There Be in the Exam?
1)	Describe the term scope and explain four techniques for developing project scope, including a diagram.
2)	Describe the use of a RAM (or RACI) chart and the benefits of doing so. Make five points in your answer.

Assessment Criteria

9.2 Explain how to manage scope through requirements management and configuration management

Requirements Management Process

So, given we are in the area of understanding the stakeholders' requirements and trying to make sense of them we will need some form of process and the following one is suggested. Each of the steps has a particular purpose and collectively they will ensure that the stakeholders have their requirements documented and properly managed through to completion.

The manner in which requirements are captured should be specified in the organisation's governance or portfolio management procedures. It is inappropriate for a project to generate its own requirements; they are totally reliant upon stakeholders to provide the necessary 'need'.

Requirements Capture

There are a number of generic techniques that can be used here and also some specific techniques. The project may consider:

- Brainstorming sessions.
- Questionnaires and data collection.
- Analysis of pre-project documentation.
- Review of any relevant legislation.
- Contract requirements.
- Prototyping.
- Written requirements specification based on the outgoing system / product.
- A 'user case', where we try and identify the use to which a product will be put.
- User forums and focus groups around new products.

Requirements Analysis

Once we have been able to identify what the stakeholders require of the system, we can begin to build an idea of how they may be achieved. We might need to build a preliminary database (computerised or otherwise) of what these requirements look like and then commence evaluating them in an orderly and systematic way.

There are a large number of tools to help evaluate requirements but they all concentrate on a few key issues:

- **Value** — does the requirement have any value in the market place into which it will be introduced? This area has a large degree of overlap with that of benefits management.
- **Priority** — is the requirement of sufficient priority to be considered as needing to be within scope of the project and is this particular requirement more or less significant than others?
- **Time** — at what point does this requirement need to be met? Sometimes where there is a nondiscretionary project to be undertaken, having the product ready by a certain time is the fundamental requirement.
- **Process** — How can these requirements be met, are they routine or innovative.? What can we do to understand how they can be satisfied?

The analysis process will be charged with understanding all of these topics and weighing them up in sympathy with the organisation's strategic objectives. The analysis may have to consider when people will be available, which subcontractors are in the market and so on.

Document Requirements

The analysis will be preceded and succeeded with a period of documentation, such that everyone concerned is clear about the nature of the requirements and subscribe to them. Once documented the requirements form a fundamental starting point for the development of more refined and detailed levels of requirement. Once the high level business requirement has been identified, it will need to be decomposed (a part of the scope definition activity) into lower levels and different types of requirement. Very often we encounter the terms 'functional requirement', 'system requirement', 'technical requirement', 'user requirement', etc. Basically, the project manager is going to have to identify the components that will work on their project and document them in the project management plan.

Once they have been so documented then the configuration management process applies, as they are effectively part of the projects baseline. Any changes to the requirements can have a huge knock on effect to other aspects of the project and the integration of all of these discrete components therefore is of paramount importance. If we decide to build the bridge 20m longer, having already built the foundations, we will experience a high degree of cost and time delays.

Requirements Test

The requirements are tested both after being first constructed and thereafter throughout the project. There needs to be a structured flow down between the various levels of requirements and each lower level may need to be validated by a different audience. This process is often demonstrated through a V-shaped diagram model:

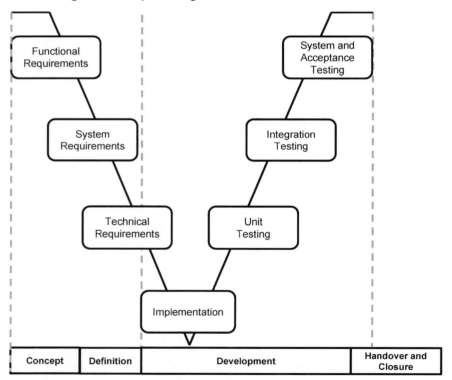

FIGURE 20 THE V SHAPED MODEL FOR UNDERSTANDING AND TESTING REQUIREMENTS

This one might apply to a software system, but others that are available will relate to engineering, petrochemical, retail and so on. The principle is that the relevant level of specification is tested and validated by the relevant level of user. As the life cycle develops then so we analyse and test the various requirements at ever increasing levels of detail as the technology becomes more specific and then towards the end of the project we revert back to the original 'need' and compare our products with it. The test we use for the functional requirements (e.g. Processing 10,000 records per hour) will not be the same as the tests applied to the hardware itself.

Requirements Linkage with Quality

For the project to be perceived as a success then it will need to be able to demonstrate that it has delivered according to the requirements. Therefore, quality and requirements must go hand in hand. The Quality Management section will focus on the achievement of quality, but suffice to say that if you do not understand what is required there is very little chance of being able to deliver it.

Work based exercise
How does your organisation collect requirements and how does it record them?
Is there an automated system?
How do you know if all relevant stakeholders have been consulted?

Configuration Management Process

The purpose of configuration management is to ensure that at any time throughout the life cycle the project manager can be confident that all of the products that have been produced conform to their own specifications, but also that they have been demonstrated to have worked with all of the products with which they interact.

Consider a building; if the design calls for a distance between two walls to be 10m, all the drawings and specifications will be geared around this fact. The foundations will have been dug and poured, the roof beams ordered and sufficient roof tiles purchased for the necessary span. We will have checked the drawings, the surveyors will have calculated the quantities and everything will be going to plan.

Let us assume that the person fabricating the roof beams was given an older version of the drawings that was made earlier in the project before the design was finalised but showed the walls to be 9m apart. When the beams arrive they will not be long enough. Whose fault would this be? The beam supplier has done what they have been told, the people building the walls similarly. Who ends up with the problem? The project manager will, and to avoid being in this position they need a configuration management system that will make sure that everyone is working to the same drawings.

Configuration management can often be overlooked as the benefits are not immediately obvious and it is also not very easy to implement configuration management later on in the project once problems have started to occur.

If the configuration management system is not in place and being operated correctly, we run the risk of:

- Individual products not working together (as per the building example above).

- Poor quality of deliverables (we will not be able to test the product against the requisite specification).

- A lot of rework (the beam supplier will need to build new beams).

- Confusion, to the detriment of morale (the tradesmen have all done their job, but the end result is incorrect).

- Unsafe products in operation (especially in safety critical software systems).

- A high degree of warranty work and bug fixes (especially software).

- Other suppliers having difficulty interfacing with the project (we cannot describe what our finished product will look like).

In the above example the simplest of configuration management systems might do. If someone on the project was charged with looking after the various drawings, who made sure that they had a reasonable version control, that a list of people who needed them was maintained and that those people got a revised version as and when it was changed, then the problem could well have been avoided. In its simplest form, this document control would have satisfied our need for a configuration management process. Please note that the area of document control overlaps quite a lot with that of information management and quite a lot of organisations will have a document management system that may well satisfy a lot of the requirements of a configuration management system. Because of the implications on the ability to produce a quality product, configuration management is often seen as a quality technique and should arguably appear as part of the project quality plan.

The Activities Contained in a Configuration Management Process

If a more comprehensive configuration management process is required then there are a number of accepted steps that can be adopted that together represent a configuration management procedure.

Configuration Planning (P)

The Project Manager — will make sure that an appropriate configuration management procedure is in place and is being followed. In practice they will work very closely with the configuration librarian in this regard. They will make sure that the procedure is briefed out and that all the stakeholders are aware of the implications of the system in operation. They will need a configuration management plan which defines all of the project specific configuration management activities, roles and responsibilities. Some of the roles include:

Configuration Identification (I)

This activity is concerned with the correct and consistent identification of all the various components that go to make up the whole 'configuration'. Each component and sub-component should have an easily identifiable and recognisable label so that it can be quickly and easily discernible where the component fits and how it may or may not interact with other components. A product breakdown structure can help here with its hierarchical numbering system; it is a key component of the cataloguing effort. The products classified in this way are also termed configuration Items.

Configuration Control (C)

Configuration control is concerned with the process to be adopted in the management of the library. There should be clearly documented procedures to be followed by all involved in the project. The project manager will be instrumental in prescribing this as part of the quality plan and thereafter will need to make sure that suitable assurance is being undertaken.

Typical steps in the configuration control processes might include:

- Interaction with the change control process as this is the source of potential configuration item amendments.
- The checking in and out of items to the project team for amendment.
- Checking to make sure other configuration items are not affected (and if they are potentially raising another change request).
- Approvals from the configuration controller to implement the change.
- Notifying all interested parties of the change.
- Making sure all records are up to date.

Configuration Status Accounting (S)

This is the recording and reporting of all information relating to each configuration item in order that the various versions can be tracked. This enables the tracking of modifications to configuration items. A status account would include for each configuration item:

- Its identifier (from the PBS)
- Its owner (the person who created it and manages it
- The date of last update
- Its current status (e.g. is it being updated at present)
- Its latest version number
- Any other products that might be affected if this item is updated.

> **Configuration Audit (A)**
>
> Configuration audit is a key component of configuration management. It is carried out at regular predetermined stages to ensure that all the planned configuration items are where they should be in terms of their life cycle (i.e. the correct version is being used) and that there is sufficient evidence to demonstrate that all the change configuration and testing processes have been completed.

The Roles Associated with Configuration Management

- The Configuration Librarian — this person is the custodian of the configuration library. The will be responsible for the proper management of the library and liaise with other team members and the project manager to ensure that the procedures are followed.

- The Project Manager — will be ultimately accountable for the proper execution of the configuration management process as indeed they are for all of the processes in the PMP. The Project Manager may need to prepare the team for an audit of the process (undertaken by impartial auditors). They will also be instrumental in championing the process as very often it is seen as onerous and unnecessary.

- The Configuration Item Controller — will have responsibility for individual configuration items. They own the technical specifications and are responsible for producing a product that conforms to the specification. If changes are to be made to a configuration item, then it is the configuration controller who will have responsibility for making sure that all the other items have been checked and updated as necessary.

- The Change Control Board — in a large project with complex inter-dependencies it might be appropriate to convene a change control board (comprised of at least the configuration controllers) to make sure that the entire scope of the change is understood, acknowledged and approved (if appropriate).

- The Project Team — by and large the project team will need to follow the process. They may see this as a hindrance to their work, but if communicated properly they can see that it is in the best interests of the project.

	Use this space to make some notes

_____

_____

_____

_____

_____

_____

_____

Quick Quiz (Answers In Section 18)

	Question	Options	Your Answer
1	The requirements are the same as benefits.	True or false?	
2	The configuration management plan forms part of the project PMP.	True or False?	
3	The ways in which requirements are gathered are usually driven by....?	a) The project manager making it up b) The organisation's governance framework c) The procurement process d) The sponsor	
4	When should the requirements be tested?	a) At the beginning b) At the end c) All the way through d) Once	
5	Which of these is not a component of configuration management	a) Work breakdown structures b) Control c) Assurance d) Planning	
6	Changes to the requirements are instigated by....?	a) The project sponsor b) The project manager c) The procurement department d) The users	
7	Which of these roles is not associated with configuration management?	a) Procurement specialists b) Configuration item controller c) Configuration librarian d) Project Manager	
8	Which of these is not a step in the requirements management process?	a) Identify b) Analyse c) Reiterate d) Test	
9	The configuration librarian checks products out and into the configuration library	True or False?	
10	A status account would not include	a) WBS number b) Owner c) Latest version d) Id number	

	What Kind of Questions Might There Be in the Exam?
1)	List and describe four key steps in a requirements management process.

	Assessment Criteria

9.3 Explain the different stages of change control

9.4 Explain the relationship between change control and configuration management

9.5 Explain the advantages and disadvantages of a change control process

What are Changes and Why do they Need Controlling?

A change is something that will affect any of the key criteria associated with a project — the time, cost, quality, risk exposure or benefits case. Some changes may be welcome, some not. Either way, they need to be managed.

Change comes about for a number of reasons:

- External influences, for example, a change of government or organisational strategies.

- A new and innovative technique or process apparent after the business case has been agreed.

- Efficiencies of process and changes associated with getting things done quicker / cheaper.

- Changes to the benefits model, perhaps doing a little more may have a huge return.

- Evolving designs and emergence of new information.

- Contractual changes generated by the client or other stakeholders.

A large proportion of the Body of Knowledge is devoted to the construction of plans of one form or another. Having gone to so much trouble to make sure that the plans are coherent, viable and communicated, it would be very counterproductive to allow uncontrolled change to undermine all of the good work. One of the major causes of problems with projects is uncontrolled change, because ultimately it ends up with no one knowing what is going on. The purpose of a change control process is to make sure that the baselines of the project are secured and only changed with appropriate controls, checks, agreement and communication.

One of the reasons that so much time is spent planning is to counteract the effects identified in Figure 21. As time progresses, the ability to have an impact on the shape and direction of a project diminishes. Similarly, as time goes by, the cost of any changes will rise. We have examined these issues earlier in this guide.

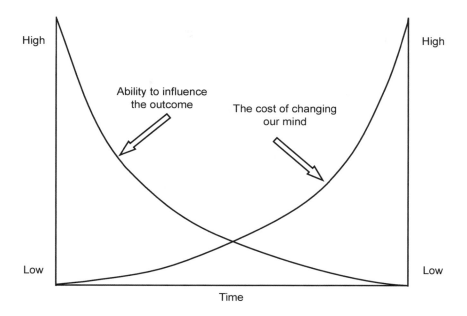

High   High

Ability to influence
the outcome

The cost of changing
our mind

Low   Low

Time

FIGURE 21 THE COST OF CHANGE CURVE

Other key aspects of projects, examined in a number of earlier sections, are that of the role of the sponsor and the business case. Once commissioned, a project is coherent in terms of understanding what will be done when and why. The cost is also fully considered and understood. Any changes to these parameters may call into question the viability of the project as a whole.

The emphasis is on control and the ability of the project manager to keep track of and make sure that proper authorisation has been received for changes to any of these key criteria.

An Example Change Control Process:

Figure 22 describes the minimum steps that should be included within a change control process to be sure to control a project's scope.

Change Request

A change can be requested from a number of sources. They can emanate for any of the reasons described above. Stakeholders generally will instigate a change and the project manager must make sure that they are recorded. A simple change control log should include a minimum of fields to properly record it. Generally fields to consider are:

- Number — some form of identifier to uniquely identify the request.

- Originator — who requested the change?

- Description — a brief overview.

- Date — date it was raised.

- Status — has it been accepted, rejected, deferred or approved?

- Impact — what will the effect be on the time, cost, quality, benefits and risk parameters for the project?

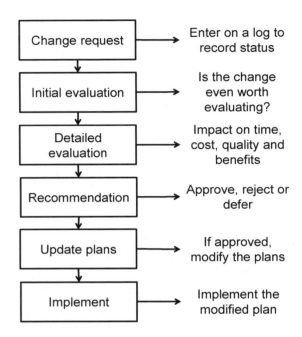

FIGURE 22 STEPS IN A CHANGE CONTROL PROCESS

Initial Evaluation

An initial evaluation is carried out to determine whether or not the change is viable, potentially acceptable and has the support of a quorum of stakeholders. This initial evaluation should be relatively short and focused. There is a potential for change requests and the analysis of them to derail a project simply because that while the team are analysing them, they are not doing the work on the plan. The initial evaluation therefore is a form of filter to ensure that only sensible and viable changes should be taken forward to the next stage with the cost and effort implications of a full scale review.

The configuration librarian, change control board (if there is one) and the configuration item controller may all need to be consulted to ensure that any changes to other parts of the system or product are scoped. This will help in the initial stages to understand the scope of the change and how much work may be involved.

Detailed Evaluation

The main use of the change control log (or register) is to keep track of the various changes which will be recorded on the change control forms. These will generally be more detailed and will usually have a significant amount of reference documents associated with them. A change control form would carry detailed analysis of the material in the change control log. They will in essence be a 'mini business case' for the change. All of the aspects of a business case need to be considered when reviewing a change control because of the potential to change the business case. The sponsor will need to have enough information on the impact of the change to make rational decisions about whether to approve them or not.

During the detailed evaluation, all the product specifications from the configuration libraries are analysed and the impacts of changes to the products are properly evaluated to make sure that any impacts are properly understood and any subsidiary change requests are raised. Once again a good proportion of the configuration management process will be exercised.

Recommendation

The person with the authority to approve a change is the project sponsor (possibly taking advice from a duly appointed change control board). They have the responsibility to make sure that the stakeholders are consulted and any differences are resolved. They will liaise with the project manager and any other advisors to make sure that they are in essence 'doing the right thing'. The options for the sponsor are:

1)   Approve the change and authorise its inclusion into the plans.

2)   Reject the change and not approve its implementation.

3)   Defer the change until later.

At all stages the stakeholders need to be communicated with and kept up to date with progress and decisions. Ultimately, the project manager will need to co-ordinate the implementation of the change to make sure that it is done seamlessly and incorporated into the plans.

Update Plans

This stage involves the project manager introducing the new tasks into the plan. Most of the normal planning process would already have been carried out during the detailed feasibility, but now the live schedules, budgets, specifications and risk registers will need to be formally updated and managed through the configuration management procedures. Changes must be considered alongside the existing frameworks of product descriptions and specifications. Once again the configuration librarian will be involved to make sure that the appropriate version number, modification levels and releases are coordinated.

Everyone who needs to know must be told about the change or else errors due to incorrect information may creep into the system. It should not be forgotten that a prospective change is substantially easier to implement than a retrospective changes to products already completed.

Implement

The implementation of a change is concerned with actually carrying out the approved work. At this point, the change control process merges with the normal managerial activities of the routine management of the plan. The project manager should maintain any changes within the main project. Once approved, the changes will be absorbed into every level of planning and the new activities will be undertaken in exactly the same way as the original task load.

The relationship between Change Control and Configuration Management

Whenever a change is considered there may be an impact on the products the project is seeking to produce. The totality of these products is described as the Project Configuration. These principles are discussed in section 9.2. However for the purposes of change control it is worth noting here that the two processes are inextricably liked and the failure to consider one without the other may result in the following problems:

- Changing a product may have an effect on other products. This may lead to a mis-match between the two and potentially causing problems later on when two components are to be connected for example.

- Uncontrolled changes undertaken by configuration item owners without reference to the controlling influence of the configuration librarian and their library will cause major problems later on when others are using the wrong versions.

- Although the checking out and checking in procedures can add time to the changes being enacted. In a live environment it is not uncommon to find conflict between those trying to get changes enacted and the configuration librarian and their staff.

Change Freeze

As the project progresses from one stage to another and as the requirements begin to be collected and converted into products, so the necessity for change also rears its head. It is virtually inevitable that the stakeholders will have forgotten something or changed their minds. The change control process is designed to protect the project from uncontrolled changes.

However there will come a time when more changes cannot be considered and this is called a 'Change Freeze'. It is implemented so that the products as they are currently specified can be finished and delivered. It is not uncommon for products (especially software) to be delivered at various stages of modification. These interim stages are usually referred to as a 'release' and most people will be familiar with the process of mobile phone software for example.

The need to freeze the design (and therefore the products to be build in conformance with them) is paramount as although some functionality may not be included in the release the release must function in its own right.

Quite often when considering the contents of a release the team will consider a mechanism for prioritising those requirements such as a MoSCoW list

M - Must have - these are things that are vital to the acceptability of the product at this release.

S - Should have - these are things that are high priority that should be included if time and resources allow. If not possible then a work around may be needed to compensate for its absence.

C - Could have - These are desirable but strictly speaking can be done without. They can wait for later releases.

W - Won't have - these are things that definitely will not be in this release and most likely no other releases.

It is quite easy to see how this method could relate to software but with a construction job (building a bridge for example) it is not so easily understandable. In this case it is the drawings that are fixed and the construction work commences based on those 'frozen' drawings. In this situation it is far less feasible to re-work the entire bridge to accommodate emerging requirements and so the change freezes are usually quite significant events requiring top level approval.

	WHIRLWIND BIKES **Consider the following circumstances and decide whether they represent a change or not.**
The customer has asked that the schedule be advanced by six weeks so that the launch can coincide with the visit of the Culture Minister who is visiting the factory.	
Exchange rates $ to £ have fallen fast (less $ for your £).	
During a road test, a wheel appears to have disintegrated and the road tester was seriously injured.	
One of the large European bike manufacturers has taken out a claim in the European courts questioning the legality of the tendering process and your response to it.	
The customer has asked that the weight of the bike must not exceed 20kg.	

Use this space to make some notes

_____
_____
_____
_____
_____
_____
_____
_____
_____
_____
_____
_____

Quick Quiz (Answers In Section 18)

	Question	Options	Your Answer
1	The steps in a change control process include request, _____, detailed evaluation, recommendation, _____, implement.	a) Initial investigation; control b) Changes; configuration c) Initial investigation; update plans d) Update; appraisal	
2	A project sponsor has ultimate authority to approve changes.	True or false?	
3	The project manager has ultimate authority to approve changes.	True or false?	
4	Which of these does a change control process not seek to deal with?	a) Morale b) Quality c) Cost d) Benefits	
5	How many times can a change be submitted?	a) Once b) Twice c) Three times d) As many as is justified	

	Question	Options	Your Answer
6	Which of these is not an outcome from the recommendation stage?	a) Deferral b) Rejection c) Absorption d) Approval	
7	Which of these is not an entry on a change control log?	a) Date b) Number c) Impact d) WBS number	
8	On a change control form, the project manager would want to record everything except...?	a) Who raised it b) Costs to implement c) Was it approved d) The probability of it happening	
9	Configuration management is tightly linked to change control.	True or false?	
10	A configuration librarian would be consulted during the initial investigation of a change control.	True or false?	

What Kind of Questions Might There Be in the Exam?

1)	List and describe the main steps in a change management process; make five points in your answer.
2)	Explain five consequences of not adequately managing change on a project.
3)	Describe five key causes of change on a project.

SECTION 10
PLANNING FOR SUCCESS

	Assessment Criteria

10.1 Explain the purpose of a business case and its importance during the life cycle

10.2 Describe who has authorship and ownership of the business case

The Need For The Business Case

The development of the business case can be viewed as a funnelling arrangement, whereby the problems or opportunities can be analysed and reviewed in order that the organisation can be assured that they are performing the correct project in response.

Figure 23 describes this 'funnel'. The ideas, problems and opportunities enter into the system as a result of some initiative on the part of the sponsoring organisation. These may be problems the organisation faces (such as rising maintenance costs on existing equipment) or capitalising on an opportunity (such as a new product launch).

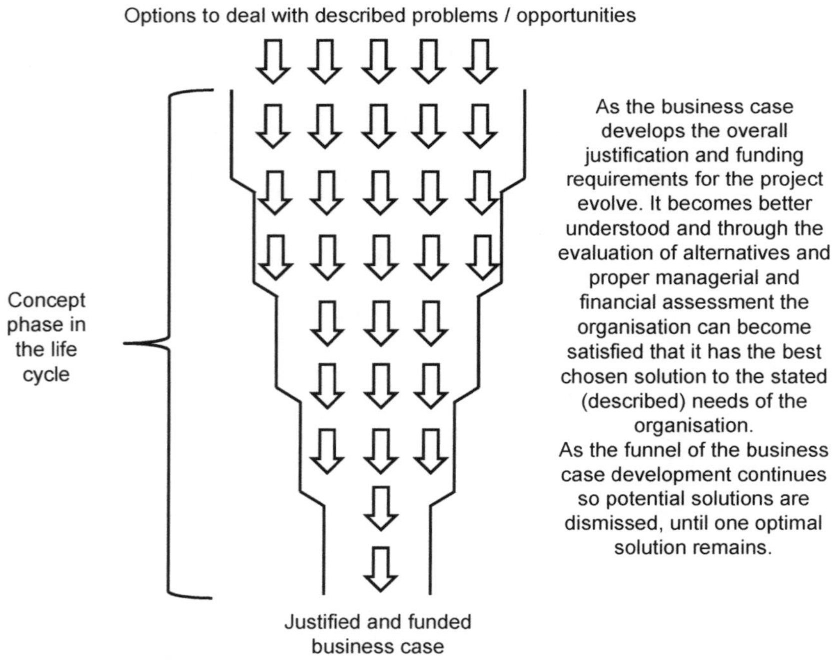

Options to deal with described problems / opportunities

Concept phase in the life cycle

As the business case develops the overall justification and funding requirements for the project evolve. It becomes better understood and through the evaluation of alternatives and proper managerial and financial assessment the organisation can become satisfied that it has the best chosen solution to the stated (described) needs of the organisation.
As the funnel of the business case development continues so potential solutions are dismissed, until one optimal solution remains.

Justified and funded business case

FIGURE 23 BUSINESS CASE DEVELOPMENT

Contents of a Typical Business Case

The business case balances the following three major topics:

Benefits — How much might be recovered from the investment, who might witness it and when will it be evidenced?

Costs — How much will it cost to produce the products that will collectively deliver the benefits?

Risks — What might go wrong with either of the above, a business case is mostly concerned with strategic risks (what might cause problems for the business)?

In doing so a Business Case also includes a number of key headings:

- Reason for the project (what problem or opportunity has it been commissioned to deal with).

- Benefits to be derived from the project, which can be financial or non financial.

- Risks — initially the strategic risks will be covered such that they can be dealt with through suitable mitigating actions well before the project proper gets underway.

- Options evaluation and justification of the chosen option (see financial investment appraisal below). As the funnel forces a gradual filtration and selection process so the various options will be discarded in favour of ultimately just one. This one option is then developed in the definition phase.

- Investment appraisal — generally an assessment of the relative costs and benefits of the project using financial and statistical modelling to understand how these balance.

- Constraints (the things that constrain our thinking) — an example might be being unable to gain access during certain hours. They are generally things over which the project has little or no control.

And for the chosen project option

- High level description of the project scope (what's included and what isn't).

- Estimated costs — these will evolve over time and it is not unusual to witness high level budgetary estimates in the business case with an ever increasing level of accuracy and detail emerging over time.

- Target schedule (key dates and milestones) — this again will be a high level schedule, possibly just a list of key deadlines to be met and further decomposed in the PMP later.

- Assumptions (the things we have taken to be true in order to proceed) — all through the business case development there is a need to use assumptions but care is required later on as these will inevitably lead to risks being created.

- Dependencies (what else needs to happen) — these need to be captured, recorded and managed to make sure that any external factors (mayoral elections, perhaps) do not impede progress.

- Success criteria are in the business case to make clear those things that the project is seeking to achieve. They are the end points, not the measure of progress (KPIs).

- Impact on business as usual. This is the disruption that may interfere with the normal operations of the business; for example, replacing a school hall may mean problems for the staff who need to hold large examinations there.

Roles in the Preparation of the Business Case

The question is always asked — who writes the business case?

The answer is not certain; the sponsor owns the business case, but they quite often will not be able to physically write the document as they will probably not have the time, the knowledge or the data. So who does contribute?

- The Sponsoring Group (Steering Group or Project Board) are the representatives of the organisation for whom the undertaking is being carried out. They oversee the construction of the business case in collaboration with the nominated Sponsor. They will be able to approve it and thereafter the Sponsor will use the business case as the reference point for the project.

- The sponsor oversees the construction of the business case in collaboration with the Sponsoring Group. They may well have specialised knowledge but must remember to use the experts that work for them and not presume too much based on their own expertise (or lack of it).

- The project manager may physically write the business case, or more likely (on a large project) will manage a 'mini project' to write it and in doing so may employ other staff.

- The suppliers may well have significant detailed knowledge to make the writing of the business case possible; for example, they may be experts in a particular process that the client is unaware of thus placing them in a good position to add value.

- The users know what they require by way of products and benefits; they need to separate musts from wants, prioritise the relevant aspects of the specification and provide advice to the sponsor as to the exact details of some of them.

- Subject matter experts, such as procurement specialists, management accountants, marketing professionals, drawn from within the organisation. These staff can be co-opted onto the team to enable proper analysis and decisions to be made.

- Often external consultants will be engaged to prepare the business case for a project. This has the distinct advantage of making the decision making process dispassionate.

How Business Case evolves through the Life Cycle

- During the Concept phase the business case is developed by the Project Manager and their advisers and once approved by the Sponsoring Group it will represent a 'one stop shop' where the primary justification for the project can be found and referenced. The original estimates generated during concept will be fairly high level and will be in need of further refinement. The business case is quite open minded at the start and will reflect the need to consider a number of options before narrowing down thinking to arrive at the recommended solution.

- During Definition, the business case needs to be reviewed alongside the evolving PMP. In truth the PMP is probably started during concept as the business case development will be subject to some of the procedures in the PMP and so they ought to go hand in hand to a large degree. As the PMP develops it will take a guide from the business case and will feed off some of the risk, success criteria and assumptions therein.

- During Development, the business case will form the cornerstone of the project evaluation. The PMP will govern the project but the business case sets out the benefits. If anything in the project has a potential to render the business case unachievable then the project manager and the sponsor will need to take remedial action (potentially even terminating the project if this mismatch is serious and significant enough). The business case benefits need to be reviewed during the Gate Reviews, this is in addition to the project performance and progress data.

- During Handover and Closure the business case needs to be checked to ensure that the products as delivered are suitable for acceptance as capable of yielding the anticipated benefits. The users will be in a position to advise the project teams and sponsor about this.

- During Benefits Realisation, the business case will form the main point of reference for the business to be assured that the benefits are being realised and to the value and timing anticipated.

WHIRLWIND BIKES

Think about the case study in Section SECTION 16. See if you can write a draft business case using the template produced here.

What are the Key Time scales

What are the Business Risks

What are the Main Costs

Quick Quiz (Answers In Section 18)

	Question	Options	Your Answer
1	Who owns the business case	a) The Client b) The Sponsoring Group c) The Project Manager d) The Project Sponsor	
2	A project will only be justified if the benefits outweigh the costs.	True or false?	
3	A project will always require a business case	True or false?	
4	When are benefits realised?	a) During operations b) During Termination c) During definition d) During implementation	
5	Suppliers may be able to provide specialist knowledge to help construct the business case	True of False?	

Use this space to make some notes

_____
_____
_____
_____
_____
_____
_____
_____
_____
_____

	What Kind of Questions Might There Be in the Exam?
1)	List and describe five key components of a Business Case
2)	List and describe the primary purpose of a Business Case and explain five key roles in the development of the Business case.

	Assessment Criteria

10.3	Explain benefits management

Success

Success is the satisfaction of the stakeholders' requirements stated at the start of the project. Benefits management is the mechanism for understanding what organisational benefits will accrue from the project and the systematic management of them until they are realised.

There are two complimentary views of success here.

Take the sponsor's perspective; they are tasked with the realisation of benefits because they own the project business case. The project manager is focused on delivering to time, cost and quality. These do not compete, but it is important to understand the nature of the differences.

Take an example of a new road bridge over a river. The project manager can build the most cost effective structure possible on time and to budget (as per their project management plan) but if nobody uses the bridge then there will be no practical benefit and any benefits inserted into the business case will obviously not be realised.

Question — is it possible to have a successful project which delivers to time, cost and quality that does not deliver benefit? Or conversely, is it possible to have an unsuccessful project (one that overspends, perhaps) that does realise benefit?

The answer, of course, is yes to both. The difficulty comes though if we do not have a sufficiently well-developed understanding of each, we find ourselves unable to really classify the project as a success or failure.

Fear not, the APM Body of Knowledge has a solution, but it does involve some terminology. Consider the introduction of a new high speed rail service:

Term	Definition	Example
Success Criteria	Those things, identified by the stakeholders, that need to be achieved in order for the project to be a success.	<ul><li>Was the project finished on time?</li><li>Can we operate at the advertised speed?</li><li>Is the system safe?</li></ul>

Term	Definition	Example
Benefits	The quantifiable and measurable improvement resulting from completion of project deliverables that is perceived as positive by a stakeholder. It will normally have a tangible value, expressed in monetary terms that will justify the investment.	▪ People travelling get to their destination quicker. ▪ The train operator makes a profit. ▪ Stations on the route encourage regeneration. ▪ N.B. It will be necessary to put a value on these if we want to fully conform to the definition.
Key Performance Indicators	Measures of success that can be used throughout the project to ensure that it is progressing towards a successful conclusion.	▪ During the project we might want to measure the rate at which we are laying the track. ▪ We might want to make sure that we have a happy team environment (survey, perhaps).
Success Factors	Factors that, when present in the project environment, are most conducive to the achievement of a successful project.	▪ A good and capable contractor with enough expertise and resources. ▪ A motivated team. ▪ A clear set of objectives. ▪ Timely decision making. ▪ Open and hones communication.
Critical Success Factors	The success factors that if absent would cause the project to fail.	▪ Failure to obtain planning permission would be a major blocker and potentially stop the project.

So there are a few things to remember about the terminology and definitions. If you grasp the principles of these here then the production of other project management material, such as the PMP, will be easier.

Once you have defined the success criteria for your project, it ought to be possible to produce a set of deliverables and plans to enable you to satisfy yourselves that you can meet them. Thus the success criteria ought to be a natural outcome.

Benefits Management Process

The Body of Knowledge recommends the following three stages: identify and agree, monitor and manage, and realise. These are explained in Figure 24.

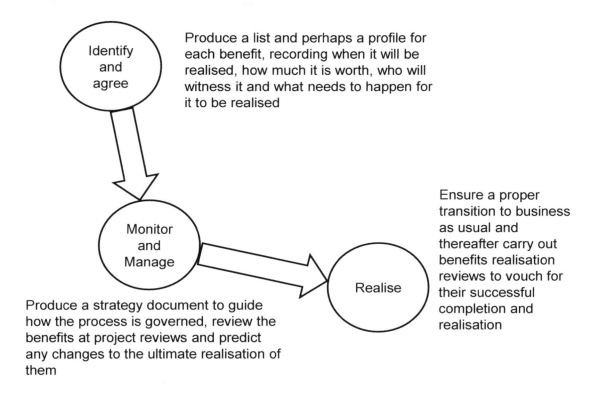

FIGURE 24 A SIMPLE BENEFITS MANAGEMENT PROCESS

There is a danger in presenting benefits management as a systematic and procedural technique, because some of its importance and implications are lost. The only reason a project is undertaken is to achieve a change. It is highly unlikely that an organisation would embark upon any project in the ready anticipation of things being worse afterwards. The role of benefits management is crucial to being able to quantify the benefits so that they can be tracked throughout the project and actually realised thereafter.

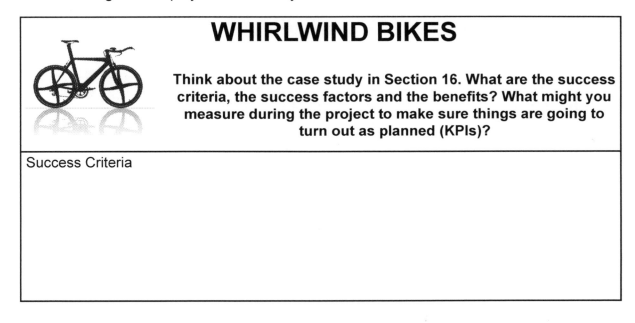

WHIRLWIND BIKES

Think about the case study in Section 16. What are the success criteria, the success factors and the benefits? What might you measure during the project to make sure things are going to turn out as planned (KPIs)?

Success Criteria

Success Factors		

Benefits (identify two and fill in the boxes for each)		
	Benefit 1	Benefit 2
Name of benefit?		
How much is it worth?		
Who will perceive it?		
When will it be realised?		
What risks might affect its realisation?		

Quick Quiz (Answers In Section 18)

	Question	Options	Your Answer
1	The benefits management process includes _____, Monitor and Manage, Realise	a) Identify and Agree b) Shape and Agree c) Populate and Agree d) Decide and Agree	
2	Benefits should be measurable	True or False?	
3	The business case will include the project benefits	True or false?	
4	Benefits are used to outweigh the costs of a project to make sure it is viable	True or False	
5	The business case is always one great big document	True of False?	

Use this space to make some notes

_____
_____
_____
_____
_____
_____
_____
_____

What Kind of Questions Might There Be in the Exam?

1)	Describe the term 'Benefit' and explain a simple process for the management of benefits.
2)	Describe the term 'Success Criteria' and explain how they are instrumental in managing a project.

Assessment Criteria

10.4 Explain the use of Payback, Internal Rate of Return and Net Present Value as investment appraisal techniques

Financial Investment Appraisal

During the development of the business case, the organisation can deploy some key financial appraisal techniques to help understand the financial aspects of the project's viability. The three that the APM would like you to consider are described below.

Payback Method

Using this method a project's projected income can be compared with its initial cost to help understand when the initial investment will be recovered. The payback is expressed as a number of years.

Year	Investment £	Income £
0 (now)	16,000	0
1	0	3,000
2	0	3,000
3	0	4,000
4	0	4,000
5	0	4,000
6	0	5,000
7	0	10,000
Total	16,000	33,000

This project will pay back its investment during year 5 (i.e. when the net income equals the investment — 4.5 years in this case)

FIGURE 25 THE PAYBACK METHOD

Benefits of the payback method	Disadvantages with the payback method
Quick to calculate.	It assumes that money is worth the same now as in the future.
Simple to calculate.	Does not take into account any income after the payback period.
Easily understood.	Does not take into account the future value of money (see NPV later in this section).

Net Present Value

Using the net present value (NPV) method it is possible to make allowances for how the value of money changes over time. Would you for example prefer to have £100 now or £100 in five years time? The answer to this is dependent upon a whole raft of data, some of which we are unaware of at the time we make the choice. To a business, cash now is much more valuable than cash in the future, partly because businesses often have to borrow money to invest in projects. To adjust for this cost of capital we reduce the value of further returns by a discount factor. These are set for each organisation based on its own policies. An accountant in each organisation will define multipliers (discount factors) to apply to the future income and investments. These adjustments seek to normalise the future values to today's prices so we can compare each to the investment. Taking our project from earlier, consider the following:

You do not usually need to calculate the rates of multipliers when carrying out these sorts of calculations; they are usually provided by the organisation's management accountants.

Taking the example from above if we assume a Discount Rate of 10% the multipliers appear in the table below as the 'Discount Factor'. The resultant perception of the Present Value of each of these appears in the right hand column

Year	Investment (£)	Income (£)	Discount factor	Present Value (£)	
0 (now)	16,000	0	1	(16,000)	The discount factors used here are derived from the assumption of a 10% discount rate
1	0	3,000	0.909	2,727	
2	0	3,000	0.826	2,478	
3	0	4,000	0.751	3,004	
4	0	4,000	0.683	2,732	
5	0	4,000	0.621	2,484	
6	0	5,000	0.564	2,820	
7	0	10,000	0.513	5,130	
Total	16,000	33,000		21,375	
			Net Present Value	21,375 − 16,000 = 5,375	

FIGURE 26 NPV DEMONSTRATED WITH A DISCOUNT FACTOR OF 10%

As mentioned earlier, the calculation of a net present value is very heavily reliant upon the choice of discount factor. If the wrong one is chosen a very different conclusion can be drawn about the viability of the project. Suppose we used a 20% Discount Rate to drive the same calculations as in Figure 26 above. We would arrive at the figures as in Figure 27 below.

In the case of the NPV calculation above, the profitability of the project is £5,375. Watch what happens if we choose a 20% discount factor:

Year	Investment (£)	Income (£)	Discount factor	Present Value (£)	
0 (now)	16,000	0	1	(16,000)	The discount factors used here are derived from the assumption of a 20% discount rate
1	0	3,000	0.833	2,499	
2	0	3,000	0.694	2,082	
3	0	4,000	0.597	2,388	
4	0	4,000	0.482	1,928	
5	0	4,000	0.402	1,608	
6	0	5,000	0.335	1,675	
7	0	10,000	0.279	2,790	
Total	16,000	33,000		14,970	
			Net Present Value	14,970 − 16,000 = minus 1,030	

FIGURE 27 NPV DEMONSTRATED WITH A DISCOUNT FACTOR OF 20%

If we compare these two tables side by side the conclusion must be that if we use a 10% rate the project is worth doing, if we use a 20% rate it is not. A reasonably profitable project has turned into one that will make a loss. This is purely and simply down to the choice of the discount rate. These variables can have a huge impact on the decisions an organisation may make about which project to pursue and indeed whether to pursue any at all. There is one final mechanism of analysis that can help remove this problem and it is referred to as the Internal Rate of Return or IRR.

Benefits of the NPV method	Disadvantages of the NPV method
Takes into account the future of money.	Quite complex to calculate.
Looks at the whole project life cycle.	Reliant on which percentage is used as the discount rate.
Yields a single figure for profitability.	The more detailed calculation implies greater certainty that is not justified.

Internal Rate of Return

If we consider the present values of the two scenarios above (i.e. Assuming 10% and 20%), then we have some data to analyse using the internal rate of return (IRR) method of investment appraisal.

The Internal Rate of Return is defined as the discount rate at which the present value of the future cash flow is equal to the initial investment or, in the other words , the rate at which the investment breaks even.

Year	Present Value (£) @ 10%	Present Value (£) @ 20%	
0 (now)	(24,000)	(24,000)	
1	4,091	3,749	
2	3,717	3,123	We can plot the two figures from the NPV row on the previous two tables
3	4,506	3,582	
4	4,098	2,892	
5	3,726	2,412	
6	4,230	2,513	
7	7,695	4,185	
NPV	8,063	1,545	

FIGURE 28 NPV VARIABILITY DEPENDING ON RATE

When we look at this on a graph we can demonstrate the IRR for this project. There is a mechanism to calculate the exact figure, but for the purposes of this guide it is merely necessary to describe the principle rather than opt for 100% accuracy.

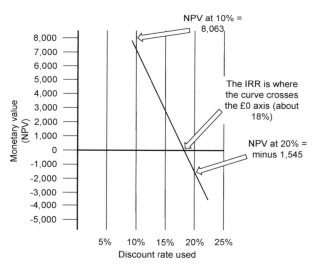

FIGURE 29 INTERNAL RATE OF RETURN

Benefits of the IRR method	Disadvantages of the IRR method
Takes into account the future of money.	Quite complex to calculate.
The choice of discount factor is not relevant.	Difficult to calculate with accuracy.
Can compare with an organisation's flat rate expectation of return.	Can result in multiple results in some particular circumstances.

Managerial Judgment

There are a number of ways in which an organisation judges its investments that is not necessarily based on sheer weight of financial evidence. In some circumstances an organisation may choose to do a project even though the investment does not appear to be worthwhile, or indeed vice versa. The managers of an organisation have the final say over how their investment capital is spent. If projects have a business case that is not positive (i.e. the benefits outweigh the costs), great care is needed throughout to ensure that incorrect decisions are not made through the life of the project predicated on incorrect financial assumptions.

 Quick Quiz (Answers In Section 18)

	Question	Options	Your Answer
1	A weakness of the payback method is what?	a) It is simple to calculate b) It requires a complicated graph to understand it c) It is hard to calculate d) It does not take into account the future value of money	
2	A weakness of IRR is that it is quite complex to calculate	True or False?	
3	A strength of the Payback method is that it is simple to calculate	True of False	
4	The discount rates used to calculate NPVs will normally be provided by whom?	a) The project manager b) The project sponsor c) The users d) The company's accountants	
5	Financial Investment Appraisal takes precedence over managerial judgement	True or False?	

 Use this space to make some notes

_____
_____
_____
_____
_____
_____
_____
_____

	What Kind of Questions Might There Be in the Exam?
1)	List and describe three investment appraisal techniques and the strengths and weaknesses of each

	Assessment Criteria
10.5	Explain an information management system
10.6	Explain a typical project reporting cycle

Information Management Systems

Accurate information is the life blood of any organisation; in its absence, it is impossible to operate. Project information begins to be accumulated right from the start. The project manager needs to make sure that all the information that is collected (whether planned or not) is stored securely. In the modern world we often think of information as being electronic; our servers replace filing cabinets, our PCs our ring binders. There is still a huge amount of information that is stored physically , but most organisations now have computerised workflow and document management processes and systems at their disposal.

Consideration must be given to some of the legislative arrangements around information and how it is used, such as the Data Protection Act, Freedom of Information Act, and perhaps the Official Secrets Act. These are also components of the project context or environment.

A typical information management system ought to be able to accommodate the following key aspects:

Information Management Plan

As a subsidiary plan in the project management plan, the information management plan would contain the following:

- Scope — what information will be covered in the plan?

- Roles and responsibilities — who on the project does what, regarding information?

- Tools and techniques — what systems are available to be used?

- Process — what processes are going to be followed?

- Audit — how will assurance and verification of the plan be carried out?

Information Collection

The project manager needs to think very carefully about how much information is collected and processed. The less that is collected, the less needs to be analysed and processed. The principle generally is that only the information actually needed should be gathered. Reports should be kept to a minimum, in a standard format, recording only the information that is needed on which to act properly. It is relatively easy to gather information, the trick is to gather only the right information. Information now falls into many different categories:

- Written — words, reports, specifications, memos, correspondence.

- Video — marketing material, training material, etc.

- Audio — pod casts, voice mail, recorded conversations.

- Web-based or streamed — You Tube, Twitter, e-learning, etc.

- Physical — such as models and prototypes.

- Biological — such as samples or DNA.

All of these might need to be captured and stored. There is no need to go too far, but care may be needed if evidence is required.

Stakeholders may introduce unsolicited information and this is perhaps the most difficult to deal with. The project (as a result of its information management plan) will be able to classify and assimilate the information it knows about, it will be far more difficult to do so with information that it is not or has not been aware of.

Information Storage

In its simplest form electronic storage is very easy with modern tools and techniques. Care should be exercised though, as there are a number of issues that can, if not dealt with appropriately, cause difficulties. As a minimum, the project should have standards associated with naming conventions, access security, backups, version control and accessibility. Document management systems have the potential to resolve a lot of these issues if used sensibly, but are not a replacement for a sound set of management controls.

Information Dissemination

The project will need to keep careful records of who needs what information and when. When something changes, who needs to know? How will the information be sent out — is it via email, paper, etc? What security arrangements need to be wrapped around these processes?

Information Storage

A lot of information needs to be kept for a minimum period of time, for example, tax information, security clearances and training records. The project may need to negotiate with the organisation within which it is operating to understand these constraints and make appropriate arrangements to conform to them. It is not really very useful to archive information without a very good cataloguing system so that information can be retrieved when necessary. Where physical information is concerned, then clearly larger expensive and controlled environments will be required.

Information Destruction

Most information may be retained for periods of time without too much difficulty, but care should be exercised so that it is not retained excessively or in breach of any legislative arrangements. The cost of retaining information indefinitely is enormous and regular audits and housekeeping is vital.

Information Reporting

Information management is not an end in itself, but a mechanism to ensure the probity of data for the purpose of dissemination. The process of transmitting formal data is via an information reporting process. There are some basic principles around information reporting.

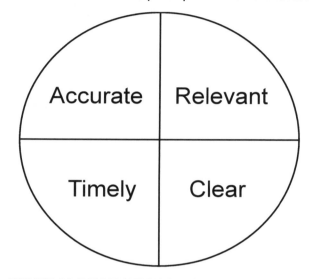

FIGURE 30 INFORMATION REPORTING PRINCIPLES

Keep it relevant — try and keep your information volume to the minimum to achieve the objectives. Examples are template reports, such as highlight reports or exception reports. Make sure you understand the audience.

Keep it clear — use graphs and charts to get the message across without 'clutter'. Examples are the milestone slip charts and Gantt charts.

Keep it timely — monthly reports can report on data up to eight weeks old; on a three-month project, this is not useful. Make sure you know the important cycles and conform.

Keep it accurate — be prepared to be challenged and that you can substantiate any data submitted. The principle of making decisions base don accurate data is well established. If there is any doubt about the accuracy of any of the key data then these concerns will need to be raised.

(Project) Reporting Cycle

Typically organisations as part of their governance framework will impose a rigid reporting cycle. If they do not it is good practice for project managers to follow a standard approach each week/month/quarter/year.

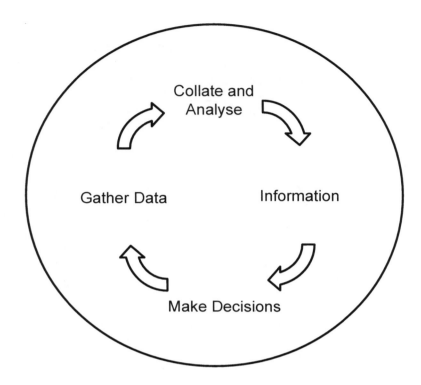

FIGURE 31 A REPORTING CYCLE

For example

- Friday afternoon - Time sheets for the project team collected and analysed by the project office who analyse them and make sure the time booked goes into the correct bucket against the correct WBS codes.

- Monday morning the Project Office produce a summary sheet for the project manger to review and approve.

- The project office then update the relevant schedules to make sure that an accurate reflection of progress is portrayed and all of the project percent complete figures are up to date.

- The project manager holds a team meeting to review progress and consider the schedules in conjunction with the teams verbal updates the meeting.

- Any corrections are made and the project progress report is produced incorporating all other data necessary such as earned value, quality reviews, changes, forecasts etc.

- The report is used at the Wednesday customer meeting where the progress is discussed and any remedial action considered and instigated.

- Each month the latest aggregated weekly reports are considered at the project board meeting where strategic decisions are taken based upon the progress to date and any new matters that need to be undertaken.

- The cycle then repeats itself and so it goes on. This process is not exhaustive and certainly not necessarily fit for all purposes but it is indicative of the kind of process that underpins many projects.

WHIRLWIND BIKES
Consider the case study and what would the reporting arrangement be?

What regular reports would you produce?

What would they contain?

Who would the audience be?

What decisions might they support?

Quick Quiz (Answers In Section 18)

	Question	Options	Your Answer
1	Which of these components is not a component of information management	a) Collection b) Retrieval c) Archiving d) Change Control	
2	Personal information can be kept forever regardless if it is needed or not	True or False?	
3	Every project needs a IT server	True of False	
4	Who is responsible for writing the Information Management Plan	a) The project manager b) The project sponsor c) The users d) The company's accountants	
5	Information management is only important on the largest projects	True or False?	

Use this space to make some notes

What Kind of Questions Might There Be in the Exam?

1)	List and describe five main components of an information management process

	Assessment Criteria

10.7   Explain the purpose of the project management plan and its importance throughout the project life cycle

10.8   Describe typical contents of a project management plan

10.9   Outline the authorship, approval and audience of a project management plan

Why Do We Need a Project Management Plan?

A project management plan or PMP creates a document that can be used by everyone to help:

- Explain the nature of the project. Be able to prescribe its scope, the material deliverables, time scales and roles and responsibilities.

- Communicate the various strategies and plans to a wider audience. The document needs to be a working document, such that its contents are known, it is up to date and visible to everyone.

- Provide a baseline from which further measurement and analysis of variation can take place. It is the key document when it comes to recording and reporting variations from the plan.

- Form a 'contract' between the project manager and the project sponsor. In a client/supplier relationship the PMP may well be part of the contract, but even in an inhouse environment, the PMP represents an agreement between the project manager and the sponsor.

- Provide a mechanism for continuity throughout the project life cycle. There is no guarantee of continuity of staff and the PMP provides the single document that provides the ability to make sure that all the relevant information necessary to run the project is available and up to date.

The PMP is finalised at the end the definition phase. However, it may well exist in draft form during the concept phase to keep a record of processes and tools as the thinking develops. Clearly the PMP is finalised after the business case is issued. Much of what is in the business case feeds the PMP and provides much of the overall strategy and background details. The business case will need to have a comprehensive understanding of the environment of a project and, as a result, heavily influences the project strategy.

For example, a business case, during its feasibility studies, will determine whether to make or buy a particular component. Having made that decision, the organisation's decision will need to be reflected in the PMP. The PMP will then take forward this principle further and develop the specific activities needed to implement this approach. It will turn the businesses strategic decisions into practical steps and define the delivery strategy for the project.

Contents of a PMP

FIGURE 32 THE CONCEPT OF THE PROJECT MANAGEMENT PLAN

The PMP has potentially a large number of contents that basically fall into the categories of:

WHY	The project management plan is built on the work done in the project business case. The reason for the project will be reproduced or referenced from the business case. Basically, it provides an explanation to the project team as to why the project is important enough for the organisation to invest time, money and effort. The business case 'sets the scene' for the PMP. It is very often a separate document (or series of documents). As a minimum, it contains: • Description of benefits • Statement of requirements • Project objectives.
WHAT	This section describes the nature of the project deliverables created to satisfy the project requirements and organisation needs. Particularly, it helps to describes the: • Project scope of the project, including being specific about what is included and excluded. • Product specifications for each of the main products to be delivered by the project. • Acceptance criteria, which define how the 'customer' will approve the deliverables. • Constraints, such as critical time slots or limitations on resources. • Assumptions, of which the plan has been formulated, such as the availability of access to a system or site to complete the project.

WHO	This is defined by an organisation chart showing who is involved in the project. Also called a organisational breakdown structure (OBS), it can be used to map the various roles to the individuals using a responsibility assignment matrix. This yields a valuable document for the project manager to control the project. Contents relating to this typically include: ▪ Responsibility assignment matrix, which defines who is responsible for the completion of each product. ▪ Organisational breakdown structure, which shows the organisational hierarchy of the project. ▪ Authority and delegation schedules, which define the delegation of authority within the project for the approval of documents, expenditures and acceptance. ▪ Role descriptions, which clearly define the overall responsibilities within the project.
HOW MUCH	This section summarises the project budget, the mechanisms for cost management and how variances are to be dealt with. Being able to predict with some certainty the rate at which the project will be spending its funds is crucial to knowing whether we are on track or not. ▪ Budget, including a time phasing, which shows when the funding will be required. ▪ Earned value arrangements for tracking actual cost and progress against the plan. ▪ Cash flow forecasts showing the balance of income vs costs for the project. This is of particular importance to contracting organisations. ▪ Variation actions, describing the procedures for agreeing changes in cost. ▪ Cost management procedures, including procedures for reviewing the estimated costs and maintaining up to date forecasts.
WHEN	The project schedule is a key document within a PMP. This may be limited to a high-level summary Gantt chart of the key milestones and stages. This is supported by a range of other scheduling information. Specific contents include: ▪ Precedence Diagrams. ▪ Resource Histograms. ▪ Gantt Charts. ▪ Project life cycle.

	This section describes the strategy for running the project. It contains the various subsidiary plans and strategies that will be deployed to arrive at the desired outcome. These ancillary plans are very often separate documents. Indeed a lot of project-based organisations may already have well-developed template plans that can be adopted by the project, rather than inventing new ones from scratch. Specific contents might include: • Project methods, which include standards for design work and review of products; • Health and safety plan, which includes the roles and responsibilities for health, and a description of how those specific risks will be managed; • Quality plan, which includes responsibilities for quality and how it will be controlled; • Procurement strategy, which includes a summary of how goods and services will be acquired, for example, through competitive tendering; • Communication plan, which describes the different communication methods that will be used for each group of stakeholders, such as public meetings for local residents; • Risk management plan, which describes the overall approach to risk, and how risk will be identified and managed; • Change control procedures, which describe the detailed process for identifying, assessing and approving changes.
HOW	

The PMP has two distinct types of content

Policies (how the project will be run)	Schedules and Plans (what exactly will we produce, when, for how much and who will do it)
Stakeholder Management Plan	Stakeholder Analysis
Risk Management Plan	Risk Log
Change Control Process	Change Control Log
Configuration Management Process	Configuration Library
Issue Management Plan	Issue Log
Quality Plan	Quality (defects log)
Resource Management Plan	Resource Plan
Monitoring and Control Procedures	Earned Value Reports
Health and Safety Plan	Health and Safety Log
Planning and Estimating Processes	Gantt Chart

PLEASE NOTE - the above table has been produced to indicate the difference between the processes that are followed to run the project on a day to day basis and the various schedules or plans that are consequential upon running those processes. There is no one to one mapping between the processes identified and the schedules on the right. They are for example only. You will notice though that these 'processes/policies/procedures' on the left are all dealt with within the syllabus. They are the things a PM must do to ensure their project is properly managed.

Use of the PMP Throughout the Life Cycle

It is quite easy to contemplate the use of the project management plan at the start of the project. Maintaining it throughout the project, however, is perhaps a bit more challenging. The PMP is a controlled document. The project manager will own the PMP and ensure that it is continually reviewed and used. The purpose is not to simply just create one and then leave it languishing on a shelf.

- The PMP should be used as a communications tool and be circulated to those who have a need to see it.

- It should be regularly reviewed to ensure it is still accurate and continues to reflect the needs described in the business case.

- Each of the contents can refer to other ancillary documents (such as a risk log). It is important that these linkages are correct and maintained.

- Changes must be conveyed to the audience of the document.

- It can be used as the basis for audits and reviews.

Work based exercise	
See if you can find an example of a project management plan and have a look at the contents. Does it have the following in it?	
Definition and Information	**Policies and Procedures**

Definition and Information		Policies and Procedures	
Scope		Risk management plan	
Success criteria		Stakeholder management plan	
Assumptions		Change control procedure	
Risks		Configuration management procedure	
Project Schedule		Communications plan	
Organisation chart		Quality plan	
Project life cycle		Health and safety plan	
Acceptance procedure		Monitoring and control procedures	

 Use this space to make some notes

_____
_____
_____
_____
_____

Quick Quiz (Answers In Section 18)

	Question	Options	Your Answer
1	Who owns the project management plan?	a) The project sponsor b) The project manager c) The procurement department d) The users	
2	Which of these is not contained in the project management plan?	a) The business case b) The risk management plan c) The project objectives d) The success criteria	
3	Changes to the project management plan are approved by who?	a) The project sponsor b) The project manager c) The procurement department d) The users	
4	If a subsidiary plan (e.g. a risk management plan) already exists, you can use that instead of writing your own.	True or false?	
5	The circulation of the PMP is limited to…?	a) The project manager and the sponsor b) The project manager, users and sponsor c) Anybody who has an involvement in the project d) Anybody with a direct involvement with the project	

What Kind of Questions Might There Be in the Exam?

1)	List and describe five main components of a Project Management Plan

Assessment Criteria

10.10 Explain estimating techniques

10.11 Explain the reasons and benefits of re-estimating through the project life cycle and the concept of the estimating funnel

Estimating Accuracy

There are numerous published works on the problems associated with estimating. The only truth when considering estimating is that you know exactly how much something is going to cost just after you have finished it. Project managers, though, are likely to get two questions asked of them fairly frequently — how much is it going to cost and when will it be finished?

The graph below demonstrates the findings that estimating accuracy improves as we get further into the project. Here at the end of concept we are +20% to -10% out from the eventual cost. The detailed estimates that we get improve as time goes by.

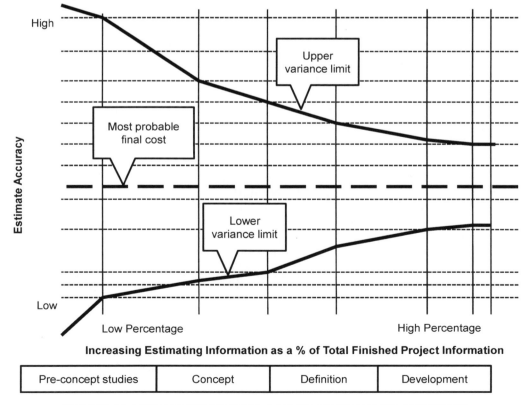

FIGURE 33 THE WAY ESTIMATING ACCURACY IMPROVES OVER TIME

They key factor in accuracy of the estimate is our knowledge about the project as represented by the bottom axis. By the time we commit to the project implementation we ought to be in possession of about 85% of the available information and this will mean our estimates are roughly +10% to -4%. This will be only true if we have made the investment to collect the information needed for a valid estimate.

Difficulties Obtaining Estimates

There are a number of reasons for poor estimates. Predominantly we are trying to predict the future and it is inherently unpredictable. We can improve our chances of getting a more refined and accurate estimate but there are counter forces at work that mitigate against this.

- **Subjectivity** — almost all estimates contain an element of subjectivity because they rely on an individual's experience and knowledge to help obtain a reasoned estimate. Those individuals will have their own bias and prejudices and probably bitter experience. This will inevitably sway their judgment. The project manager needs to understand what the individuals have taken into account to try and peel back the layers to get to the root of the estimate and discount any bias.

- **Assumptions** — we make these during a project with the objective of moving things forward. There is a huge opportunity for these to be erroneous and as a result any deductions are incorrect. If these are documented then they can be analysed to give a true picture of the problem. The project manager can challenge these assumptions to establish the facts rather than proceeding on unfounded assumptions.

- **Not knowing who will do the work** — if we make an estimate for a piece of work, we often use our own knowledge and skill and do not make adjustments to compensate for the uncertainty introduced because another person may actually do the work. Wherever possible the project manager will get the estimate from the person who is going to do the work. Where this is not possible the project manager can eliminate the bias through challenge and by seeking different views on the estimate.

- **Risks** — in project work, the element of risk is critical to a good estimate. Inherent risk means that we cannot fully understand the potential for problems delay or over-run. This in itself is not an estimating issue but our attempts to allow for risk occurrences can merely introduce a further layer of uncertainty. We need to be clear how risks are included within the estimate. Often people will add 'contingency' into a task estimate without declaring it. This is quite dangerous and can inflate some estimates unnecessarily and is usually not systematic, understood or based on any real information.

- **Lack of previous data** — if we have never undertaken this type of project before we will have little or no knowledge of how to do it. We will be unable to arrive at a considered estimate without significant up front work and even then the element of risk will be increased. Where this data is available then it will clearly be of paramount importance. It should be collected from the actual out-turns of earlier projects and must be used intelligently in case mistakes of the past are not replicated.

Despite all of this there are a number of recognised estimating techniques that allow us to systematically understand the problem and provide some tools to help us get better at estimating.

Comparative Estimating

A comparative estimate is where we take a single known project and simply scale it up and make any allowances that we can to help arrive at a better value. For example, if we built a warehouse last week and it was 300,000m³ and we are building another next year which is 400,000m³, we can scale up the cost proportionately by 4/3. We would then have to take into account any variables that were not proportional; for example, although bigger, the new building may be higher and so the same (or even possibly less) land area may be used thus affecting the cost.

Bottom Up Estimating

If we know the component parts through a process of scope definition we can build up a more thorough and detailed idea of the top level cost. This type of estimate relies on a very well-developed understanding of the various components and is therefore not really possible during the early stages of a project. The diagram in Figure 34 seeks to demonstrate how a top level project cost can be derived by adding up all the constituent parts from the developed product breakdown structure (PBS). The same principle can be applied to a WBS in the same manner.

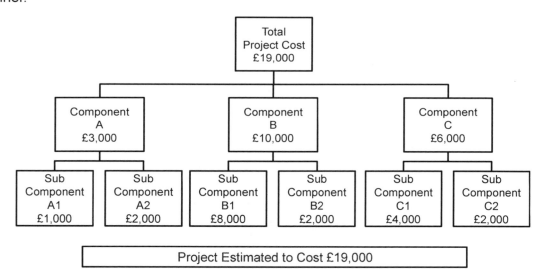

FIGURE 34 AN EXAMPLE OF BOTTOM UP ESTIMATING

Parametric Estimating

This form of estimate relies on multiplying out a known number of units by the price of those units. For example, if we wanted to lay 100 miles of railway track and we knew how much it was per mile (say £1m) then 100 miles of track would cost £100m. It is simple and quick. However, of course, the problems are that if there is a small error in the base data then it will cause significant errors later on. It also relies on a very well-developed body of data on which to draw, which would have been built up over a long period of time and they must be representative of the job we are doing now. We could not rely on the price for a mile of road and use that for our railway estimate. Parametric is relatively quick though, as all we need are the raw numbers to put into our model. We might also run into the problem whereby that PARTICULAR mile of track costs a lot more while ANOTHER PARTICULAR mile costs a lot less. There will be elements of 'swings and roundabouts' at play.

Three Point Estimating

A three point estimate seeks to remove some of the vagaries of calculating a single point estimate. It can be easier to estimate a minimum and maximum cost within which the true cost lies. The estimate can be improved further using a three point estimate for the best case, most likely and worst case estimate for a cost or duration, consider Figure 35.

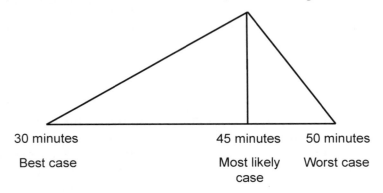

| 30 minutes | 45 minutes | 50 minutes |
| Best case | Most likely case | Worst case |

FIGURE 35 AN EXAMPLE OF THREE POINT ESTIMATING

In fact, we can combine these estimates using a PERT formula:

Best estimate = (1 x best case) + (4 x most likely case) + (1 x worst case) / 6

For example, consider your journey to work:

Best case (if no traffic) = 30 minutes

Most likely Case (normal traffic) = 45 minutes

Worst case = 50 minutes

The best estimate would be 43 minutes, slightly better than the most likely. This is equivalent to the time it would take you to get to work, assuming your travel pattern followed a PERT distribution. However, your boss would not be very happy because you would be late most of the time if you predicted 43 minutes and always more often than not achieved 45 (the most likely case).

The second use of three point estimating is to use multiple estimates to run a statistical modelling technique using a computer. This provides the ability to arrive at a statistical estimate by combining a lot of individual three point estimates together. This is called Monte Carlo modelling. In a number of industries you may come across the term Quantitative Modelling and three point estimating is the root of that technique. It is not in the APMP syllabus, but is mentioned only as an extension to the three point technique as above.

 Use this space to make some notes

_____

_____

_____

_____

_____
_____
_____
_____
_____
_____
_____

WHIRLWIND BIKES

If you had to estimate how long the road testing might take, how might you do it? There are a specific number of miles to be covered and a period of time. What do you need to know? How might you calculate it?

Quick Quiz (Answers In Section 18)

	Question	Options	Your Answer
1	A comparative estimate will compare one project with another.	True or false?	
2	A comparative estimate may be most useful at which point in the project?	a) Beginning b) Middle c) End	

	Question	Options	Your Answer
3	What other technique is fundamental to the creation of a bottom up estimate?	a) WBS b) OBS c) PBS d) Gantt chart	
4	Who should the project manager consult in the creation of estimates?	a) The suppliers b) The users c) The sponsor d) All of the above	
5	Where would the high level estimates first be recorded?	a) Business case b) PMP c) Risk management plan d) Lessons learned report	
6	Input to parametric estimates might not include what?	a) Price per tone b) Man day cost c) Mile of road d) PERT	
7	A PERT calculation has a divisor of 6	True or False	
8	It is easier to calculate the estimate as the life cycle progresses.	True or false?	

	What Kind of Questions Might There Be in the Exam?
1)	List and describe three types of estimating technique and give examples of where two of them might be used in the life cycle.
2)	List and describe four elements that can cause estimates to be inaccurate and what the project manager can do to try and prevent these problems.

	Assessment Criteria

10.12 Describe stakeholder management processes

10.13 Explain the importance of managing stakeholder expectations

Stakeholder Management Process

The definition of a stakeholder is someone who has a vested interest in the outcome of a project. This is based on the fact that each stakeholder may have a differing view about the project and may support it (or otherwise). They may also have an opportunity to exert influence over the project in a positive or negative manner. There are key stakeholders who may not want a project to go ahead. History is littered with projects that have failed to understand the magnitude of hostility towards their project or indeed the wave of enthusiasm and support that can be tapped.

There is a danger that the identification of stakeholders is the end of the story. In fact it is only the start. A stakeholder management process appears below: This once again would normally be embedded within the overall Project Management Plan.

Identify	We need to come up with a way of identifying stakeholders. If you work in a well-understood organisation and have been there for some time, you may well have come into contact with all the existing stakeholders. Teleport yourself to a new project with a new customer and you might need to start from scratch. Company organisation charts, web sites, interviewing people, brainstorming sessions, talking to peers and colleagues, and generally working the system will reveal a whole host of people who may or may not have power and/or influence over what happens on your project.
Assess	Having got a list of the stakeholders, your next challenge is to understand which ones are important. The grid the APM advocate is a two by two matrix as appears here. The principle is that you should be able to identify who are the influential people and position them in their relative positions. It is always difficult when doing these to know whether you are plotting them as at the start of the project or during it. The answer is that you need to be able to produce a management plan. The plan implies that you will want to take action over some of the stakeholders. The action will cause a change of position for some of them. Therefore it is important to place them where they are now and the plan will describe how you will get them to where you want them to be (or possibly stay where they are).

	## Stakeholder Analysis 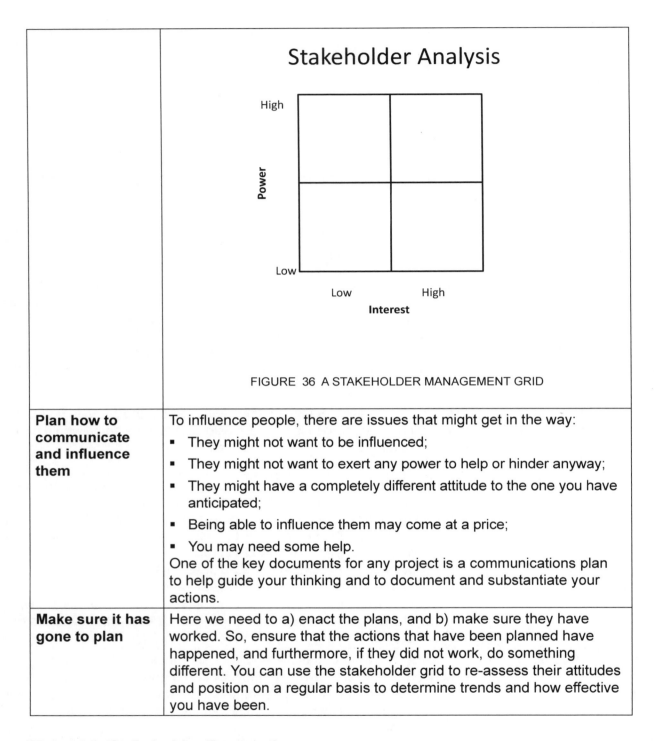 FIGURE 36 A STAKEHOLDER MANAGEMENT GRID
Plan how to communicate and influence them	To influence people, there are issues that might get in the way: ■ They might not want to be influenced; ■ They might not want to exert any power to help or hinder anyway; ■ They might have a completely different attitude to the one you have anticipated; ■ Being able to influence them may come at a price; ■ You may need some help. One of the key documents for any project is a communications plan to help guide your thinking and to document and substantiate your actions.
Make sure it has gone to plan	Here we need to a) enact the plans, and b) make sure they have worked. So, ensure that the actions that have been planned have happened, and furthermore, if they did not work, do something different. You can use the stakeholder grid to re-assess their attitudes and position on a regular basis to determine trends and how effective you have been.

Managing Stakeholder Expectations

The importance of managing cannot be underestimated. The project manager will need to ensure that not only are the stakeholder community properly analysed and categorised bu that the appropriate amount of attention is applied to each, depending on their relative power and interest. Failure to do this may result in

- Inability to fully understand the requirements. The users represent a significant element of the stakeholder community. Without their input it will prove difficult to obtain sufficient information relating to nature of the requirements and what acceptability might look like.

- The risks may be difficult if not impossible to determine, because we would not have had the opportunity to engage with sufficient stakeholder to properly understand them.

- Their may be significant pressure groups or parties against the project such that the progress would be delayed and potentially prevented

- The benefits cannot be fully understood. The beneficial aspects of the project are understood by the stakeholders and they are the ones who will be the recipient of those benefits

- We cannot truly acknowledge the influence of our own organisation on our success. Internal stakeholders can be just as fundamental to progress as external ones

WHIRLWIND BIKES

Carry out a stakeholder analysis for the case study and recreate a stakeholder grid and populate the various boxes with names or job titles. You might need to use your own experience to help in some of the areas.

Stakeholder Analysis

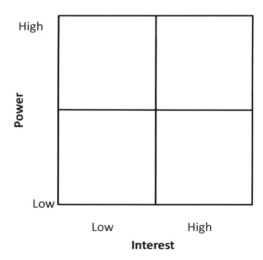

Use this space to make some notes

Quick Quiz (Answers In Section 18)

	Question	Options	Your Answer
1	The axes of a stakeholder grid are what?	a) Power and influence b) Interest and knowledge c) Commitment and power d) Brains and help	
2	Which of these is not a stage in stakeholder management?	a) Identify b) Assess c) Plan d) Negotiate	
3	Which of these is classified as a stakeholder	a) The Sponsor b) The Client c) The Team d) All of the Above	
4	Some of the problems associated with stakeholder management are that in assessing relative power and influence, personal judgment can take a big part.	True or false?	
5	Understanding the stakeholders on a project will be key to understanding which project manager to appoint.	a) True b) False c) Will certainly help	

What Kind of Questions Might There Be in the Exam?

1)	Describe five main components of a stakeholder management process

 Assessment Criteria

10.14 Describe advantages and disadvantages of earned value management

10.15 Perform earned value calculations and interpret earned value data

These are covered in Section 11 of this Study Guide as they are far more easily explained after the concept of scheduling has been discussed.

SECTION 11

SCHEDULE AND RESOURCE MANAGEMENT

This section contains the description of project scheduling. It needs a bit of introduction to try and help put all of the subsequent sections into context. Each of the sections builds on the previous one and the following diagrams help us to understand where these fit into the whole.

We saw in earlier sections how a Work Breakdown Structure is created and the concept that it includes all the components required to deliver the project.

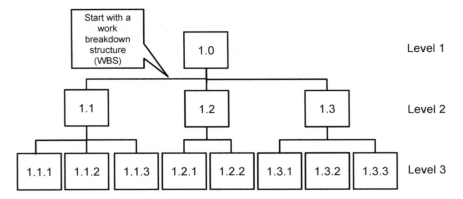

We have taken the WBS and considers the scheduling and logical dependency relationships in order to produce a precedence diagram.

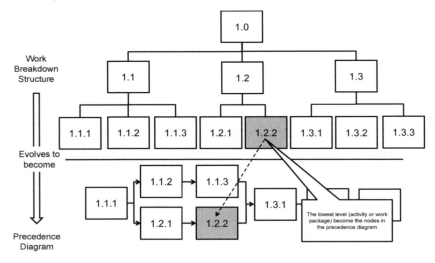

We then go on to consider the construction of the Gantt chart, probably the most recognisable aspect of modern project management.

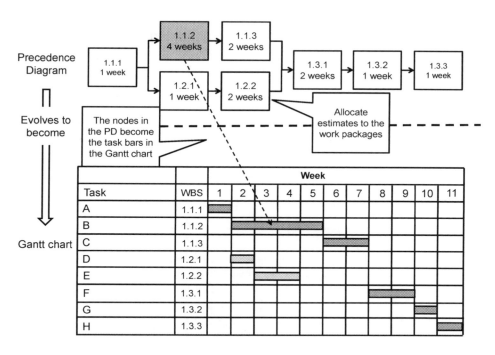

The precedence diagram and Gantt chart are developed to begin to consider how resources will be consumed and what kind of resources they may be.

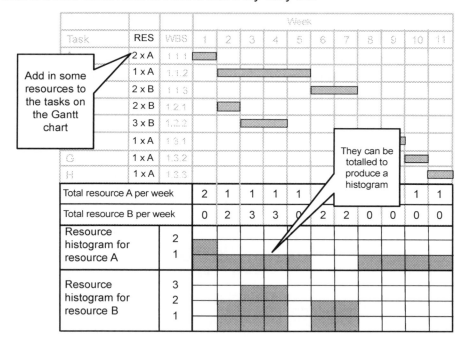

Lastly the overall profiled resource curve is transformed into a project budget by adding actual costs to the volume of resources.

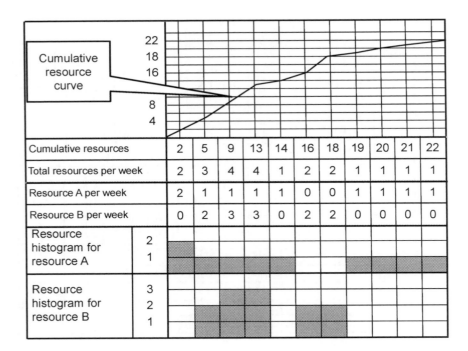

Cumulative resources		2	5	9	13	14	16	18	19	20	21	22
Total resources per week		2	3	4	4	1	2	2	1	1	1	1
Resource A per week		2	1	1	1	1	0	0	1	1	1	1
Resource B per week		0	2	3	3	0	2	2	0	0	0	0

If we assume that these resources cost money, then the total number of them per week multiplied by their respective cost rate (per week) will result in a curve that effectively demonstrates the anticipated cost as it rises over the life of the project. Here we have assumed that both resource type A and B each cost £100 per week. This is called the project budget or planned cost.

Cumulative cost curve showing how costs rise over time

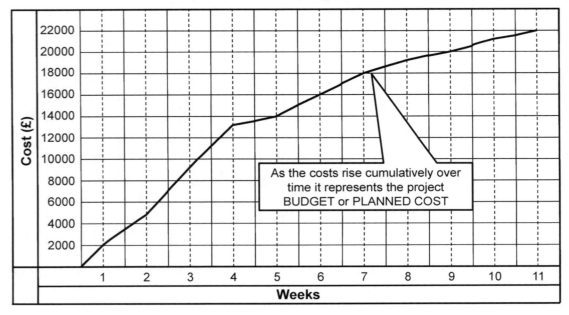

These diagrams help to explain the overall process, but there is a lot more to it than meets the eye. So read on, for the next few sections you will be exposed to the principles of how to produce a schedule and a fully costed budget.

| | **Assessment Criteria** |

11.1 Explain the process for creating and maintaining a schedule

11.2 Describe different techniques for depicting a schedule

11.3 State advantages and disadvantages of using software scheduling tools

The Creation of a Project Schedule

We saw in earlier sections how the project Work Breakdown Structure was created. The next diagram demonstrates how a work breakdown structure is used to generate a precedence diagram. The method for doing this is called the precedence diagram method (or PDM). Each of the lowest levels (work package or activity) are placed into a logical sequence working from left to right. The lines between the nodes indicate a relationship and the normal relationship is that of finish to start as in Figure 38. This is the most common way of linking tasks and will usually be sufficient for simple plans, although there are more complex relationships available which are documented in Figure 39.

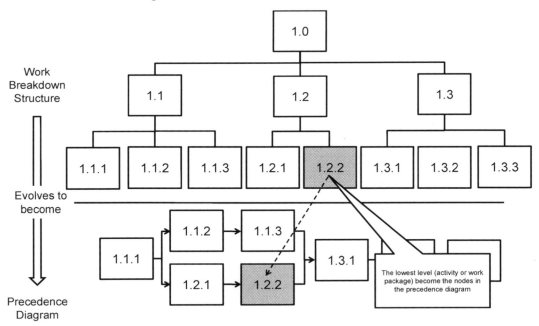

FIGURE 37 THE CREATION OF A PRECEDENCE DIAGRAM FROM A WBS

Types of Network Node Relationships

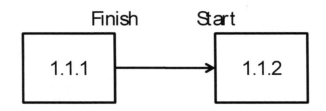

FIGURE 38 FINISH TO START RELATIONSHIP

This relationship simply means that 1.1.2 cannot start until 1.1.1 has finished. It does not have to start immediately but merely that it is able to start. This latter factor is quite important as it means that in theory a gap in time can appear between the end of one task and the start of the next. This gap is referred to as 'float'. There are other types of relationships, two of which are commonly used as below:

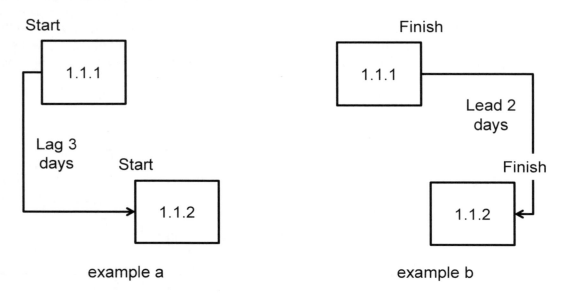

FIGURE 39 START TO START AND FINISH TO FINISH LINKS

The examples of the use of these might be:

1)   **Start to Start** — (example a) 1.1.2 can only start once 1.1.1 has started; so, for example, we can only start testing the software once the software has begun to be produced.

2)   **Finish to Finish** — (example b) 1.1.2 can only finish, once 1.1.1 has finished; so, for example, the project management activities can only finish once the final acceptance has been achieved.

Once again it is important to note that the start(s) and finish(es) do not have to coincide in time, merely that they are dependent upon each other.

Any of these connections can have a modification with either a lag (delay) or a lead (concurrency) introduced.

In these two examples, the raw connectivity has been modified through the insertion of a Lag of 3 in a) and a Lead of 2 in b). The effect of this will be:

1)   That 1.1.2 can only start at least three days after 1.1.1 starts (Lag 3);

2)   That 1.1.2 can finish up to two days before 1.1.1 finishes (Lead 2).

So, utilising these various connections, we can start to 'hook up' all of the 'nodes' to provide a complete picture of the end to end logic of the project. If all the connections are made, the project will appear as a diagram similar to the one below (Figure 40). The 'nodes' in the diagram have now been expanded into a recognised format which is as follows.

ES is the earliest that a task can start   EF is the earliest that a task can finish

LS is the latest that a task can start   LF is the latest that a task can finish

D is the duration   TF is the total float (discussed later)

Precedence Diagramming

If you apply these terms and complete a fully developed network, you can build up a working knowledge of the earliest the project can finish as well as a number of other key facts relating to the project such as total float, free float and the critical path through the network.

So, we have taken the WBS from the earlier section (ignoring the level 4 work packages) and applied some fictitious durations to the work packages, and by using those durations we can produce an updated network as appears below in Figure 40 We need to assume that the relationships between the nodes have been clarified and are correct:

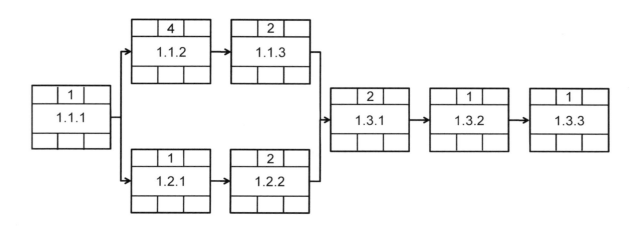

FIGURE 40 A BASIC DIAGRAM TO USE AS AN EXAMPLE

Forward Pass

In this example the duration box (middle top of each node) has been completed. The first thing when calculating the critical path through the network is to carry out a 'forward pass' through the network.

We do this by commencing far left and populating the early start, then we add the duration to calculate the early finish. In practical terms, think about a task that starts on Monday first thing, We know from our estimates that it should take 1 week, so the task should finish end of business on the Friday. In our network, we choose to start at week 0, add the 1 week of the task duration and arrive at week 1 for the earliest finish.

If we apply this principle to the network, we will end up with something like this (for the first node):

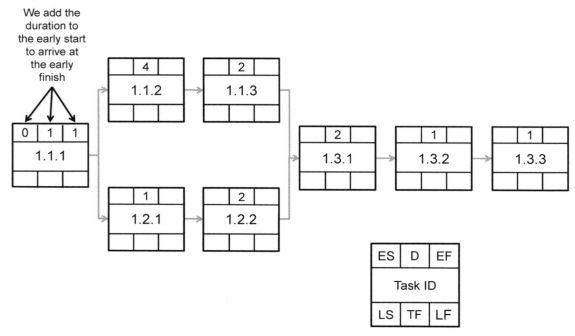

FIGURE 41 NETWORK DIAGRAM SHOWING EARLY FINISH CALCULATION

When we have done the first, we can continue with the forward pass and populate the top rows of all the nodes. There are two tricky bits:

- The early finish from the predecessor node gets transposed into the early start in the subsequent node(s).

- In the forward pass, if you have a choice about which number to take from the early finish to the early start, you always choose the higher number.

To move on, take a look at the next diagram. The grey areas are the numbers we are worried about.

Forward Pass

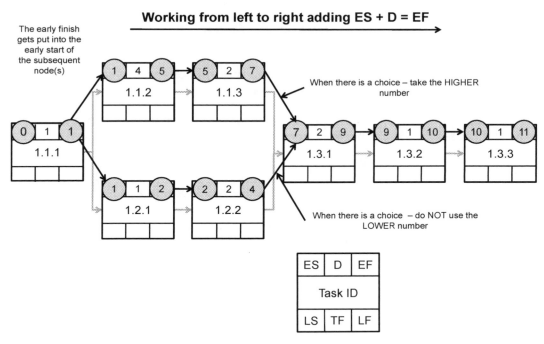

FIGURE 42 NETWORK DIAGRAM SHOWING EARLY START AND EARLY FINISH

When you have finished adding all the way through, the last early finish box is the earliest date on which the project will finish. It is the sum of all the longer durations through the network.

Backward Pass

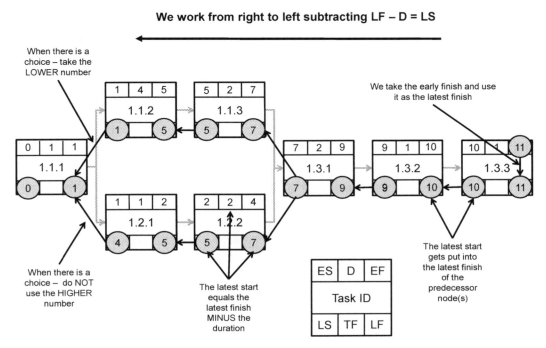

FIGURE 43 NETWORK DIAGRAM SHOWING LATEST START AND FINISH CALCULATIONS

The next job is to carry out the backward pass. Working from right to left this time, we subtract the duration from the latest finish to arrive at the latest start. Again, there are a few tricky bits:

- The latest start from the successor node gets entered into the latest finish for the predecessor node.

- In the backward pass, if you have a choice about which number to take backwards from the latest start into the latest finish of the predecessor task, you always choose the lower number.

- In the cases for the exam and to make life a bit easier in these examples, the earliest finish from the last node in the network becomes the latest finish for that (last) node.

Total Float and Critical Path

What the diagrams have shown so far is that if we assume the latest finish is the same as the earliest finish and we work back from right to left we get back to a zero as the latest start in the first node. There is still a blank box in the middle on the bottom row of each of the nodes. This is reserved for the calculated total float. Total float is arrived at by subtracting the early finish of a given node from the latest finish of the same node. In the case of 1.1.3 above this equals 0, as it does for most of the other nodes, except 1.2.1 and 1.2.2, which both have 3 in the total float box. Let's take a look at the finished diagram:

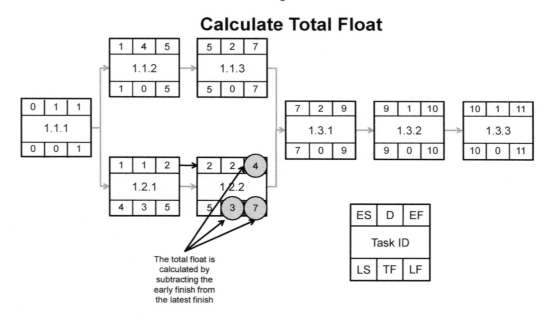

FIGURE 44 NETWORK DIAGRAM SHOWING TOTAL FLOAT CALCULATIONS

The definition of the term total float is "*the amount of time by which a task (node) can be delayed before it affects the end date of the project*". In the diagram above, if 1.1.3 takes 3 weeks instead of 2 weeks the end date will be delayed. This is because it has 0 weeks total float, therefore no option to be lengthened or delayed.

In the diagram, if 1.2.2 is delayed by a week it will not affect the end date because it has 3 weeks total float.

The critical path through the network is that path that demonstrates the LEAST TOTAL FLOAT. In the case of our example, it follows the path as defined in Figure 45. It is also the longest in terms of duration (it defines the end date).

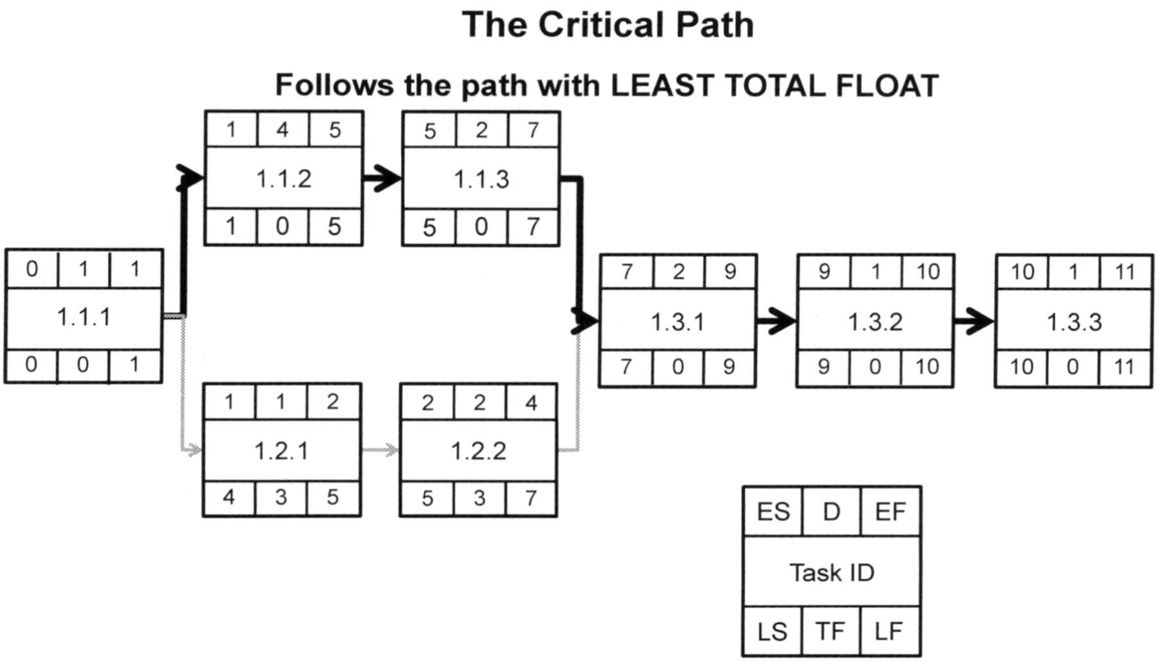

The Critical Path

Follows the path with LEAST TOTAL FLOAT

FIGURE 45 NETWORK DIAGRAM SHOWING THE CRITICAL PATH

Free Float

Free float is one more term defined in the syllabus for the APMP. It is defined as being *"the amount of time by which the end of a task can be delayed before affecting any subsequent tasks"*.

Free float is therefore concerned with the gap between the end of one task and the start of the next one(s), but here we are just concerned with affecting the next task and not the project end date as we were with total float considerations. If we want to gauge the gap between two tasks, we need to consider the gap between the earliest one task can finish and the earliest the next can start. So, for example in Figure 46, 1.2.2 can be delayed by three weeks before it 'bumps into' 1.3.1. Therefore, if we take the earliest finish of 1.2.2 away from the earliest start of the successor task (1.3.1) we arrive at 3 (weeks). This is said to be the free float of 1.2.2. If we carry out the same exercise with 1.2.1, however, and take the earliest finish of 1.2.1 from the earliest start of 1.2.2, we end up with 0 weeks free float — even though 1.2.1 has three weeks total float.

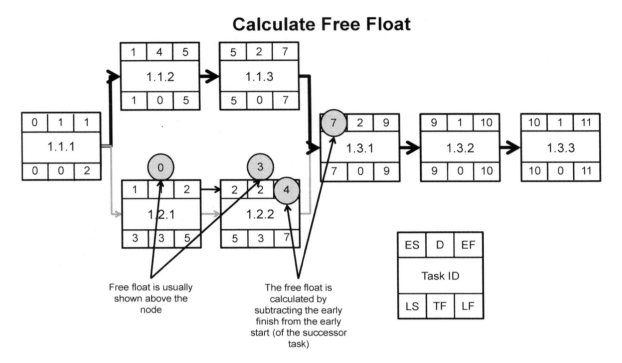

FIGURE 46 NETWORK DIAGRAM SHOWING FREE FLOAT CALCULATIONS

The Purpose of Critical Path?

Critical path analysis (as described in Figure 40 to Figure 46) is the accepted method for calculating the optimal end date for a project. In doing so, it reveals the total float and free float values. These are important because:

1)   Tasks with the lowest combined total float describe the critical path. If we understand which tasks are going to affect the end date we can pay a little more attention to them than some of the others. They are at the top of the project manager's list.

2)   Tasks that affect another task need to be understood, as their delay will affect another task and as such may need managerial intervention. They won't affect the end date of the project though, and so are not as key as the ones with little or no total float.

3)   Tasks with total float and free float have a fair degree of flexibility in their timings and therefore do not need to be as closely scrutinised and managed as the others. They may also represent those task that can have resources reduced to redeploy elsewhere, as extending them may not have ramifications for the end date.

4)   By drawing the network we are actively engaged in thinking about the detail of the interdependencies, the estimates, the relationships between tasks, the implications of delays and so on. If the team are engaged in the process the quality of the planning will improve dramatically.

Once the networks have been produced, the next step is usually to convert it into a bar chart. The most common term used is that of the Gantt chart, as it is the one most widely reproduced in planning software. The principle is quite simple. A Gantt chart has the tasks down the left hand axis and the timescale across the top and the tasks are represented by a bar or line going from left to right covering the start and end of that task. The migration of the network to a Gantt chart is described in Figure 47. They are really useful at

- Providing a communication tool for portraying progress to others.

- For being able to relate the relative timings of the network diagram into absolute timings with reference to actual dates.

- They are able to be colour coded thus showing the relevant relationships and for example critical / non critical activities.

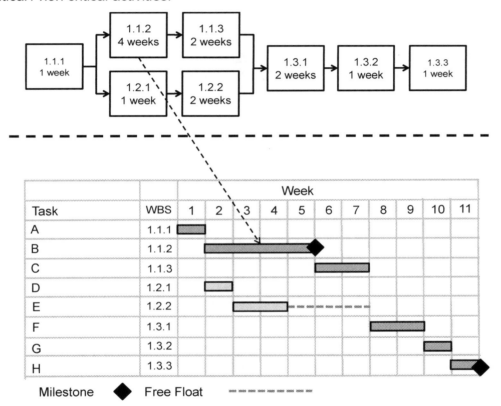

FIGURE 47 SHOWING THE EVOLUTION OF A NETWORK DIAGRAM INTO A GANTT CHART

The Use of Software Systems for Planning

Over the last twenty years or so, the use of personal computers and the availability of corporate systems has increased dramatically. This ready availability of processing power has caused an explosion of software tools in many industries and project management is one of them.

The continual recalculation, storage of data and excellent rendering of the various charts and diagrams has led to a huge uptake of their use. There are a number of recognised advantages and disadvantages to their deployment.

ADVANTAGES

- Quick to use and relatively inexpensive. Most modern systems are intuitive and have a flexible user interface supported on most platforms and supported by widely available training.

- Able to support 'what if' modelling. It is possible to dynamically change the resource loadings, the dependencies and so on, to provide quick and easy manipulation of numerous potential scenarios.

- Able to continually recalculate as circumstances change. They can be used throughout the project to continually review and update the thinking without laborious changes and detailed recalculations by hand.

- Easily customised to conform to most standards. Most packages will integrate into corporate standards and will be flexible enough to be adapted to most needs.

- Can be used in multi-user mode to support large workgroups. Enterprise planning software can be hosted on a server and is a quick and relatively easy way of ensuring that corporate planning standards are followed.

- Excellent range of reports and displays are available. These help to make sure that the monthly and other regular reporting is relatively quick and painless.

- Corporate systems can usually be readily interfaced with financial and other systems. This means that financial and other data can flow up and down the managerial hierarchy of the organisation.

DISADVANTAGES

- Can 'dumb down' the area of planning, leading to poor plans. This can lead to people just following the software blindly without really thinking through the implications of what they are doing.

- Can be seen as authoritative simply because of the use of a computer. Garbage in means garbage out.

- Can be overly systemised, requiring large amounts of data simply to operate them and sometimes the plan can become the project.

- Corporate systems can limit the flexibility of the project manager who has to conform to standards that do not add value to their role.

 Quick Quiz (Answers In Section 18)

	Question	Options	Your Answer
1	The top axis of a Gantt chart contains the…?	a) Time periods b) Tasks c) Resources d) Work packages	

	Question	Options	Your Answer
2	Total float is the difference between latest finish and…?	a) Early start b) Latest start c) Early finish d) Free float	
3	Free float is the difference between the early start of the successor activity and the early finish of the activity in question.	True or false?	
4	A lag shows the time a task must be delayed after the preceding task.	True or false?	
5	A milestone has what amount of time associated with it?	a) One day b) One week c) Nothing d) Depends	
6	The critical path is the longest path through the network.	True or false?	
7	The early finish is the early start plus…?	a) Duration b) Latest start c) Latest finish d) Early finish	
8	Milestones can be used to trigger payments.	True or false?	
9	Work packages become nodes in the network.	True or false?	
10	The middle box on the bottom row of a network node contains…?	a) Total float b) Free float c) Early start d) Early finish	

Use this space to make some notes

What Kind of Questions Might There Be in the Exam?

1)	Describe five major examples of how a software tool can help in planning a project and give examples of where three of them might be helpful in solving common planning problems.
2)	Analyse the following network and answer the questions below: a) What is the earliest finish of the project? b) What is the total float for task D? c) What is the free float for task B? d) What is the critical path? e) What is the latest finish for task C? f) Describe the term critical path. g) Explain the use of the critical path and how it might be used when running a project. 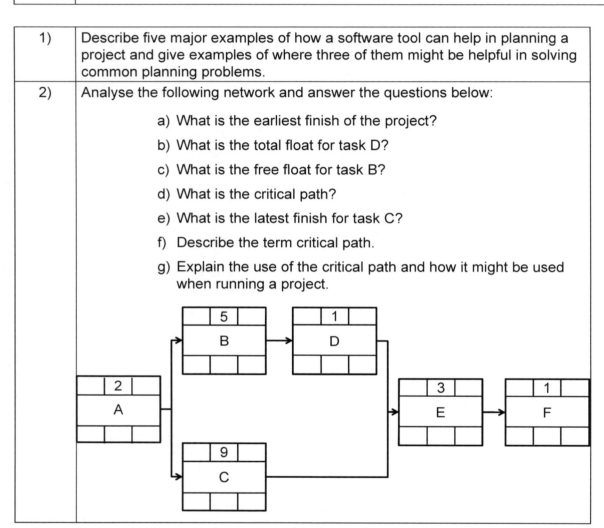

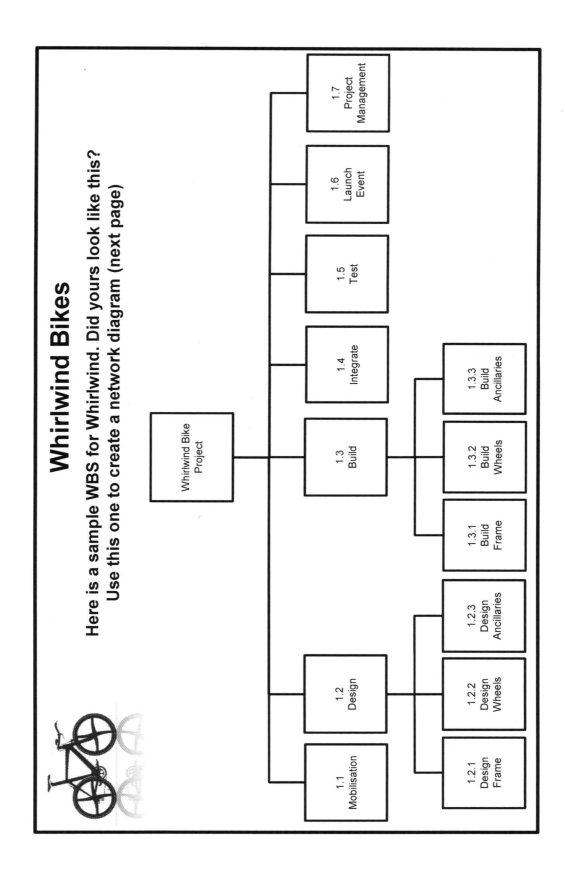

Whirlwind Bikes

Here is a sample WBS for Whirlwind. Did yours look like this? Use this one to create a network diagram (next page)

Whirlwind Bike Project

- 1.1 Mobilisation
- 1.2 Design
  - 1.2.1 Design Frame
  - 1.2.2 Design Wheels
  - 1.2.3 Design Ancillaries
- 1.3 Build
  - 1.3.1 Build Frame
  - 1.3.2 Build Wheels
  - 1.3.3 Build Ancillaries
- 1.4 Integrate
- 1.5 Test
- 1.6 Launch Event
- 1.7 Project Management

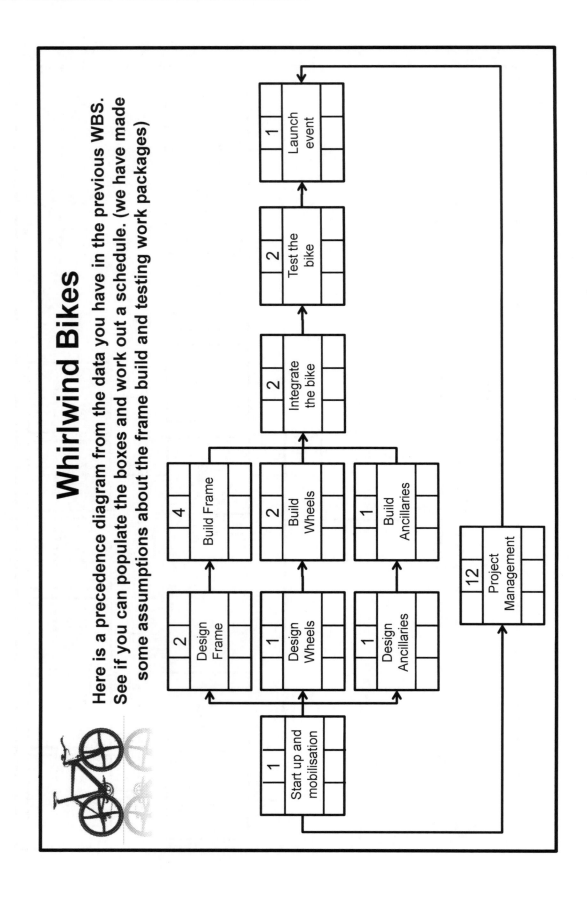

Whirlwind Bikes

Here is a precedence diagram from the data you have in the previous WBS. See if you can populate the boxes and work out a schedule. (we have made some assumptions about the frame build and testing work packages)

	Assessment Criteria

11.4 Explain categories and types of resource

11.5 Describe how resources are applied to a scheduling process

11.6 Differentiate between smoothing and levelling

Resource Management

Resource management is the term used to describe the proactive management of the various human and other resources in an efficient manner. In doing so, the project manager will need to consider a large number of different things, including:

- The availability of the resources in terms of timing and quantity. There might be a limit on how many people can contribute to the task in hand at any one time.

- Awareness of any specific individual or scarce components that will be critical to the ability to deliver the project. For example, sometimes there is a certain piece of equipment of which there is only one in existence, such as a super sized crane, perhaps.

- Limits and constraints that might impinge upon the totally flexible deployment (and redeployment) of resources. For example, there is no point in having three tunnel-boring machines if there are only two access points to the tunnel (each end).

- The costs involved and creative ways of profiling the project budget to minimise any impacts from cash flow or the availability of funds.

There are a number of types of resource to consider. Each will be treated differently

Consumable resources are those things that once used need to the replaced. Examples of these are fuel and money. The project manager must make appropriate arrangements for these to be replaced one used up. They do this by creating budgets and plans to ensure that all stakeholders are aware of the implications of their use and what the consequences are when they are used up.

Re-usable resources can be redeployed when no longer needed, examples include people, accommodation, vehicles, etc. The project manager will need to make appropriate arrangements for the re-use of resources especially human resources. Care should be taken of any materiel that can be re-deployed to avoid scrappage costs and unnecessary expense.

Equipment used on the project needs to be allowed for. If a tunnel is being dug then a boring machine may be required. This is not a direct cost to the customer (we will not provide the machine at the end of the job) but we need it in order to fulfil the project activities.

Materials are used in the same way as Equipment except they contribute directly towards the finished product. If we are building a railway, we will lay the tracks and they become part of the finished article and a deliverable of the project. They are a direct cost.

Space is usually required to house the project teams, for an IT project office space will be required to accommodate the machines, people and support services.

Creating a Resource Histogram

The major mechanism for the project manager to understand the resources available and to pro actively manage them is the resource histogram. The principle being that each resource can be charted showing the time scale on the x axis and the number of resources on the y axis.

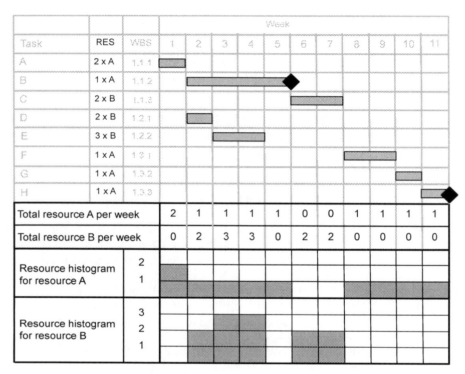

FIGURE 48 EXAMPLE RESOURCE HISTOGRAM

The diagram above demonstrates the principles of the resource histogram. The Gantt chart appears at the top of this diagram only to help describe the bottom half, which is the resource histogram itself. The grey areas in the bottom half are there to reflect the value of resources planned week by week. Varying amounts of resource type 'A' and 'B' have been allocated to each task and require two B's in week 2 and three in week 3 for example.

The purpose of this is to see at a glance where resources are planned to be used, such that action can be taken to make sure that they are available according to the plan and if this is impossible, to take steps to deal with it before it becomes a problem.

Resource Smoothing

In some circumstances it may be possible to swap resources around and increase the number on one particular task at the expense of others. It may also be possible to simply allocate more people to the task thus making it shorter.

For the purposes of explaining resource smoothing let's assume that there are only 2 resource type B's available. There would therefore be an over allocation of these resource types during weeks 3 and 4. On the face of it, the project plan is not viable simply because we cannot go into the project knowing that we cannot resource it. The project manager should therefore undertake a process of resource smoothing.

The purpose of smoothing is to seek to resolve any over allocation issues without affecting the end date. The presumption is that the end date is paramount and should not be compromised. However, if we assume that all of the network and task interdependencies are correct, and the estimates and allocation of resources is similarly accurate, then there is not much that can be done without modifying the schedule.

The potential solution to this dilemma is through the use of float. Total float is the amount of time by which a task can be delayed before it affects the end date. The dotted line on the Gantt chart demonstrates the float that is available for task E, which has three resources of type B used for two weeks. At the end of this task there is a gap before it starts to interfere with the task that follows it (task F). Task E is responsible for the limit of resources being breached, but because there is some float there are a couple of things that we could consider doing to solve the problem (assuming we definitely cannot get more resource B's).

The project manager investigates the nature of task E and after discussions with the team decides that instead of three resources for two weeks, an alternative might be to have two resources for three weeks. The resultant plan might look like this:

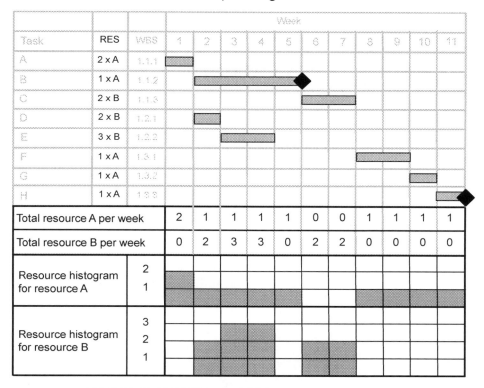

FIGURE 49 EXAMPLE OF RESOURCE SMOOTHING

Notice how task E now takes three weeks, but the limit of two resource type B's has been adhered to. This now represents a viable project schedule. The end date has not been compromised and the project can proceed on this basis. The total float for E has been reduced by a week to accommodate the extended duration.

Splitting Tasks

One other technique a project manager may be able to deploy when coming up with a viable schedule is that of splitting tasks. By doing this, a task is started, stopped and restarted, leaving a break in the middle possibly to conform to any resource availability constraints. There are certain instances where in the real world splitting tasks is inevitable (during public holidays, factory shutdowns, etc.), but the project manager may choose to split a task at other times simply to conform to resource constraints.

Generally speaking though, splitting tasks is not to be recommended as it inevitably introduces a demobilisation and remobilisation overhead. Individuals will put one task down and then pick it up again sometime later. This usually introduces delay and risk. It is an option but not one that should be considered until all other smoothing options have been discounted.

Resource Levelling

Consider Figure 48 again. Let us assume this time that there is only one of resource type A available. There is an over allocation in week one as the plan is showing the need for two A's in that week. The project manager can do some investigation, but the problem with the over allocation is that it is caused by task A, which is on the critical path. By definition, therefore, task A cannot be extended or delayed because it will cause a delay to the end date of the project. If task A can be extended and the resources reduced (in the same manner as we looked at for smoothing above), we will delay the project by a week, making it a 12-week project instead of an 11-week one.

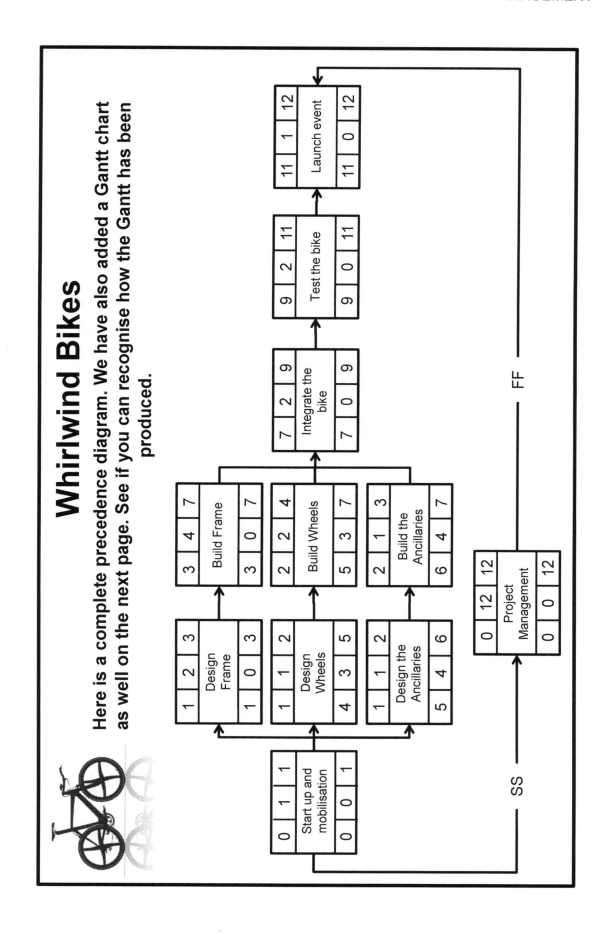

Whirlwind Bikes

Here is a complete precedence diagram. We have also added a Gantt chart as well on the next page. See if you can recognise how the Gantt has been produced.

Whirlwind Bikes

Here is the project Gantt chart. See if you can produce a resource histogram on the template on the next page.

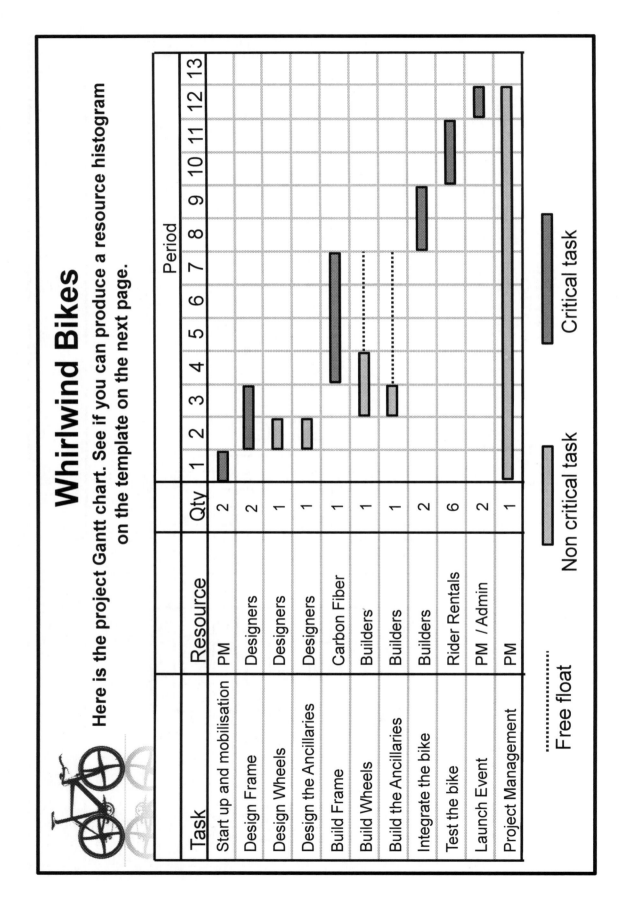

Task	Resource	Qty	1	2	3	4	5	6	7	8	9	10	11	12	13
Start up and mobilisation	PM	2	▮												
Design Frame	Designers	2		▮											
Design Wheels	Designers	1		▯											
Design the Ancillaries	Designers	1		▯											
Build Frame	Carbon Fiber	1				▮▮▮▮									
Build Wheels	Builders	1				▯									
Build the Ancillaries	Builders	1				▯									
Integrate the bike	Builders	2								▮					
Test the bike	Rider Rentals	6										▮			
Launch Event	PM / Admin	2												▮	
Project Management	PM	1	▮▮▮▮▮▮▮▮▮▮▮▮▮												

Period

········· Free float

▮ Non critical task

▮ Critical task

Whirlwind Bikes

Here is a blank resource histogram template. Have a go at populating it from the data in the Gantt chart.

Resource Histogram

	7	6	5	4	3	2	1

Per period												
Period	1	2	3	4	5	6	7	8	9	10	11	12

Whirlwind Bikes

Here is an example answer to the resource histogram.

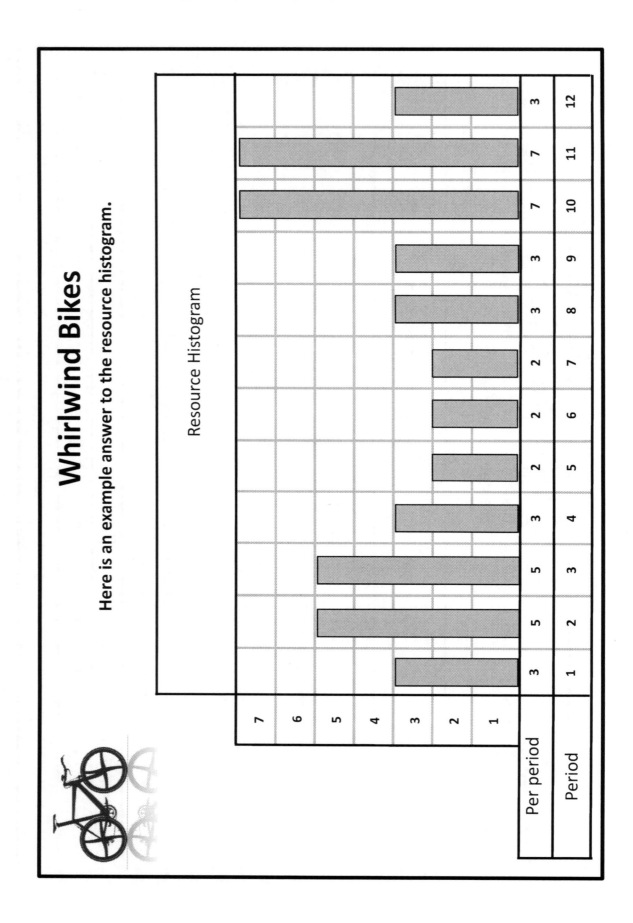

Resource Histogram

Per period	3	5	5	3	2	2	2	3	3	7	7	3
Period	1	2	3	4	5	6	7	8	9	10	11	12

Use this space to make some notes

_____
_____
_____
_____
_____

Quick Quiz (Answers in Section 18)

	Question	Options	Your Answer
1	The two ways of dealing with resource over allocation are…?	a) Levelling and settling b) Lightening and strengthening c) Levelling and smoothing d) Building and moving	
2	Resource levelling has the potential to extend the project end date.	True or false?	
3	Resource smoothing has the potential to extend the end date.	True or false?	
4	Resource planning can be iterative.	True or false?	
5	Which technique provides the precursor to producing a resource histogram?	a) Precedence Diagram b) WBS c) RAM Chart d) Gantt Chart	
6	Which of these is a type of resource?	a) Fixed b) Cost based c) Replenishable d) Unused	
7	Splitting a task will incur which kinds of overheads?	a) Mobilisation and demobilisation b) Total float c) Free float d) Lag	
8	Examples of replenishable resources are all of these except…?	a) Fuel b) Labour c) Money d) Time	

	Question	Options	Your Answer
9	Which of these is NOT a consideration that the project manager would take into account when producing an initial resource histogram?	a) Costs b) Availability c) Constraints d) Skills	
10	A resource histogram can apply to all types of resources separately or collectively.	True or false?	

What types of questions might there be in the exam?

1)	Describe the term resource management and from the Gantt chart below draw a resource histogram.

Task	RES	1	2	3	4	5	6	7	8	9	10	11
A	2 x A											
B	1 x B											
C	2 x A											
D	2 x A											
E	2 x B											
F	1 x A											
G	2 x A											
H	2 x A											

2)	Explain the terms 'resource levelling' and 'resource smoothing' and describe three potential consequences of splitting tasks.

Assessment Criteria

11.7 Explain budgeting and cost management

The use of the resource histogram is to help identify and understand where the peaks and troughs are. An extension of this principle would be to consider the resources together and arrive at a total figure for time period and then combine them all to provide a cumulative figure for the life of the project. Consider Figure 50 (we have reverted to the pre-levelled schedule from earlier).

This shows how these two different resources have been added together to provide a single cumulative value, which is translated in the upper part of the diagram as a cumulative (or summation) curve.

As a principle this is going to be very useful during the project. An obvious extension to it, however, is to take the resources and apply the relative costs to each of them. Having done this, instead of merely having a number of days described by the curve, we can start to understand the costs or the budget and how it gets profiled over the project.

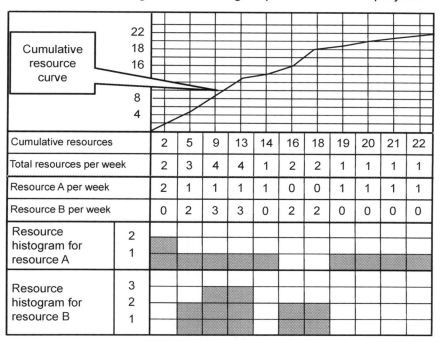

FIGURE 50 CUMULATIVE RESOURCE CURVE

Using our examples from earlier sections, if we assume that resource A costs £1000 per week and resource B costs £500 per week, we can multiply out the figures as in the following table:

Week	Resource Type	Units	Rate (£) per week	Cost (£)	Total Cost (£)	Cumulative Cost (£)
1	A	2	1,000	2,000	2,000	2,000
2	A	1	1,000	1,000		
	B	2	500	1,000	2,000	4,000
3	A	1	1,000	1,000		
	B	3	500	1,500	2,500	6,500
4	A	1	1,000	1,000		
	B	3	500	1,500	2,500	9,000
5	A	1	1,000	1,000	1,000	10,000
6	B	2	500	1,000	1,000	11,000
7	B	2	500	1,000	1,000	12,000
8	A	1	1,000	1,000	1,000	13,000
9	A	1	1,000	1,000	1,000	14,000
10	A	1	1,000	1,000	1,000	15,000
11	A	1	1,000	1,000	1,000	16,000
				Total	**16,000**	

The graphical representation of these figures has been produced in Figure 51.

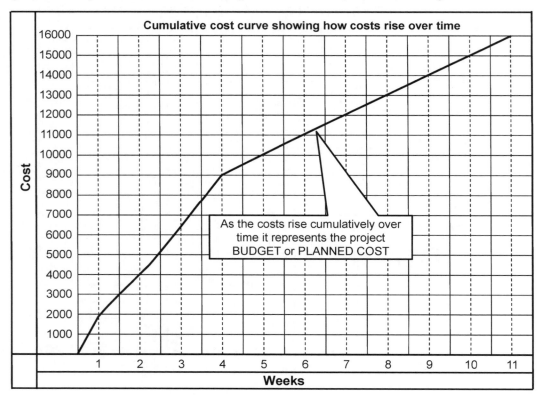

FIGURE 51 THE PROJECT BUDGET

This is the final step in the planning exercise. It provides the project manager with a definitive budget against which all expenditure can be compared and managed. When we introduce the concept of earned value later, this curve (referred to as the planned cost) will be used to compare with the actual costs and earned value amounts to provide not only the performance against cost budgets, but also an index to describe progress against the time schedule as well.

As with all the plans, an initial estimate will have been described in the business case. As the project progresses, this is further iterated, refined and developed, so that a fully considered plan can be produced. These budgets will have had an input from the risk management process (Section 12).

Benefits of Budgeting and Cost Management

By producing a budget the project manager will be better placed to:

- Record progress against a known baseline and spot early deviations and variances, thus be able to make alternative arrangements before things become too far from plan.

- Describe to others the need for project funding requirements, thus be able to justify the expenditure with clear analysis underpinning the business case.

- Introduce an effective change control procedure as there will be a definite baseline about which change can be controlled, so the changes can be clearly delineated from any variance.

- Closely link it with the cost breakdown structures and in this way the actual expenditures can be closely mapped to the estimates. This is an invaluable aspect in the ability to learn lessons for the future.

- Provide a key input into the project review cycles, making the analysis of variations possible again aiding corrective actions.

- Provide careful cost management, which is the key in the organisation understanding its own liabilities and provide information to help 'balance the books'.

Commitments

The budget is extremely useful in understanding the nature of the costs we anticipate. However, consider the following example:

We are running a project with £24,000 cost budget for accommodation. At the start of the project we commit to lease a building for a year. The costs are £2,000 per month. In month 0 we sign the lease and are contractually committed to this expenditure with no 'get out clause'. At this point in time our commitment is £24,000. Our project budget is reduced by £24,000 to £0. We have not spent anything. We are said to have a committed cost of £24,000.

At the start of month 1, for the 12 months of our project, the commitments looks like this (not including any other considerations). As time goes by (assuming the incurred costs are paid), the legal commitment reduces.

Month	0	1	2	3	4	5	6	7	8	9	10	11	12
Uncommitted Budget	24	0	0	0	0	0	0	0	0	0	0	0	0
Committed cost		24	22	20	18	16	14	12	10	8	6	4	2

The reason we need to monitor this, is because we need to be aware of our total liability so that we do not exceed our budget. These records are kept in the project accounts.

Commitments also give us the ability to understand the costs that we cannot avoid if at any point the project is halted. If you sign a mobile phone contract for 12 months, the provider will expect to receive payment for each of the 12 months even if you do not want the service. You are therefore committed to the expenditure (but only that amount you have not yet paid).

Accruals

An accrual is our best estimate of expenditure that has not been invoiced or paid in a given period. They allow expenditure to be properly estimated for that period. Without accruals, we would not get a true picture of the costs of a project at that time, because it would depend when other organisations sent us invoices and when they in turn get paid, which can be some time after the work has been completed. These accruals, when combined with the actual expenditure, give us the best estimate of our total actual costs to date.

If we consider the position of our project at the end of month 2, we will have recorded the actual expenditure from month 1 as a result of an invoice we have received and paid. The invoice for month 2 may not have been received yet so we make an accrual for this cost.

Actual expenditure is the money that has already been paid, and the convention is to record that against the period to which the costs relate by removing the accrual and replacing it with an actual.

Month	0	1	2	3	4	5	6	7	8	9	10	11	12
Budget in month		2	2	2	2	2	2	2	2	2	2	2	2
Cumulative budget		2	4	6	8	10	12	14	16	18	20	22	24
Actual expenditure		2	0	0	0	0	0	0	0	0	0	0	0
Accrual		0	2	0	0	0	0	0	0	0	0	0	0
Actual costs in month		2	2	0	0	0	0	0	0	0	0	0	0
Cumulative actual cost		2	4										
Forecast cost in month		2	2	2	2	2	2	2	2	2	2	2	2
Forecast cumulative cost		2	4	6	8	10	12	14	16	18	20	22	24

Forecasts

The budget and actual figures are very important from cash and cost management points of view, but as well as them, the other main area that project managers are frequently asked to report upon is that of a forecast. The principle here is that it is inadequate to merely report on things that have happened in the past, and the real key to effective management is to, as far as is possible, plan for the future and then seek to follow the plan. You can only manage the things you haven't done yet.

The forecasting by a project manager is crucial to the sponsoring business, as it provides key financial information so that the organisation can properly manage its portfolio.

Let's say that on our project we are aware that because of certain factors the rent will rise on the building (perhaps energy prices have risen and the contract stipulates that we will pay such increases). Without action we will encounter a problem as we have no allowance for the increase in the budget. At the end of month 7 we are told that our rent will rise by £1k per month from month 8 onwards. We cannot change what has already gone before, but we can change our perspective of the future. Our new forecasts will change to a new forecast outturn of £29k, compared to a budget (and original forecast outturn) of £24k.

At the end of month 7:

Month	0	1	2	3	4	5	6	7	8	9	10	11	12
Budget in month		2	2	2	2	2	2	2	2	2	2	2	2
Cumulative budget		2	4	6	8	10	12	14	16	18	20	22	24
Actual expenditure		2	2	2	2	2	2	0	0	0	0	0	0
Accrual		0	0	0	0	0	0	2	0	0	0	0	0
Actual costs in month		2	2	2	2	2	2	2	0	0	0	0	0
Cumulative actual cost		2	4	6	8	10	12	14					
Forecast cost in month									3	3	3	3	3
Forecast cumulative cost		2	4	6	8	10	12	14	17	20	23	26	29

In the example above, the project manager and the sponsoring organisation have a choice as to whether they change the budget (perhaps call down some contingency) and effectively change the cost baseline to avoid showing any variances, or simply record it as a variance, which, if within tolerance, can be managed through any existing arrangements. They may of course have alternative courses of action, such as renegotiating leases, use less energy, etc.

Cash Flows

Think about your bank account. It is preferable to be paid at the start of the month and pay all the bills and hopefully have a credit balance at the end, rather than the opposite i.e. when you pay all your bills during the month and get your salary at the end. The latter situation leads you to run up an overdraft which costs money in interest. Organisations are precisely the same. It is preferable to be paid before expenditure is incurred.

Consider the diagrams in Figure 52.

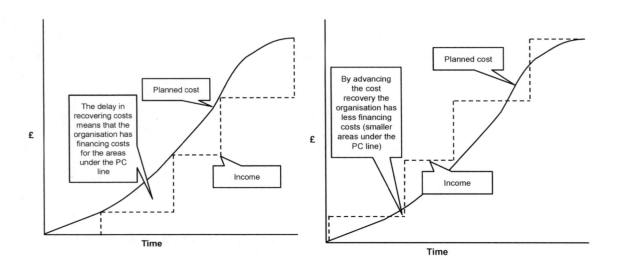

FIGURE 52 TWO TYPES OF CASH FLOW SITUATIONS

Of course not all projects are funded by genuine income (i.e. from a client), but nevertheless the money to cover the costs has to come from somewhere, and the sponsoring organisation will need to borrow from the bank if the cash is not immediately available. Either way, running a deficit will not go down well with your accounting colleagues, if it can be avoided.

Whirlwind Bikes

Use this costed Gantt chart to produce a cumulative cost curve on the template provided on the next page

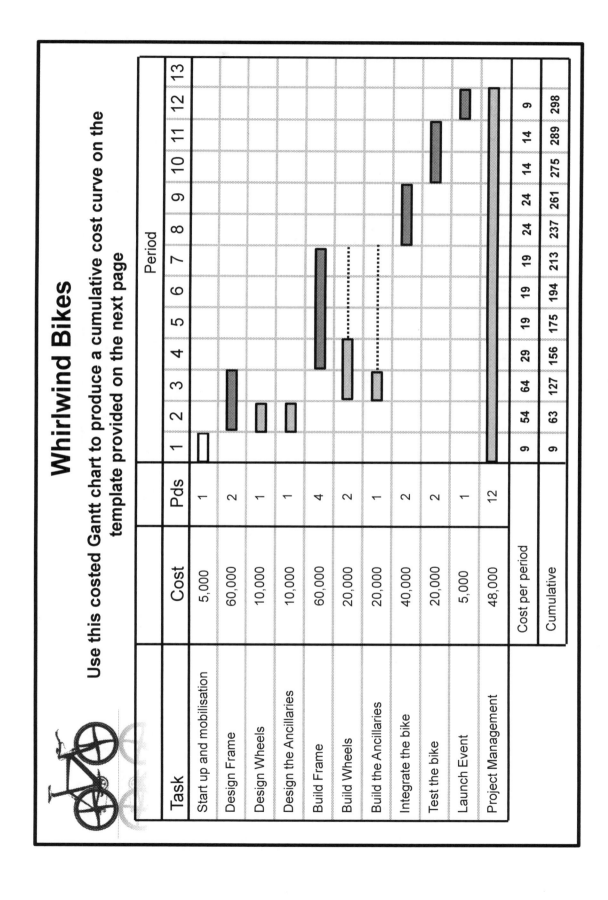

Task	Cost	Pds	Period 1	2	3	4	5	6	7	8	9	10	11	12	13
Start up and mobilisation	5,000	1	■												
Design Frame	60,000	2		■	■										
Design Wheels	10,000	1		■											
Design the Ancillaries	10,000	1		■											
Build Frame	60,000	4				■	■	■	■						
Build Wheels	20,000	2				■	■								
Build the Ancillaries	20,000	1				■									
Integrate the bike	40,000	2								■	■				
Test the bike	20,000	2										■	■		
Launch Event	5,000	1												■	
Project Management	48,000	12	■	■	■	■	■	■	■	■	■	■	■	■	
Cost per period			9	54	64	29	19	19	19	24	24	14	14	9	
Cumulative			9	63	127	156	175	194	213	237	261	275	289	298	

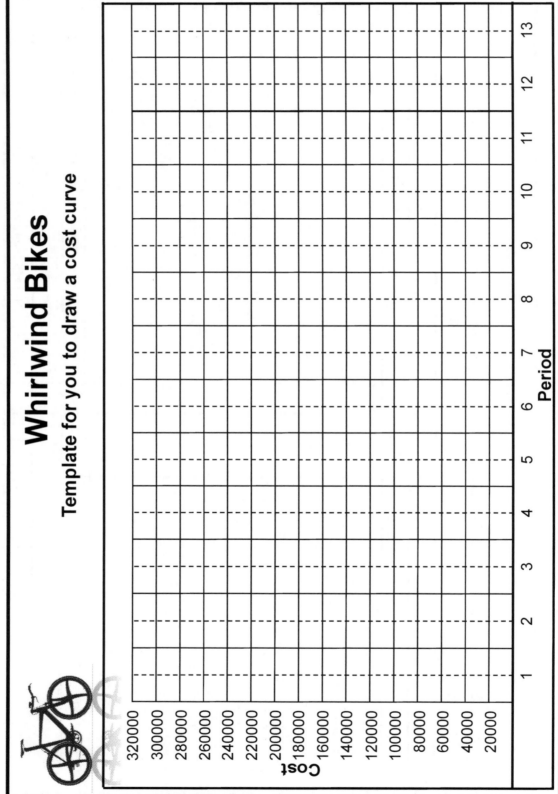

Whirlwind Bikes

Template for you to draw a cost curve

Use this space to make some notes

Quick Quiz (Answers in Section 18)

	Question	Options	Your Answer
1	A resource histogram shows the quantity of resources used over time as a horizontal bar.	True or false?	
2	The estimated cost of a project is reflected in all of these except?	a) Budget b) Planned cost c) Actual cost d) Estiamtes	
3	The objective of cash flow management is to _____ the amount of time costs exceed income?	a) Reduce b) Increase c) Normalise d) Determine	
4	What term describes the technique for making sure that predicted costs are recorded in the project accounts in the appropriate time period?	a) Budget b) Forecast c) Accrual d) Actual	
5	The project manager is responsible for identifying the predicted out-turn (forecast) for the project.	True or false?	
6	The planned cost gets carried forward into the earned value calculations.	True or false?	
7	Which term describes monies legally due on a project?	a) Actual b) Forecast c) Commitment d) Negative	

8	Who is responsible for making sure that costs are properly managed on the project?	a) The sponsor b) The project manager c) The client d) The project manager and the sponsor	
9	Budgets are only a guide and do not really matter.	True or false?	
10	Cumulative resources rise over the time of the project.	True or false?	

What types of questions might there be in the exam?

1)	List and describe five things a project manager might do to manage costs on the project.

Assessment Criteria

11.8 Describe advantages and disadvantages of earned value management

11.9 Perform earned value calculations and interpret earned value data

What is Earned Value?

Earned value is a term used to describe a value placed in a non-subjective manner, on the products that have been produced, belong to the project that cannot be taken away. It is a calculated figure derived by multiplying the budget allocated to produce the product and the percentage complete of that product.

Consider the diagram in Figure 53. In this scenario, the costs of the project were predicted at the outset to rise steadily up to the original budget at completion (BAC). Armed with this information, we can derive information about any difference between the money we had anticipated to spend (planned cost) and the money we have actually spent (actual cost), both recorded at the time now or actual time expended (ATE).

In isolation, you could draw the conclusion that the project is just fine as the actual cost is below where we thought we would be in terms of cost. On the face of it, very good news! However, if we have actually not produced anything, this graph is exceptionally bad news.

The concept of earned value can be used to help understand more about the true nature of the project and its performance, and if applied correctly can provide indicators as to a) what might be going wrong; and b) where the project might end up in terms of cost and time if it carries on as it is.

Earned value management is the proactive management of the project using earned value as a key input.

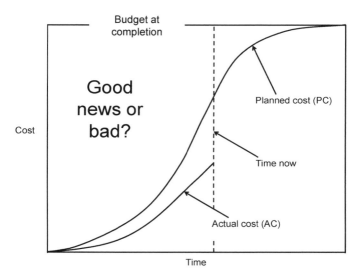

FIGURE 53 THE NEED FOR EARNED VALUE

Consider an example:

A builder is building a wall; it is 3m high, 2m long, is intended to take three weeks to build and we pay the builder £100 per week while he is working for us building it. We have to pay the builder even if he is off sick.

The budget at completion is £300; the planned completion is 3 weeks.

After two weeks, we measure the wall and find it is only 1m high (but 2m long) so we can clearly tell we are behind schedule. We have paid the builder £200 as he has been working for two weeks and we would expect it to be 2m high. In a simple case like this, a subjective analysis may be sufficient to spot the problem. Earned value gives us the tools to do more than that.

We can take an objective measure (using a tape measure) of the height of the wall (1m). It is demonstrably one third finished (33%). On the basis that the wall cannot be taken from us and it belongs to us we can classify this as having earned value equalling 33% x the budget at completion or 33% x £300 or £100. **The earned value we have on our project is £100 even though we have spent two thirds of the schedule and £200 getting it**.

Using this example therefore, we would appear to have a problem. We are now going to be late as the builder needs to build 2m of wall in one week, which probably won't happen if past experience is anything to go by, and this means we will probably go over budget. On the face of it, 1m in two weeks may well mean 3m in six weeks. If this turns out to be true, we will take twice as long and spend twice as much. This we can do in our head. On a large project, with many work packages, these relatively simple principles need earned value techniques to help us keep track.

Earned Value Terminology

The following terms will be used consistently from here on in this guide.

Acronym	Term	Definition
ATE	Actual time expended	The time now (at which the earned value calculations are done, including all the data up to that point).
EV	Earned value	The value of the useful work done at any given point in a project. The value of completed work expressed in terms of the budget assigned to that work. It is calculated by multiplying the original budget at completion for the given wok package by the % complete (for that work package). **EV = BAC (for that work package) x %complete (of that work package)**
PC	Planned cost	This is the rate at which the project expects to spend its costs. It is effectively the sum of the period phased BAC's for the work packages rising to the project BAC at the planned completion.
AC	Actual cost	The costs incurred by the project up to the ATE in carrying out the planned activities. AC is derived as part of the normal project accounting procedures and is a record of cost incurred to date.
BAC	Budget at completion	Describes either the individual work package BAC or the sum of all of the individual work package budgets at completion.
EAC	Estimate at completion	The final estimated cost at completion (derived from the earned value calculations). **EAC = BAC / CPI**
	Planned completion	The date the project was originally planned to be finished
	Actual completion	The date at which it is predicted, as a result of the earned value calculations, that the project will finish. Actual completion = planned completion / SPI
CV	Cost variance	The difference between the earned value of the products produced to date and the actual cost incurred in doing that work to date. **CV = EV – AC**
SV	Schedule variance	The difference between the earned value of the products pro-duced to date and the planned cost of doing that work to date. **SV = EV – PC**
CPI	Cost performance Index	The ratio of the earned value and the actual cost (both as at the ATE) expressed as a decimal. **CPI = EV / AC**
SPI	Schedule performance index	The ratio of the earned value and the planned cost (both as at the ATE) expressed as a decimal. **SPI = EV / PC**

It is usual to demonstrate the earned value principles in a diagram such as in Figure 54.

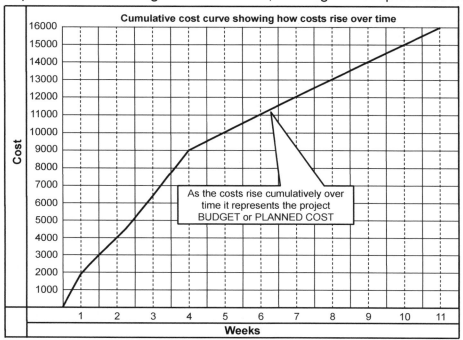

FIGURE 54 EARNED VALUE ANALYSIS TERMINOLOGY

A More Complex Example

We considered earlier the construction of a cumulative cost curve for a sample project and called it the planned cost or budget. As a reminder, the diagram is reproduced here.

This is the basis for our earned value calculations. It is the planned cost curve. When we calculated it earlier we used the weekly figures to plot the curve. In the table below we have re-analysed the data to give us a perspective based upon the work package details, rather than on a weekly basis. The curve will remain the same. By doing it now this way around, we are able to attribute progress figures to individual WP's, so that a true picture of progress can be calculated.

Work Package	Duration	BAC
A	1	2,000
B	4	4,000
C	2	2,000
D	1	1,000
E	2	3,000
F	2	2,000
G	1	1,000
H	1	1,000
Total		16,000

So let's now move to the end of week 5, check the graph and you can see we should have spent (according to the planned cost curve) £10,000. We are going to introduce some more figures so we can work through an earned value calculation for our project.

Let's say that we have gone through the project and, as part of our regular record keeping (undertaken by the project office perhaps), we have ascertained the following progress and cost data relating to the project at the end of week 5.

Don't forget that the earned value = BAC for the work package x % complete

Work Package	Duration	Planned Cost (£)	Earned Value % Complete	Earned Value (£)	Actual Costs Booked to WP (£)
A	1	2,000	100	2,000	2,100
B	4	4,000	25	1,000	1,800
D	1	1,000	80	800	1,600
E	2	3,000	70	2,100	2,000
Total		10,000		5,900	7,500

We are only concerned with data up to week 5 with WP's C,F,G and H yet to start.

So, we now have the data we need to plot the remaining curves and try and understand where we are on the project. You will see on the diagram in Figure 55 that the planned cost curve is above both the earned value and the actual costs. The actual costs are above the earned value. This is not particularly good, in fact it is bad. We have overspent for the things we have produced and we have delivered those things more slowly than we should. This latter fact is the bit that a lot of people have trouble grasping. That the earned value is below the planned cost means that (in this example) we should have produced £10,000 worth of products but we have only actually produced £5,900 worth of products in that time. So we need to catch up — another way of saying we are late.

Earned Value Displayed Graphically for the Example Project

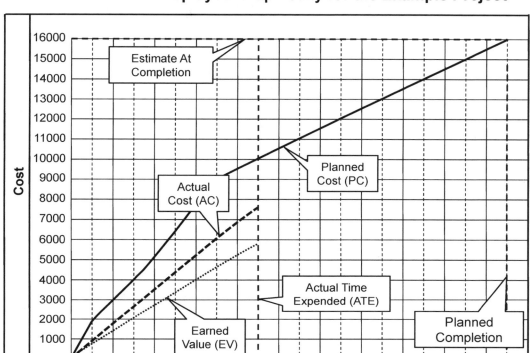

FIGURE 55 EARNED VALUE FOR THE EXAMPLE PROJECT

We can now consider the formulae we need to know to be able to analyse this in more detail.

Formula	From the example	Value
CV = EV − AC	CV = 5,900 − 7,500	£-1,600
SV = EV − PC	SV = 5,900 − 10,000	£-4,100
CPI = EV / AC	CPI = 5,900 / 7,500	0.79 (or 79%)
SPI = EV / PC	SPI = 5,900 / 10,000	0.59 (or 59%)
EAC = BAC / CPI	EAC = 16,000 / 0.79	£20,200
Actual completion = planned completion / SPI	Actual completion = 11 (weeks) / 0.59	18.6 (weeks)

A **negative CV or SV is BAD. An SPI or CPI less than 1 is also BAD.**

CPI and SPI can sometimes be thought of as schedule and cost 'efficiencies'. If something is running at less than 100% it might be considered to be inefficient.

We are going to need a bigger graph to demonstrate graphically what is going to happen with this project (see Figure 56).

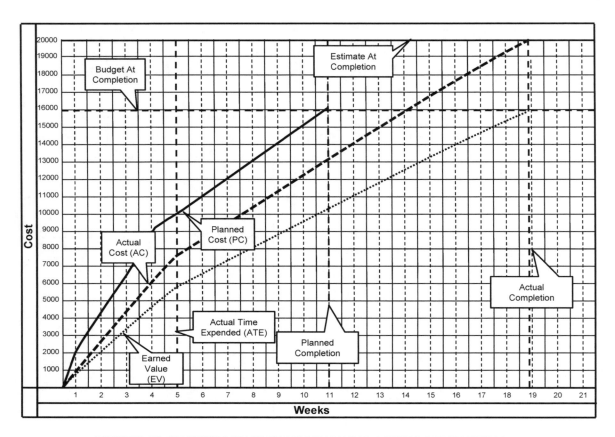

FIGURE 56 EARNED VALUE GRAPH SHOWING ACTUAL COMPLETION

Note: the earned value NEVER exceeds the original budget at completion, but will be achieved at the new actual completion.

In essence, the example project is not doing very well at all. It is late (projected to finish in week 19 and not week 11 as planned) and will overspend (£20,200 instead of £16,000 as planned). The project manager will have quite a bit of work to do to pull this back.

Interpreting Earned Value

In the example used above, the project is in a fairly sorry state. It will require significant activity and effort to pull back on track. This, of course, is not true of every project, indeed very often quite the opposite in fact. Earned value is a well-developed and objective mechanism for understanding what is going wrong (or right).

Consider the following graphs. Can you work out whether the projects are in good (or bad) shape and what might be going wrong (or right)?

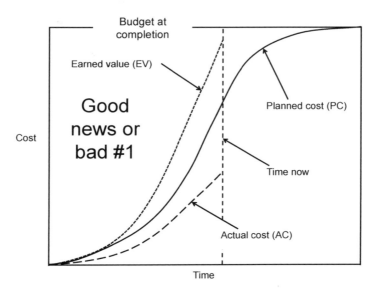

FIGURE 57 GOOD NEWS OR BAD #1

The project is storming ahead, the earned value is relatively high and the actual costs relatively low (below the PC and EV). The project has nearly finished with dramatically lower costs than estimated. There can be down sides to this though, as dramatically poor estimating can cause organisations to take on less risk than they might otherwise do, thereby potentially missing out on opportunities. The team may just be very efficient, which should be applauded.

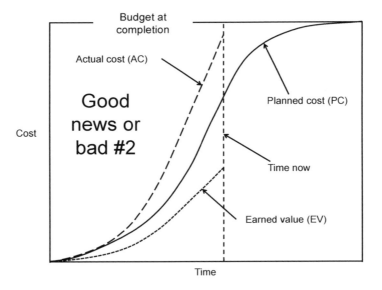

FIGURE 58 GOOD NEWS OR BAD #2

Completely the opposite of example #1. The actual costs are way above budget and the delivery is very late. There are inefficiencies in here; the team are exerting a lot of effort but not getting very far. Again, perhaps the estimates were wrong, or perhaps we need some training or a good hard look at how to speed things up and save costs. This could also be an indicator of poor morale.

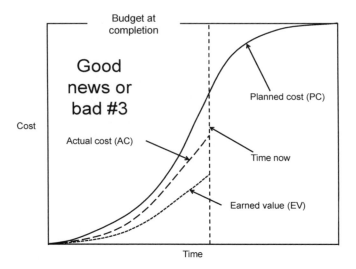

FIGURE 59 GOOD NEWS OR BAD #3

The actual costs are below the planned costs but above the earned value. Here we are delivering slowly and spending more than we should for what we deliver. Once again, the team may be in need of motivation or possibly some re-enforcement. Perhaps we have too junior members of staff and could do with some more skilled people to recover the schedule and utilise the under spend. We might consider overtime working.

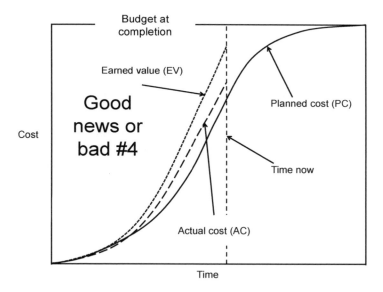

FIGURE 60 GOOD NEWS OR BAD #4

The earned value is above the actual cost and way above the planned cost. This means once again that the project is roaring ahead. Perhaps it could slow down a little, maybe redeploy some of its staff to cut back on costs as it can afford to deliver a bit more slowly.

The Advantages of Using Earned Value

- It provides an index that can be used to help understand whether the project is going to fulfil its success criteria and parameters.

- It provides an insight into how the project has been performing to date.

- Helps provide clues as to what needs to change in order that corrective action can be taken.

- Helps communicate the situation through the use of graphs and diagrams.

The Disadvantages of Using Earned Value

- Needs rigour and tight control of costs.

- Requires a properly established baseline WBS so that costs can be tracked accurately.

- Requires openness and honesty and not hiding things 'under the carpet'.

- Has a huge reliance on the assessment of percent complete, which in physical products is relatively straightforward, but presents a huge challenge where the products are less well-defined (for example, software).

Use This Space to Make Some Notes

_____
_____
_____
_____
_____
_____
_____
_____
_____
_____
_____
_____
_____
_____
_____
_____
_____
_____

WHIRLWIND BIKES

For Whirlwind, we have introduced some data and 'rolled the project forward' to period 6 at which the planned cost is £194k (derived from the earlier cost curve calculations). Calculate the earned value, the CPI, SPI and actual completion, and estimate at completion based on the data provided. Draw the other two curves (EV and AC) on the template provided.

Work Package	Duration	Work Package BAC	Earned Value % Complete	Earned Value	Actual Costs Booked to WP
Start up and mobilisation	1	5,000	100		5,000
Design frame	2	60,000	95		57,000
Design wheels	1	10,000	100		12,000
Design the ancillaries	1	10,000	100		15,000
Build the frame	4	60,000	0		
Build the wheels	2	20,000	70		14,000
Build the ancillaries	1	20,000	90		17,000
Integrate the bike	2	40,000	0		
Test the bike	2	20,000	0		
Launch the bike	1	5,000	0		
Project management	12	48,000	50		22,000
Total		**298,000**			**142,000**
CPI =					

SPI =

SV =

CV =

Actual completion

Estimate at completion

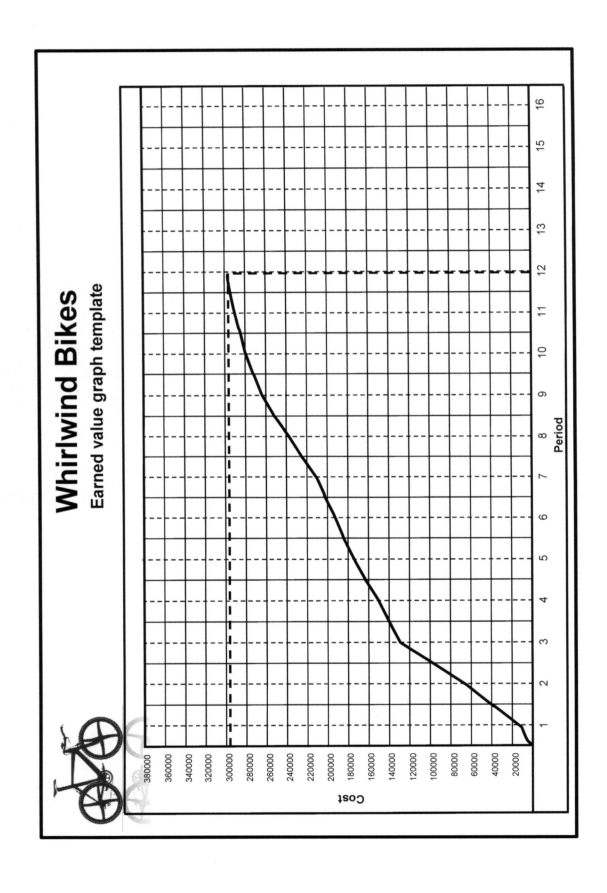

Whirlwind Bikes

Earned value graph template

Use This Space to Make Some Notes

Quick Quiz (Answers in Section 18)

	Question	Options	Your Answer
1	An SPI more than 1 is bad.	True or false?	
2	A CPI less than 1 is good.	True or false?	
3	Earned value management cannot be used to tell whether we are...?	a) Ahead or behind of schedule b) Ahead or behind on cost c) In control of costs d) None of the above	
4	CV = EV – ?	a) SV b) CPI c) AC d) PC	
5	BAC stands for...?	a) Budget at cost b) Budget after completion c) Bonus at completion d) Budget at completion	
6	Earned value management needs a very well-considered WBS in order to be operated effectively.	True or false?	

	Question	Options	Your Answer
7	Which of these is NOT a disadvantage of using earned value management Techniques?	a) It needs accurate data b) It needs a very granular WBS c) It is inaccurate d) It needs resources to operate it	
8	If the EV is above the AC, is this …?	a) Good b) Bad c) Maybe d) Can't tell	
9	The actual costs are usually provided by the accounts department (or project accountants).	True or false?	
10	Changes to the budgets will affect EV calculation.	True or false?	

What Kind of Questions Might There Be in the Exam?

1)	From the data supplied below, calculate the SPI, CPI, estimated price at completion and actual completion, and comment on the state of the project's health.

Work Package	Duration	Planned Cost (£)	Earned Value % Complete	Earned Value (£)	Actual Costs Booked to WP (£)
A	1	2,000	100	2,000	2,100
B	4	4,000	25	1,000	1,800
C	2	2,000	10	200	600
D	1	1,000	90	900	1,000
E	2	2,000	90	1,800	2,000
Total		11,000		5,900	7,500

2)	Explain the term 'earned value' and explain four advantages or disadvantages of using it.

SECTION 12
PROJECT RISK AND ISSUE MANAGEMENT

 Assessment Criteria

12.1 Explain each stage in a risk management process

12.2 Compare the responses to risk in terms of risk as a threat or opportunity

12.3 Explain the benefits of project risk management

What is a Risk?

> "Project Risk is the exposure of stakeholders to the consequences of variations in outcome. It is the overall risk affecting the whole project, defined by components associated with risk events, other sources of uncertainty and associated dependencies, to be managed at a strategic level.
>
> A Risk Event is an uncertain event or set of circumstances that, should it occur or they occur would have an effect on the achievement of one or more of the project's objectives.". (APM Project Risk Analysis and Management Guide)

The Body of Knowledge focuses attention on the overall impact of risk to the whole project outcome, including the benefits. This overall risk is made up of specific project risk events, such as 'possible failure of acceptance testing', which we would record on the risk register, AND other sources of uncertainty, such as estimating. These latter are areas we suspect may be potential risks that may need more investigation but are not quantifiable at this stage.

It is important to differentiate between the causes of risks, the risk itself and the effect of a risk. Take a simple example. There is a risk that we may not have enough of a specific resource for a critical stage in the project, such as commissioning or going live with a system. The causes may be failure of the transport system due to extreme weather, inability to recruit sufficient people with the right skills or that there is a flu pandemic. Because of one or all of these causes, the risk transpires and the effects occur which might be that we are unable to deliver the critical stage product on time, we get sued by the client and we all lose our jobs.

We need to focus on the causes and the effects rather than the terminology of the risk itself. Causes may in themselves have other causes (extreme weather may (or may not) be caused by global warming). The causes also have a probability associated with them. If they have already happened then they are not a risk but an issue. All risks have to have an element of uncertainty associated with them. We describe this uncertainty as their probability.

If the risk matures there will be an impact, which we measure in terms of time, cost or failure to meet performance criteria.

There is a tendency to merely think of risks as threat-based (i.e. what might go wrong). The APM encourage thought about the opposite (i.e. what might go better than right) and these are referred to as opportunities.

Why Do We Need a Proactive Risk Management Process?

A risk management process is intended to encourage the team to identify and pre-empt the things that might affect the project. Using a formal process allows thought and energy to be applied at the time when it has the most value — at the beginning.

- The process will define the way in which risks are dealt with, the objectives and the roles of the various stakeholders.

- The mechanism to achieve continuous improvement through a proper feedback loop throughout the process itself.

- It will help make sure that a proper contingency is in place by calculating the relevant allowances against a quantified and fully considered risk profile.

- A process ensures that everyone is doing the same things in the same way as it is documented in the PMP.

- It provides a common reference point for any audit and assurance processes.

- It will make sure that the sponsoring organisation enters into projects with a clear perspective of the risks, in the knowledge that all the avenues have been covered and due process has been followed, and the resultant data on which decisions are made is accurate.

The PRAM Process

The Project Risk and Management (PRAM) guide published by the APM advocates a generic risk management life cycle and it is reproduced in Figure 61 below. The arrows around the boxes are significant and imply that the steps are not isolated but are in fact iterative in a number of ways. Following the process blindly is not going to be sufficient to manage risks effectively on the project. It is merely a framework around which the project manager and teams will need to use their skill, knowledge and ingenuity on an on-going basis to pre-empt the things that might interfere with the achievement of objectives.

These stages are discussed below.

Initiation

The main output from the initiation phase is the risk management plan. This document describes the following key elements of how risk management will be implemented on the project:

- Scope — of the risk management process, what are the objectives of having the process and which elements of the project are in (and which out) of scope of the process. For example, a risk study may focus on the risk to a particular milestone, such as a product launch, in isolation from the rest of the project.

- Objectives — what is the process trying to achieve, what level of risk reduction are we trying to achieve? What are the legislative or industry standards applicable to the industry in which we are operating?

- Roles — who has a role in the risk management process; who are our advisors? Is there a corporate component to be taken into account; is the project part of a programme or portfolio? If so, there are probably already roles in place.

- Process — what steps will we follow for the identification, assessment and management of the risks (i.e. what is the process and how can we demonstrate we are following it)?

- Tools — what tools are available and what techniques are going to be supported in the process?

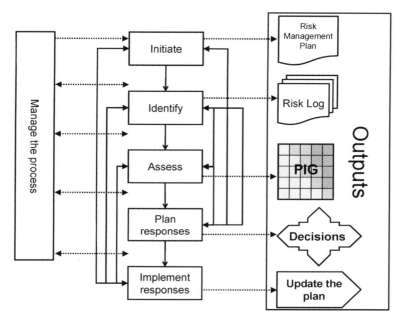

FIGURE 61 THE APM RISK MANAGEMENT PROCESS (ANNOTATED)

These stages are discussed below.

Identification

- **Brainstorming** is the use of facilitated workshops to elicit 'blue sky' ideas from participants with a view to identifying risks that may be significant. Brainstorming gets a lot of good ideas out in the open quickly, but because of the number of people involved it can be expensive and requires careful management.

- **Interviewing** is where specific subject experts in their respective fields are interviewed to help focus in on specific components or activities in the project. Experts will tend to use their own subjective perspective of what are risks and what are not. These views may differ from other 'experts'. They do yield a lot of detailed data and insights though and capitalise on experience.

- **Delphi** This is a form of expert analysis where a number of 'experts' are consulted about a specific problem or set of circumstances and they then discuss and debate within groups or plenary what the nature of the resultant risks may be. This is easily done remotely using email or web based technology and will provide a large amount of expert input but will doubtless cost quite a lot of money and will be tricky to co-ordinate.

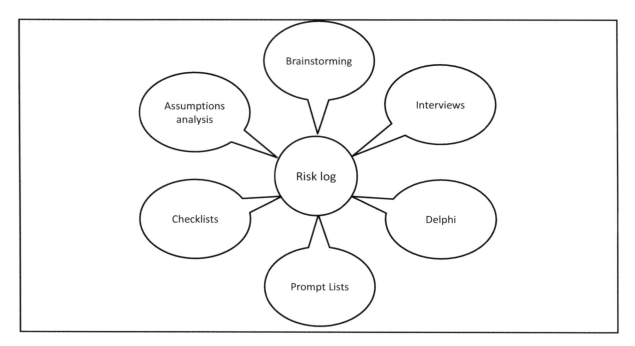

FIGURE 62 RISK IDENTIFICATION TECHNIQUES

- **Prompt lists** these are a form of checklist but more generic in nature and are used to help identify the nature of a risk rather than provide a preexisting 'category' as such. They can include things like a categorisation (e.g. technical, commercial, etc). They do in some cases limit thought and creativity though as time can be consumed discussing the headings rather then the risks themselves.

- **Checklists** are widely used to help identify risks. They appear in all walks of life and are borne out of a systematic process done once to analyse potential areas of risk and deployed into repetitive situations to speed up the identification process. They are quick and relatively cheap, but sometimes it can be felt that doing the checklist is doing the risk management and significant risks are overlooked simply because they are not on the list.

- **Assumptions analysis** is a mechanism of going through previous lists of assumptions and breaking them down to understand which risks may be a consequence of them. This is relatively quick and easy, and draws on work that has gone before; there is a danger that assumptions are not managed otherwise.

Risk Log

Once a risk has been identified, it must be recorded on a risk log and be annotated with some basic information, such as:

- **Identification number** — usually sequential within a given project or programme.

- **Description** — a long-hand description, which should include the cause and effect.

- **Category** — this aids communication and might include: strategic (risks that would interfere with the organisation's interests); project (those that might cause the project to fail); operational (risks that would interfere with the organisation's business); and technical (potential problems with the products and their manufacture).

- **Potential impact** on the project objectives pre-mitigation (only possible after the assessment step — see below).

- **Probability pre-mitigation** (only possible after the assessment step — see below).

- **Potential actions** to mitigate the risk (only possible after the plan response step — see below).

- **Assignment of an owner** — a risk owner is the person or individual who is best placed to manage the risk.

Typically, there may also be an indication of the effect of the actions and a post-mitigation score so that the effect of committing resources is visible.

Assesment

The most recognisable and common output from the risk assessment process is called the probability and impact grid (PIG), an example of which appears in Figure 63. The use of this example is to show that a risk is evaluated on two axes; that of probability (how likely is it to happen) and that of impact (what will happen if it does).

Each of the two axes has two forms of scale. The VHI, HI, MED, LO, VLO is an example of a **qualitative** scale. This is a subjective scale and cannot be processed easily using an automated tool. Whether a risk is a very low probability is a personal evaluation. One person's view of very low is different from another person's view. This is a perfectly viable scale though and should not be dismissed. It has the advantage of being accessible to lay people and encourages individuals to become engaged in the process, which can sometimes otherwise be seen as complicated and obscure.

The numbered scale on the other hand is an attempt to put a more **quantitative** assessment on the risks and it encourages thinking about specific numbering, providing potential to input these numbers into some form of modelling and analysis tool.

It is normal to take the probability score and multiply it with the impact score to arrive at what is often termed the Severity. It is usual at this time to also record their ranking on the risk log, and in an automated system the most significant risks will 'bubble to the top'. So on the grid below, the following maths can be exercised:

Risk A = 0.5 x 0.1 = 0.05
Risk B = 0.9 x 0.8 = 0.72
Risk C = 0.1 x 0.8 = 0.08
Risk D = 0.9 x 0.05 = 0.045

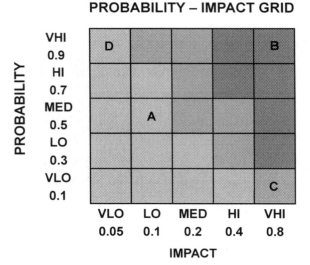

FIGURE 63 PROBABILITY IMPACT GRID

Note that the impact score is nonlinear. This is because the impact of a risk is usually considered to be more significant than the probability. If a potential impact has a calamitous outcome (e.g. nuclear core meltdown) we want to see it much higher up the ranking (probably at the top) than it might otherwise do if the scores were simply linear (1–5 perhaps).

Plan Response

Having arrived at a severity score for the risk, it is now necessary to determine a potential response to the risk. There are two things to do here. One is to determine what can be done to reduce the probability of the risk occurring (thereby reducing its probability). The second is to determine a plan and set aside contingencies to deal with it if it does. Some examples appear in the following table:

Risk Event	Consequence	Mitigation Action to reduce probability	Contingency actions to deal with it if it still does occur
Bad weather	There may be delays in replacing the roof, thereby causing delays and potential overspend	Do roofing work during the drier months.	Erect protective sheeting above roof while work takes place. Stop work and move workers inside during bad weather.
The new server does not arrive in time	The software testing cannot take place	Make sure it is purchased from a reputable supplier.	Provide a delay between planned delivery and testing starting. Purchase two, one as a spare.
The staff do not accept the new working practices	Poor customer service and morale	Make sure staff are communicated with early in the process.	Have a long transition phase. Hire temporary staff while changes and alterations are made.

Generally speaking there are eight potential responses to risks (four for threats and four for opportunities) described here. There are more but these are the main ones:

Threats:

- Accept — Here we accept the risk and take no proactive action other than put monitoring processes in place to make sure that the potential for damage does not change. Once risks are accepted it is generally necessary to provide for some form of contingency to provide funds or time to accommodate the risk should it happen (despite its lower probability / impact).

- Avoid — The only real way to avoid a risk is to change the project scope or approach — what we do or the way we do it. Remove a particular chemical from the process, for example.

- Transfer — We seek to move the risk from our risk log onto someone else's risk log. We seek to transfer the potential for harm to another, usually through an insurance policy or a contract.

- Reduce — Either the probability or the impact (or both). For example, provide training to staff so they know how to operate a process (reduces probability) or perhaps test all output so that if a poor quality product is produced, we do not deliver it to the client (reduces the impact of the risk).

Opportunities:

- Reject — Choose not to take advantage of the opportunity, possibly because it is worth too little or requires too much work to capitalise upon.

- Enhance — Take proactive steps to make sure that not only is the risk made more likely to happen but also that the consequences are made more valuable. If there is a chance of finishing the hotel refurbishment early, then we can seek to sell the rooms earlier.

- Exploit — Take no steps to enhance probability or impact and merely allow it to mature. We then take advantage of the consequences. This perhaps would be where their value is fair, but perhaps not worth exposing more risks involved in Enhance.

- Share — seek partners with whom we can actively capitalise on the circumstances. Often a joint venture, perhaps where an opportunity exists for an extra retail outlet in the bus station, but as it is not core business, we may seek a partner to help capitalise on it.

Care is needed when arriving at any response to risk because whatever action we take has the potential to generate other risks. For example when changing the type of chemical used in a particular process with another to avoid risks of corrosion to the containers, we may introduce the secondary risk of that replacement chemical not being as efficient as the original, leading to a risk of a less than optimal result. This is an example of a secondary risk.

Implement Responses

Once the specific responses have been decided upon they should be included within the project plan. A project does not have a risk plan and a separate project plan. It simply has a new version of the plan. Therefore, once the responses have been scoped and planned, they are included within the work breakdown structures, schedules, budgets, and so on.

You also need to establish a separate activity if there needs to be a contingency or fall back plan created to make sure that there is a proper course of action to be followed in the event of a risk materialising. This plan does have a separate budget formulated from the calculated contingencies for the project. If a risk occurs, then the contingency is disbursed by the sponsor when required. Contingency is only set aside to deal with the known and quantified effects of risk.

Make sure that the process is alive and continually reviewed. Risk reviews should take place at prescribed intervals, proper records kept, and escalation and advice sought where necessary. Make sure the team are engaged and that all available information is utilised where practical to improve the quality of the evaluations.

 Use This Space to Make Some Notes

 Quick Quiz (Answers on the Website)

	Question	Options	Your Answer
1	The axes of a risk assessment grid are	a) Power and influence b) People and information c) Probability and influence d) Probability and impact	
2	Which of these is not a response to a threat-based risk?	a) Accept b) Avoid c) Share d) Reduce	
3	If a risk has a probability score or 0.4 and an impact score of 0.05, its risk score (severity) is...?	a) 0.01 b) 0.02 c) 0.04 d) 1.01	
4	Which of these is NOT a stage in the APM risk management process?	a) Initiate b) Plan response c) Quantitative d) Asses	
5	The risk management plan may be part of the overall project management plan.	True or false?	

	Question	Options	Your Answer
6	Brainstorming is a way of identifying risks.	True or false?	
7	Expert judgment will never affect an individual's view of a risk probability.	True or false?	
8	Throughout the project, risk scores will never change.	True or false?	
9	Which of these is not a risk identification technique?	a) Brainstorming b) Expert judgment c) Assumptions analysis d) Guesswork	
10	A risk owner is the person who carries out the risk mitigation actions.	a) Yes b) No c) Manages them	

What Kind of Questions Might There Be in the Exam?

1) Consider the diagram below and rank the risks in order. Describe four responses to risks or opportunities.

2) List and describe the stages in a risk management process, making five points in your answer.

Assessment Criteria

12.4 Distinguish between risks and issues

12.5 Explain the benefits of the escalation process

This is one of the key roles of a project manager. The APM has a particular interpretation of the term 'issue', however, and you should note well that:

> "A formal Issue occurs when the tolerances of delegated work are predicted to be exceeded or have been exceeded. This triggers the escalation of the issue from one level of management to the next in order to seek a solution" (APM Body of Knowledge 6th edition)

A project manager would normally be allowed a tolerance to make decisions to keep the project going along. They are not required to resort to a sponsor decision as soon as something minor occurs. One of the key pieces of judgement a PM will need to apply is that of when to seek assistance to sort out a problem and when to make that decision themselves. This has a lot to do with the relationship between the PM and the Sponsor but also needs to be recorded in a manner of formal process. The Issue Management Plan is one of those documents that finds its way into the PMP.

The Issue Log

Recognition of an issue should be swiftly followed by the recording of it on some form of template, maintained by the project manager (potentially supported by the project office). An example of such a template (the issue log) appears in Figure 64:

			Impact				
ID	Description	Date	Time	Cost	Owner	Status	Agreed actions

(Issue Log)

FIGURE 64 ISSUE LOG

The headings are very similar to those on a risk log and there are a lot of synergies. One significant source of issues is simply risks that have occurred. Issues can appear under other circumstances, but it can be argued that this is simply a failing on the part of the risk management process having not predicted them!

A couple of things to note on this sample issue log are:

There is no probability column. An issue has a probability of 100% (i.e. it has happened)

The status would reflect whether it was perhaps Open or Resolved. These headings would be spelt out in the issue management plan.

However, given that they have occurred, they need to be managed in a systematic way. Key failings in this process are often:

- Not recognising an issue for what it is and not escalating it, believing it can be resolved by the project manager.

- Failing to track an issue once escalated to make sure it has or is in the process of being resolved.

As well as the project manager, the sponsor and steering group have a key role in dealing with issues as they will be the bodies to whom the issues are raised. Failure on the part of the steering group or sponsor to deal with the issue leaves very little other option. The project manager needs a good solid network of support from these two entities.

The Benefits of Issue Management

If left unattended, issues will slowly grow in number and build up to be a wave of difficulty that can submerge a project. Issues must be dealt with as soon as they become apparent (or at least identify how they will be resolved).

Stakeholders will be properly informed, as potential threats can be shared amongst the individuals or groups that can best deal with them, possibly through the use of specialist support.

Contingencies allocated in the risk management process need to be drawn down to deal with the issues as they present themselves.

There is a clear hierarchy of responsibility required to be sure where responsibility lies.

Allocation of an owner is an important process in itself and it will ensure that a suitably capable person or group has the delegated to sort out the issue.

 Use This Space to Make Some Notes

_____
_____
_____
_____
_____

Quick Quiz (Answers in Section 18)

	Question	Options	Your Answer
1	An issue is a threat that the project manager cannot deal with.	True or false?	
2	To whom would an issue NOT be escalated?	a) Sponsor b) Steering group c) Team	
3	Which of these is NOT a heading on the issue log?	a) Date b) Number c) Owner d) Probability	
4	Not escalating an issue early enough is a common cause of projects running into difficulties.	True or false?	
5	The project manager may chose to write the issue management process in the PMP.	True or false?	

What Kind of Questions Might There Be in the Exam?

1)	Describe the term issue management and explain four reasons why it must be practiced on a project.

SECTION 13
QUALITY

 Assessment Criteria

13.2 Define quality management

13.3 Define quality planning, assurance, control and continual improvement

13.4 Describe the benefits of the quality management process

A Definition of Quality

Quality is an objective assessment of a product's fitness for purpose. Whilst this definition appears to be limited to the products that the project will produce, importantly, quality applies not only to these products, but also to the processes and procedures deployed in managing the project itself. There is great deal of significance to the term quality and it is worth spending a little more time looking at it in more detail.

If I want to travel cheaply and easily by car, then a small hatchback may be just what is required. In this respect the car conforms to my requirements and specification and is therefore deemed to be a 'quality' product. If I wish to transport a family of six in comfort I may need some form of larger vehicle. This then would be a quality car and the hatchback would not be. Quality is a binary decision. The product either fulfils the specification, or it does not.

Often the term quality is applied to the assessment of a product without a requisite specification. In these cases, the perspective will be totally subjective and open to interpretation. Inevitably, there are occasions when a subjective analysis carries a lot more weight than the purely objective analysis against a pre-agreed specification, such as a stay in a hotel, where the customer experience is more than just the size of the room.

The nature of the product is specified as part of the work package descriptions and will carry associated acceptance criteria. It is the achievement of these acceptance criteria that formally acknowledges that the requirements have been met.

Quality pervades everything we do and what we produce. It is an integral component of professional project management directed full square at producing the right product first time, every time.

Quality Management

The term quality management applies to four main components, each of which we consider later. However, it is worth considering the interaction of quality with other components of the Syllabus. Consider the diagram below.

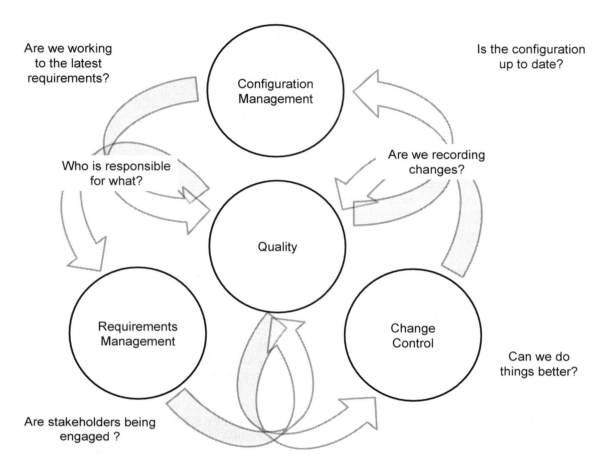

FIGURE 65 QUALITY IS NOT AN ISOLATED 'CAMEO' SUBJECT

There is a value in managing quality pro actively on a project. It can also be argued that quality is in fact free, in that it pays for itself; as the organisation becomes more mature, it makes less faulty goods that need to be replaced and repaired less often. As the prevention costs slowly rise, the failure and prevention costs fall dramatically. This concept is called The 'Cost of Quality' coined by Philip B Crosby in the 1980's.

The benefits of the quality management processes are that:

- Eventually, if followed to their ultimate conclusion, it will eradicate all problems and a perfect product will be produced. This will probably never happen in reality, but as we progress towards it, faults will occur less often.

- It engenders confidence on the part of the stakeholders that they will receive what they asked for because requirements are visibly and systematically recorded and processed. Stakeholders can therefore be more comfortable their needs will be addressed.

- It reduces rework, thus ultimately reducing costs. This is because there will be clear specifications and direction to the effort with clear statements of anticipated results that can be assured and checked.

- In safety critical systems, it provides confidence that those processes will not introduce risk through faulty deliverables. Testing will be thorough and rigorous and any deviations from the specification will be spotted and dealt with at an early stage and completely.

- With a strong ethos of continuous improvement, quality will improve efficiency and effectiveness over time as lessons will be learnt and used to provide diagnostic information and guidance for the establishment of better processes going forward.

There are four stages in quality management:

Quality Planning

The project must produce a quality plan (part of the PMP) and in it describe how the project will produce quality products and how it will manage itself. It will describe all of the following:

- The roles and responsibilities concerned with quality — these might include quality assurance, testing, supervision and management roles;

- The processes that will be followed — these will be documented in a systematic way and will govern the mechanisms for the production of the product specifications and testing procedures for example;

- How continuous improvement will be carried out — this will include making adjustments to processes where they are proven to be unsatisfactory;

- What project assurance techniques will be deployed, such as audit, supplier vetting, specification writing, etc.;

- What quality control techniques will be used, like the Pareto analysis, control charts, inspection test and measurement, etc.;

- Interactions with other processes (e.g. configuration management) and how these links will be established and managed and in a suitable manner.

The project manager owns the PMP and therefore owns the subsidiary plans of which the quality plan is one. In drawing it up, the project manager needs to draw on the organisation's existing processes tools and techniques. External influences will need to be taken into account that influence the nature of the quality environment.

- ISO 9000 — is the company an ISO 9000 accredited organisation?

- TQM — is there adherence to a Total Quality Management system?

- Are Investors in People principles in place?

- Are any Quality Maturity Models being actively managed, such as European Foundation Quality Model?

- Are there external industry standards that need to be adhered to?

- Is Six Sigma used as a quality control technique?

The project is not operating in a vacuum and, as such, all or any of the above may have a direct bearing on the way in which the project is commissioned and run.

Quality Assurance

Quality Assurance is the process associated with demonstrating and providing confidence to all stakeholders that the quality requirements will be achieved. Quality assurance will provide satisfaction that the plans are being followed and in the absence of any external distractions a quality product will be produced.

Assurance usually incorporates components of:

- **Training** — are the team properly trained? Are training records in place? Are there clear job requirements and are we able to vouch for the fact that the post holder is competent?

- **Audit** — can be used to make sure in a formal and external way whether or not the processes and principles of the PMP are being followed. Commissioned by sponsors, steering groups and others they will provide evidence of the fact that things are being executed in the way intended.

- **Lessons learned** — the assurance processes make sure that the lessons learned during the project are properly communicated and that a properly formulated feedback loop is in place, making sure that mistakes and poor quality are removed at the root of the problem; the illnesses cured not the symptoms.

- **Supplier Accreditation** — the supplier base may need to demonstrate their quality credentials. Where goods and materials are shipped in for incorporation into the project's products (steel in a building perhaps) it may be necessary to ensure that those materials are of a suitable quality and will not cause a failure of testing further down the line.

Quality Control

Quality control techniques are many and varied and are generally influenced to a very large degree by the nature of the project. For example, you would not rely on a visual inspection of safety critical software code, whereas for a small brick wall it may well be appropriate.

There are a number of these techniques, some of which are discussed below. In all cases, quality control must be undertaken using an objective mechanism comparing the finished product against a specification to confirm acceptability. Work packages will all have associated acceptance criteria relating to the products.

Inspection and Measurement — as discussed above, very often a simple sight check will be sufficient, looking through a document before it is sent out or looking at the way a playing surface has been laid may be all that is required, perhaps measuring the height of the goal posts using some form of gauge or a tape to make sure the white lines are the right distance apart. In software, the use of various levels of specification can provide the means to develop ever more precise tests to turn what might be fairly subjective requirements into testable products and systems.

Walkthroughs — are a little more in-depth and these will usually involve a group of people stepping through the lines of code in a software programme, literally perhaps walking through a finished arrivals hall to make sure the signs are in place as an example.

Pareto Analysis — involves understanding the nature of the observable faults and understanding the nature of the root cause of those problems. Once these are understood, it will be beneficial to solve the causes that result in the most number of faults. There is little point fixing the problems that never result in an observable fault. This is sometimes called the 80:20 rule; 80% of the observable faults are caused by 20% of the root causes. Focus attention on those and a big impact will be achieved. Once those are fixed the next 20% (of a smaller sample) can be tackled and so on.

Process Control Charts — A process control chart plots the measurements of how the readings taken of a sample of product varies over time. With time on the x axis and the range of witnessed measurements on the y axis, a plot can be taken that describes how the readings fluctuate. There may be upper and lower control limits (UCL and LCL) which are based on the specification requirements. The intention is to recognise that a problem is about to occur and various algorithms can be deployed to determine whether there is a significant problem or not.

Cause and effect — diagrams are used to decompose a single cause of the problem and understand as much as possible about the root causes that may have caused the problem. The intention is to 'root out' the causes and eradicate them.

Continuous Improvement

This is a fundamental principle of quality. This requires the correct use of feedback and using the lessons of the past to drive the actions of the future. Projects can evolve their processes to tune and develop their approach, improving accuracy and conformance to requirements.

Continuous improvement will require the collection of data, using some of the techniques above, such as Pareto Analysis for example. Lets take an example of a project to build a bridge. The welds between he individual beams of the bridge are inspected and a lot of them are demonstrating faults during the x-ray analysis of those welds. Work is undertaken to examine why the faults are occurring and it is determined that the welder needs better training, but also that the welding equipment has not been serviced and is performing below its expected capability. If the welder is sent on a refresher training course and the equipment serviced then the number of faults will reduce. There may still be faults but they will be for other reasons perhaps. This is continuous improvement.

The Benefits of a Quality Management Process

A well established and embedded Quality Management Process are that

- It will engender confidence in the stakeholders as the consistency of the products delivered to them will increase and they will not be engaged with continually referring things for re-work

- The costs will reduce over time as the combined costs of doing the work incorrectly, followed by re-work are more than getting it right in the first place

- Team morale will improve over time as they will become associated with a quality product rather than a poorly turned out and ill received undertaking.

- It will start to reflect on the organisation itself as being trustworthy and capable.

Use This Space to Make Some Notes .

_____
_____
_____
_____
_____
_____

_____
_____
_____
_____
_____
_____
_____

WHIRLWIND BIKES

See if you can spot some fundamental requirements in the case study and try and identify a mechanism for testing to see if they have been achieved.

Requirement	Mechanism for testing to see if it has been satisfied

Quick Quiz (Answers in Section 18)

	Question	Options	Your Answer
1	Quality is best described as what?	a) The best we can do b) Gold plated c) Posh d) Fitness for purpose	
2	Acceptance criteria are associated with work package deliverables.	True or false?	
3	Which of these is not a component of a quality management process?	a) Continuous improvement b) Planning c) Control d) Finishing	
4	An 80:20 diagram is a demonstration of the what?	a) Perverse method b) Machiavelli method c) Pareto method d) Italian method	
5	A process control chart records samples against upper and lower control limits.	True or false?	
6	Pareto analysis is a quality control technique.	True or false?	
7	Changes to specifications need to be controlled by which other process?	a) Requirements management b) Configuration management c) Change control d) Project management plan	
8	Which of these is not a quality assurance component?	a) Training b) Lessons learned c) Audit d) Resource management	
9	As the cost of prevention rises slowly the cost of failure and prevention drop dramatically.	True or false?	
10	Who is responsible for quality on a project?	a) The project manager b) The project sponsor c) The project team d) Everyone	

	What Kind of Questions Might There Be in the Exam?
1)	List and describe why it is important to manage quality on your project, make five points in your answer.
2)	List and describe five key components of a quality management process

SECTION 14

PROCUREMENT

	Assessment Criteria

14.1 Explain the purpose and content of a procurement strategy

14.2 Distinguish between different methods of supplier reimbursement

14.3 Distinguish between different contractual relationships

14.4 Explain a supplier selection process

Procurement Strategy

Procurement is the process by which an organisation acquires goods and services. It includes the development of a procurement strategy, preparation of contracts, selection and acquisition of suppliers and management of the contract.

Procurement is a process that is followed and most organisations will already have a significant amount of material and systems associated with it. The project will need to make sure that it has a clear interaction with the business components and this needs to be properly documented in a procurement strategy.

The procurement strategy is a project document that describes the mechanics of how the project will go about procuring and subsequently managing services and goods. The procurement strategy defines how the project procurement will take place and as such needs to be considered when the project is being formulated alongside the business case. There will be numerous procurement implications for the project manager throughout the life of the project, so the procurement strategy may also be a component of the PMP. There are a number of key sections that it should contain:

1) The **Make or Buy Decision** — should the goods be made in-house or could we procure them elsewhere at a lower cost or better quality? To do this, we will need a well-developed understanding of the specification, because in order to derive a solid price, we will need to be specific about what it is we want.

2) Choice of **Contractual Relationship** — Should we buy from one supplier or many? There are many types of different contractual arrangements that we can end up with and some are mentioned here. Please note that a contract type is different from a payment term (see reimbursement methods later). The following types of contractual arrangement might be considered when drafting the procurement strategy.

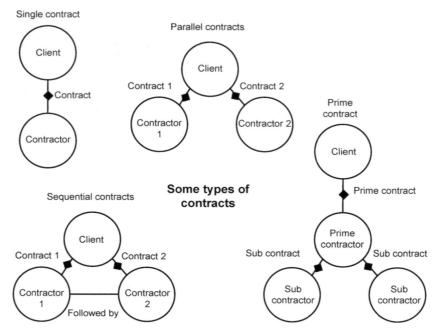

FIGURE 66 TYPES OF CONTRACTUAL RELATIONSHIPS

- Single contracts are where a single client purchases from a single supplier with a single contract between them. This is the simplest form of arrangement.

- Parallel contracts are an arrangement there are a number of single contracts with a number of suppliers all doing the same work. We may have a number of house builders all building houses on the same site to the same design for example.

- Sequential contracts are where we have one supplier doing one element of the work (e.g. design) and another doing the next (e.g. build).

- Prime and sub contracts are where we allocate one single contract to a main supplier who then 'sub contracts' that work to others.

- Turnkey contracts (no diagram) are where a single supplier undertakes to provide everything needed to meet the requirements. It is called turnkey because the principle is that the client merely turns the key and it works.

- Partnering (no diagram) is where two or more organisations agree to work together to achieve the project. They both have separate skills and areas of expertise; in isolation they are unable to deliver the finished product, but collectively they can.

3) **Reimbursement Methods** — the project and the sponsoring organisation will need to decide on the mechanism it would prefer to use to pay for the goods procured under the contract. These are referred to as payment terms and as mentioned are different from the contract type.

There are a number of factors to be taken into account when deciding which type to use. Often the decision is based on risk. If the client is unsure about exactly what is to be purchased, they would probably not be in a position to demand a fixed price from the supplier. If there are new innovative techniques involved, the client may not wish to have a fixed price and may pay the supplier to innovate, which needs a more flexible payment regime.

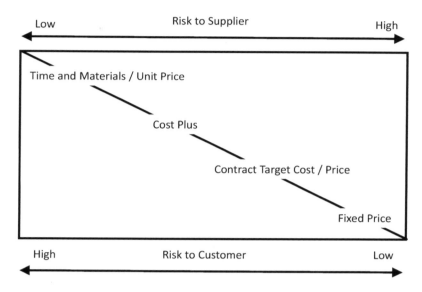

FIGURE 67 TYPES OF SUPPLIER REIMBURSEMENT TERMS

Time and materials payment or unit price — is where a price is agreed for a unit of cost (e.g. a man day, a ton of concrete) and the client pays per unit. The problem with this approach, of course, is that if the job is estimated to take 20 days and takes 30, the client will pay for 30. Thus the risk of overrun lies with the client. These can be useful, however, when the client genuinely does not have a fixed view about the costs and the specification is vague. The project management here would normally have to be a shared responsibility or rest with the client.

Fixed price payment — is where a fixed price is agreed for a fixed scope of work to be carried out by the supplier. If the job is contracted at 20 days and it actually takes 30, the client still only pays for 20. Fixed price may be appropriate if you know exactly what is required and there is a precise requirement. Fixed price contracts tend to cost more as the supplier will normally look for some form of reimbursement for carrying the risk of overrun.

Cost plus payment — this type of payment is where the supplier gets reimbursed their cost (N.B. not price) and the client agrees to pay a certain amount over the costs to cover the supplier's profit. These arrangements can include cost plus fixed fee or cost plus percentage. Both of these will have a slightly different impact on the way the supplier is motivated because cost plus fixed fee will only allow the same fixed fee regardless of actual cost, whereas the percentage fee rises at the same percentage with the cost, thus protecting the contractors margin.

Target cost/price payment — is where a target price (or cost) is agreed up front and the supplier and client agree to work to try and achieve it. It has a big impact on the way the contract is managed as usually any over or under performance is shared between the parties and they agree to share it at an agreed rate. There is potentially therefore the opportunity to provide motivation on both parties to work corroboratively to maximise under spend and minimise overspend.

4) **Supplier Selection** — a key consideration for the procurement strategy is how to go about engaging the right contractor. There are usually a number of steps to go through and most organisations will already have some rules and guidelines to help the project

on its way. These procedures will almost certainly involve most of the following key stages:

a) Define the requirement and make sure that there is a suitable level of definition for the scope of work. Document it as part of the project documentation and record it in appropriate systems for later reference.

b) Issue an Invitation To Tender (ITT) which may follow an advertising process to determine who the likely suppliers might be. The ITT usually has a response period and should include enough information for the potential bidders to respond. It should also include the criteria on which the responses will be judged, perhaps some form of compliance matrix. ITTs are sometimes referred to as invitation to bid or request for quotation.

c) Answer the bidder's queries they have raised. It is normal to make sure that if one bidder asks a question then all the bidders see the answer. Sometime a bidder's conference can be held where there is an interactive opportunity to ask questions and seek clarification.

d) Receive and evaluate bids and review against the compliance matrix. The bidders may well provide a lot of 'extras' over and above the specification and these can be considered, but straightforward compliance to the ITT is the minimum.

e) Award a contract to the successful bidder(s), making sure that the scope is as per the tender, bind in whatever documents are relevant and make sure that you and they fully understand the nature of the arrangement and their respective liabilities. There are a number of key components of a contract:

   Offer, the client offers to buy; **Acceptance**, the supplier agrees to sell; **Consideration**, money or some other form of value changes hands; **Form**, generally contracts do not need to be in writing, but best practice dictates that they are in case they need to be referenced; **Intent**, both parties need to be intent on being bound; **Legal entity** both parties need to be able to undertake a contract; **Capacity**, both parties must be in a position to fulfil the bargain.

f) Other areas that need to be considered are duration, termination, intellectual property rights, warranties, indemnities and guarantees. The advice generally is to seek advice from a qualified person before entering into any legally binding arrangements. Warranties need to be considered as do the terms of penalty if either side break their part of the bargain and breach the contract.

5) **Contract administration** should be carried out following the contract award to make sure that both parties are conforming and discharging their duties accordingly. Any recourse to enforcement of the contract will need to be supported by evidence that both parties were engaged and trying to make the agreement work as planned

Feedback and review, a key ingredient for any strategy, is a lessons learned and feedback process to understand what has gone well and what has not gone so well. Procurement departments are usually only too happy to become engaged in feedback from the 'coal face' so that processes can be improved for next time.

WHIRLWIND BIKES

Think about the case study in Section 16.
What decisions are you going to have to make when considering which contractor to use?

Use this space to make some notes

Quick Quiz (Answers in Section 18)

	Question	Options	Your Answer
1	In a fixed price arrangement, the supplier holds the risk of overrun.	True or false?	
2	Which of these is not a payment term?	a) Fixed price b) Target cost c) Unit price d) Parallel	

	Question	Options	Your Answer
3	In a sequential contract, two different suppliers can each provide their own component of the project simultaneously.	True or false?	
4	Which of these is not a component of a contract?	a) Consideration b) Termination c) Project management plan d) Duration	
5	A procurement strategy forms part of which document?	a) PMP b) Business case c) Needs to be considered for both	
6	In a unit price contract, who pays for the extra work if the actual effort goes up?	a) The client b) The supplier c) Both d) Neither	
7	In writing the procurement strategy, which of these components is most important?	a) Selection of supplier b) Payment terms c) Contract type d) All of them	
8	If a contract is not performed it is called a breach.	True or false?	
9	How many parties can there be to a contract?	a) One b) Two c) Any number d) Four	
10	Who writes the project procurement strategy?	a) The project manager b) The sponsor c) The users d) The project manager in consultation with the procurement department	

What Kind of Questions Might There Be in the Exam?

1)	List and describe five key components of a procurement strategy.
2)	List and describe five steps in a supplier selection process.

SECTION 15
GLOSSARY OF TERMS

This glossary contains terms derived from the APM Body of Knowledge 6th edition and are used with permission.

A

Accept

A response to a threat when no action is taken

Acceptance criteria

The requirements and essential conditions that have to be achieved before a deliverable is accepted.

Acceptance test

Formal, predefined test conducted to determine the compliance of the deliverable item(s) with the acceptance criteria.

Accrued cost

Costs that are earmarked for the project and for which payment is due, but has not been made.

Activity

1) A task, job, operation or process consuming time and possibly other resources. 2) The smallest self contained unit of work used to define the logic of a project.

Activity duration

The length of time that it takes to complete an activity.

Activity-on-node-network

A network diagram where the activities are represented by the nodes.

Actual cost

The incurred costs that are charged to the project budget and for which payment is made or accrued.

Actual dates (start or finish)

The dates on which activities started and finished, as opposed to planned or forecast dates.

Actual expenditure

The costs that have been charged to the budget and for which payment has been made, or accrued.

Actual progress

A measure of the work that has been completed for comparison with the baseline.

Agile

A family of development methodologies where requirements and solutions are developed iteratively and incrementally through out the lifecycle.

Analogous estimating -

See comparative estimating

Analytical estimating -

See bottom-up estimating

Actual time expended

The elapsed time from the beginning of an activity to date.

Approval to proceed

Approval given to the project at initiation or prior to the beginning of the next stage.

Assumptions

Statements that will be taken for granted as fact and upon which the project business case will be justified.

Audit

Systematic retrospective examination of the whole, or part, of a project or function to measure conformance with predetermined standards. Note: audit is usually qualified, for example, financial audit, quality audit, design audit, project audit, and health and safety audit.

Avoid

A response to a threat that eliminates its probability or impact on the project.

B

Backward pass

A procedure whereby the latest event times or the latest finish and start times for the activities of a network are calculated.

Balanced matrix

An organisational matrix where functions and projects have the same priority.

Bar chart

A chart on which activities and their durations are represented by lines drawn to a common time scale. See Gantt chart.

Baseline

Reference levels against which the project is monitored and controlled.

Baseline cost(s)

The amount of money that a project or activity was intended to cost when the project plan was baselined.

Baseline date(s)

The original planned start and finish dates for a project or an activity when the schedule was baselined.

Baseline schedule

The baseline schedule is a fixed project schedule. It is the standard by which project performance is measured.

Benefit

The quantifiable and measurable improvement resulting from completion of deliverables that is perceived as positive by a stakeholder. It will normally have a tangible value and be expressed in monetary terms that will justify the investment.

Benefits management

The identification, definition, planning, tracking and realisations of benefits.

Benefits management plan

A plan that specifies who is responsible for achieving the benefits set out in the benefits profiles and how achievement of the benefits is to be measured, managed and monitored.

Benefits realisation

The practice of ensuring that the outcome of a project produces the projected benefits.

Board

A body that provides sponsorship to a project, portfolio or programme. The board will represent financial, provider and user interests.

Bottom up cost estimating

An estimating technique that uses detailed specifications to estimate time and cost for each product or activity.

Breakdown Structure

A hierarchical structure by which project elements are broken down, or decomposed. Examples include: cost breakdown structure (CBS) organisational structure (OBS) product breakdown structure (PBS) or Work breakdown structure (WBS).

Budget

The agreed cost of the project or a quantification of resources needed to achieve an activity by a time, within which the activity owners are required to work.

Budget estimate

An approximate estimate prepared in the early stages of a project to establish financial viability or secure resources.

Budgeting and cost control

The estimating of costs, the setting of an agreed budget, and management of actual and forecast costs against that budget.

Business as usual

An organisation's normal day to day operations.

Business case

Provides justification for undertaking a project in terms of evaluating the benefits, cost and risk of alternative options and the rationale for the preferred solution. Its purpose is to obtain management commitment and approval for investment in the project. The business case is owned by the sponsor.

C

Cash flow

Cash receipts and payments in a specified period.

Cash flow forecast

A prediction of the difference between cash received and payments made during a specific period or for the duration of the project.

Change control

A process that ensures all changes to the project's baseline scope, cost, time or quality objectives are identified, evaluated, approved, rejected or deferred.

Change freeze

A point after which no further changes to scope will be considered.

Change control board

A formally constituted group of stakeholders responsible for approving or rejecting changes to the project baselines.

Change log (or register)

A record of all project changes, proposed, authorised, rejected or deferred.

Change request

A request to obtain formal approval for changes to the scope, design, methods, costs or planned aspects of a project.

Client

The party to a contract who commissions the work and pays for it on completion.

Closure

The formal end point of a project or programme, either because it has been completed or because it has been terminated early.

Collaborative negotiation

Negotiation that seeks to create a 'winwin' scenario where all parties involved get part or all of what they were looking for from the negotiation.

Commissioning

The advancement of an installation from the stage of static completion to full working order and achievement of the specified operational requirements.

Committed Expenditure

Costs that have not yet been paid but cannot be cancelled.

Committed costs

Costs that are legally committed even if delivery has not taken place with invoices neither raised nor paid.

Communication

Communication The means by which information or instructions are exchanged. Successful communication occurs when the received meaning is the same as the transmitted meaning.

Communications planning

The establishment of project stakeholders' communication and information needs.

Concept (phase)

Concept is the first phase in the project life cycle. During this phase the need, opportunity or problem is confirmed, the overall feasibility of the project is considered and a preferred solution identified.

Configuration

Functional and physical characteristics of a deliverable defined in its specification.

Configuration audit

A check to ensure that all deliverables (products) in a project conform with one another and to the current specification. It ensures that relevant quality assurance procedures have been implemented and that there is consistency throughout project documentation.

Configuration control

A system to ensure that all changes to configuration items are controlled. An important aspect is being able to identify the interrelationships between configuration items.

Configuration identification

The unique identification of all items within the configuration. It involved breaking down the project into component parts or configuration items, and creating a unique numbering or referencing system for each item, and establishing configuration baselines.

Configuration item

A part a of configuration that has a set function and is designated for configuration management. It identifies uniquely all items within the configuration.

Configuration management

Configuration management encompasses the administrative activities concerned with the creation, maintenance, controlled change and quality control of the scope of work.

Consumable resource

A type of resource that only remains available until consumed (for example a material).

Configuration status accounting

A record and report of the current status and history of all changes to the configuration. Provides a complete record of what happened to the configuration to date.

Conflict management

The process of identifying and addressing differences that if unmanaged would affect project objectives. Effective conflict management prevents differences becoming destructive elements in a project.

Constraints

Things that should be considered as fixed or must happen. Restrictions that will affect the project.

Contingency

Resource set aside for responding to identified risks

Contingency plan

Alternative course(s) of action to cope with project risks or if expected results fail to materialise.

Contract

An agreement made between two or more parties that creates legally binding obligations between them. The contract sets out those obligations and the can be taken if they are not met.

Contractor

A person, company or firm who holds a contract for carrying out the works and/or the supply of goods in connection with the project.

Control

Tracking performance against agreed plans and taking the corrective action required to meet defined objectives.

Cost benefit analysis

An analysis of the relationship between the costs of undertaking a task or project, initial and recurrent, and the benefits likely to arise from the changed situation, initially and recurrently.

Cost breakdown structure (CBS)

The hierarchical breakdown of a project into cost elements.

Cost code

A unique identity for a specified element of work. A code assigned to activities that allow costs to be consolidated according to the elements of a code structure.

Cost estimating

The process of predicting the costs of a project.

Cost performance index (CPI)

A term used in earned value management. A measure, expressed as a percentage or other ration of actual cost to budget plan. The ratio of work accomplished versus work cost incurred for a specified time period. The CPI is an efficiency rating for work accomplished for resources expended.

Cost variance

A term used in earned value management. The difference (positive or negative) between the actual expenditure and the planned/budgeted expenditure.

Critical activity

An activity is termed critical when it has zero or negative float. Alternatively, the activity that has the lowest float on the project.

Critical path

A sequence of activities through a project network from start to finish, the sum of whose durations determines the overall project duration. There may be more than one such path.

Critical path analysis

The procedure for calculating the critical path and floats in a network.

Critical success factor

See Success factors

D

Definition (phase)

Definition is the second phase of the project life cycle. During this phase the preferred solution is further evaluated and optimised. Often an iterative process, definition can affect requirements and the project's scope, time, cost and quality objectives.

Delegation

The practice of getting others to perform work effectively which one chooses not to do oneself. The process by which authority and responsibility is distributed from project manager to subordinates.

Deliverables

The end products of a project or the measurable results of intermediate activities within the project organisation. See Products.

Dependency

A relationship between activities on a network diagram

Duration

Duration is the length of time needed to complete an activity.

E

Early finish date

The earliest possible date by which an activity can finish, within the logical and imposed constraints of the network.

Early start date

The earliest possible date when an activity can start, within the logical and imposed constraints of the network.

Earned value management

A project control process, based on a structured approach to planning, cost collection and performance measurement. It facilitates the integration of project scope, time and cost objectives and the establishment of a baseline plan of performance measurement.

Earned value analysis

An analysis of project progress where the actual money, hours (or other measure) budgeted and spent is compared to the value of the work achieved.

Enhance

A response to an opportunity that increases its probability, impact or both.

Environment

The circumstances and conditions within which the project, programme or portfolio must operate.

Escalation

The process by which issues are drawn to the attention of a higher level of management

Effort

The number of labour units necessary to complete the work. Effort is usually expressed in person hours, weeks and days, and should not be confused with duration.

Estimate

An approximation of time and cost targets, refined throughout the life cycle.

Estimate at completion

The final estimated cost at completion (derived from the earned value calculations).

Estimating funnel

A representation of the increasing levels of estimating accuracy that can be achieved through the phases of the life cycle.

Estimating

The use of a range of tools and techniques to produce estimates.

Exploit

A response of an opportunity that maximises both its probability and its impact.

Extended life cycle

A life cycle model that includes the operational life and termination, including disposal and the project deliverables.

F

Financial management

The process of estimating and justifying costs in order to secure funds, controlling expenditure and evaluating the outcomes.

Fitness for purpose

The degree to which the project management process and project deliverables satisfy stakeholders' needs.

Finish date

The actual or estimated time associated with an activity's completion.

Finish-to-finish

A dependency in an activity-on-node network. It indicates that one activity cannot finish until another activity has finished.

Finish-to-start

A dependency in an activity-on-node network. It indicates that one activity cannot start until another activity has finished.

Fixed price contract

A generic category of contracts based on the establishment of firm legal commitments to complete the required work. A performing contractor is legally obliged to finish the job, no matter how much it costs to complete.

Float

A term used to describe the flexibility with which an activity may be rescheduled. There are various types of Forward pass

Forward Pass

A procedure whereby the earliest event times or the earliest start and finish for the activities of a network are calculated.

Free float

Time by which an activity may be delayed or extended without affecting the start of any succeeding activity.

Functional organisation (structure)

A functional management structure where specific functions of a business are grouped into specialist departments that provide a dedicated service to the whole of the organisation, for example, accounts department, production department, marketing department or IT.

G

Gantt chart

A particular type of bar chart used in project management showing planned activity against time. A Gantt chart is a time-phased graphic display of activity durations. Activities are listed with other tabular information on the left side with time intervals over the bars. Activity durations are shown in the form of horizontal lines.

Gate

The point between phases, gates and/or tranches where a go/ no go decision can be made about the remainder of the work.

Gate review

A formal point in a project where its expected worth, progress, cost and execution plan are reviewed and a decision is made whether to continue with the next phase or stage of the project.

Go/No go

A form of control where a decision is made whether or not to continue with the work.

Governance

The set of policies, regulations, functions, processes, procedures and responsibilities that define the establishment, management and control of projects, programmes and portfolios.

H

Handover

The point in the life cycle where deliverables are handed over to the sponsor and users. See Handover and closeout.

Health and safety management

The process of identifying and minimising threats to workers and those affected by the work throughout the project, programme or portfolio life cycle.

Host organisation

The organisation that provides the strategic direction of the project, programme or portfolio and will be the primary recipient of the benefits.

Handover and closure (phase)

Handover and closeout is the fourth and final phase in the project life cycle. During this phase final project deliverables are handed over to the sponsor and users. Closeout is the process of finalising all project matters, carrying out final project reviews, archiving project information and redeploying the project team.

Histogram

A graphic display of planned and/or actual resource usage over a period of time. It is in the form of a vertical bar chart, the height of each bar representing the quantity of resource usage in a given time unit. Bars may be single, multiple or show stacked resources.

Impact

The assessment of the adverse effects of a risk occurring.

Impact analysis

An assessment of the merits of pursuing a particular course of action or of the potential impact of a requested change.

Implementation (phase)

Implementation is the third phase of the project life cycle where the project management plan (PMP) is executed, monitored and controlled. During this phase the design is finalised and used to build the deliverables.

Incurred costs

The sum of actual and committed costs, whether invoiced/paid or not, at a specified time.

Information management

The collection, storage, dissemination, archiving and appropriate destruction of project information.

Infrastructure

Provides support for projects, programmes and portfolios, and is the focal point for the development and maintenance of P3 management within an organisation.

Investment appraisal

A collection of techniques used to identify the attractiveness of an investment.

Invitation to tender

An invitation to a supplier to tender or bid for the supply of goods or services.

Issue

A formal issue occurs when the tolerances of delegated work are predicted to be exceeded or have been exceeded. This triggers the escalation of the issue from one level of management to the next in order to seek a solution.

K

Key performance indicator

Measures of success that can be used throughout the project to ensure that it is progressing towards a successful conclusion.

Knowledge management

The systematic management of information and learning. It turns personal information and experience into collective knowledge that can be widely shared throughout an organisation and a profession.

L

Latest finish

The latest possible time by which an activity has to finish within the logical activity and imposed constraints of the network, without affecting the total project duration.

Latest start

Latest possible time by which an activity has to start within the logical and imposed constraints of the network, without affecting the total project duration.

Leadership

The ability to establish vision and direction, to influence and align others towards a common purpose, and to empower and inspire people to achieve project success. It enables the project to proceed in an environment of change and uncertainty.

Lessons learned

Documented experiences that can be used to improve the future management of projects, programmes and portfolios.

Life cycle

The inter-related phases of a project, programme or portfolio and provides a structure for governing the progression of work.

M

Management plan

A plan that sets out the policies and principles that will be applied to the management of some aspects of a project, programme or portfolio. Examples include a Risk Management Plan, a Communication Management Plan and a Quality Management Plan.

Management reserve

A sum of money held as an overall contingency to cover the cost impact of some unexpected event.

Matrix organisation

An organisational structure where the project manager and the functional managers share the responsibility of assigning priorities and directing the work. Individuals stay in their functional departments while performing work on one or more projects.

Method

A method provides a consistent framework within which project management is performed.

Milestone

A key event. An event selected for its importance to the project.

Milestone plan

A plan containing only milestones that highlight key points of the project.

Monitoring

The recording, analysing and reporting of project performance as compared to the plan in order to identify and report deviations.

N

Negotiation

A search for agreement seeking acceptance, consensus and alignment of views. Negotiation in a project can take place on an informal basis throughout the project life cycle, or on a formal basis, such as during procurement and between signatories to a contract.

Network analysis

A collective term for the different ways in which a network diagram may be analysed including, for example, critical path analysis, programme evaluation and review technique, and critical chain.

Network diagram

A pictorial presentation of project data in which the project logic is the main determinant of the placements of the activities in the drawing. Frequently called a flowchart, PERT chart, logic drawing, activity network or logic diagram.

Nodes

The points in a network at which arrows start and finish.

O

Objectives

Predetermined results toward which effort is directed.

Operations management

The management of those activities that create the core services or products provided by an organisation.

Operations phase

The period during which the completed deliverable is used and maintained in service for its intended purpose.

Opportunity

A positive risk; a risk that if it occurs will have a beneficial effect on the project. A positive aspect of project uncertainty, it may also help to negate threats.

Organisation

A single corporate entity that is undertaking a project or providing services to a project.

Organisational breakdown structure (OBS)

A hierarchical way in which the organisation may be divided into management levels and groups, for planning and control purposes.

Outcome

The changed circumstances or behaviour that results from the use of an output.

Output

The tangible or intangible product typically delivered by a project.

P

P3 management

The collective term for project, programme and portfolio management.

Parametric estimate

An estimating technique that uses a statistical relationship between historic data and other variables (for example, square area in construction, lines of code in software development) to calculate an estimate.

Path

Activity or an unbroken sequence of activities in a project network.

Payback

An investment appraisal technique.

Percent complete

A measure of the completion status of a partially completed activity. May be aggregated to sections of a project or the whole project.

Phase (of a project)

Part of a project during which a set of related and interlinked processes are performed to attain a designated objective. One of a series of distinct steps in carrying out a project that together constitute the project life cycle.

Phase review

A review that takes place at the end of a life cycle phase. See Gate review.

Plan

A plan is an intended future course of action. See Project management plan.

Planning

Determines what is to be delivered, how much it will cost, when it will be delivered, how it will be delivered and who will carry it out

Planned cost

The estimated cost of achieving a specified objective.

Planning

The process of identifying the means, resources and actions necessary to accomplish an objective.

Portfolio

A grouping of an organisation's projects, programmes and related business as usual activities, taking into account resource constraints. Portfolios can be managed at an organisational, programme or functional level.

Portfolio management

The selection and management of all an organisation's projects, programmes and related operational activities, taking into account resource constraints.

Post project review

Undertaken after the project deliverables have been handed over and before final closeout, this review is intended to produce lessons learnt that will enable continuous improvement.

Precedence network

A multiple dependency network. An activity on node network in which a sequence arrow represents one of four forms of precedence relationship, depending on the positioning of the head and tail of the sequence arrow. The relationships are:

Finish to start

Start of activity depends on the finish of the preceding activity, either immediately or after a lapse of time.

Finish to finish

Finish of activity depends on the finish of the preceding activity, either immediately or after a lapse of time.

Start to start

Start of activity depends on the start of the preceding activity, either immediately or after a lapse of time.

Start to finish

Finish of activity depends on the start of the preceding activity, either immediately or after a lapse of time.

Predecessor

An activity that must be completed (or be partially completed) before a specified activity can begin.

PRINCE2™

A project management method created for government projects. It is an acronym for Projects In a Controlled Environment (second version). It is intended to be generic.

Probability

The likelihood of a risk occurring.

Processes

A set of interrelated resources and activities that transform inputs into outputs.

Procurement

The process by which the resources (goods and services) required by a project are acquired. It includes development of the procurement strategy, preparation of contracts, selection and acquisition of suppliers and management of the contracts.

Product

A tangible or intangible component of a project's output. Synonymous with deliverable.

Product breakdown structure (PBS)

A hierarchy of deliverable products that are required to be produced on the project. This forms the base document from which the execution strategy and product-based work breakdown structure may be derived. It provides a guide for configuration control documentation.

Programme

A group of related projects, which may include related business as usual activities, that together achieve a beneficial change of a strategic nature for an organisation.

Programme management

The coordinated management of a group of related projects, which may also include related business as usual activities that together achieve a beneficial change of a strategic nature for an organisation.

Program evaluation and review technique

A network analysis technique that calculates standard deviations for the schedule based on three-point estimates of activity durations.

Programme management office

The office responsible for the business and technical management of a specific programme.

Programme manager

The individual with responsibility for managing a programme.

Programme support office

A group that gives administrative support to the programme manager and the programme executive.

Project

A unique, transient endeavour undertaken to achieve a desired outcome.

Project appraisal

The discipline of calculating the viability of a project. May be conducted at any time throughout the project.

Project board

See Steering group

Project closure

Formal termination of a project at any point during its life.

Project context

The environment within which a project is undertaken. Projects do not exist in a vacuum, and an appreciation of the context within which the project is being performed will assist those involved in project management to deliver a project.

Project evaluation review

A documented review of the project's performance, produced at predetermined points in the project life cycle.

Project life cycle

All projects follow a life cycle and life cycles will differ across industries and business sectors. A life cycle allows the project to be considered as a sequence of distinct phases that provide the structure and approach for progressively delivering the required outputs.

Project management

The process by which projects are defined, planned, monitored, controlled and delivered, so that benefits can be realised.

Project management plan

A plan for carrying out a project, to meet specific objectives, that is prepared by or for the project manager. The output of the definition phase of a project or programme.

Project manager

The individual responsible and accountable for the successful delivery of the project.

Project office

This serves the organisation's project management needs. A project office can range from simple support functions for the project manager to responsibility for linking corporate strategy to project execution.

Project organisation (structure)

The project organisation structure provides the maximum authority to the project manager. It provides integration of functional capabilities within projects. However, this leads to duplication of facilities and less efficient use of resources.

Project phase

A group of related project processes and activities that come together with the completion of major deliverable(s).

Project planning

The development and maintenance of a project plan.

Project quality management

The discipline that is applied to ensure that both the outputs of the project, and the processes by which the outputs are delivered, meet the required needs of the stakeholders. Quality is broadly defined as fitness for purpose or, more narrowly, as the degree of conformance of the outputs and process.

Project risk

The exposure of stakeholders to the consequences of variability in outcome.

Project risk management

A structure process that allows individual risk events and overall project risk to be understood and managed pro actively thus optimising project success by minimising threats and maximising opportunities.

Project schedule

The timetable for a project. It shows how a project's activities and milestones are planned over a period of time. It is often shown as a milestone chart, Gantt or other bar chart, or as a tabular listing of dates.

Project sponsorship

An active senior management role, responsible for identifying the business need or problem of opportunity. The sponsor ensures the project remains a viable proposition and that benefits are realised, resolving issues outside the control of the project manager.

Project steering group

See **Steering group**

Project strategy

A comprehensive definition of how a project will be developed.

Project success criteria

See **Success criteria**

Project team

A set of individuals, groups and/or organisations that are responsible to the project manager for working towards a common purpose.

Q

Qualitative risk analysis

A generic term for subjective methods of assessing risks that cannot be identified accurately.

Quality

The fitness for purpose for the degree of conformance of the outputs of the process.

Quality assurance (QA)

The process of evaluating overall project performance on a regular basis to provide confidence that the project will satisfy the relevant quality standards.

Quality audit

An official examination to determine whether practices conform to specified standards or a critical analysis of whether a deliverable meets quality criteria.

Quality control (QC)

The process of monitoring specific project results to determine if they comply with relevant standards and identifying ways to eliminate causes of unsatisfactory performance.

Quality plan (for a project)

That part of the project plan that concerns quality management and quality assurance strategies.

Quality planning

The process of determining which quality standards are necessary and how to apply them.

R

Reduce

A response to a threat that reduces its probability, impact or both.

Reject

A response to an opportunity where no action is taken.

Replenishable resource

A resource that when absent or used up, fresh supplies of which can be obtained. Raw materials and money are common examples. See Consumable resource.

Request for change (RFC)

A proposal for a change to the project.

Request for proposal (RFP)

A bid document used to request proposals from prospective sellers of products or services.

Requirements

A statement of the need that a project has to satisfy. It should be comprehensive, clear, well structured, traceable and testable.

Requirements management

The process of capturing, analysing and testing the documented statements of stakeholder and user wants and needs.

Resource

Any variable capable of definition that is required for the completion of an activity and may constrain the project.

Resource aggregation

A summation of the requirements for each resource, and for each time period.

Resource availability

The level of availability of a resource, which may vary over time.

Resource constraint

A limitation due to the availability of a resource.

Resource histogram

A view of project data in which resource requirements, usage, and availability are shown using vertical bars against a horizontal time scale.

Resource levelling

Resource levelling can be applied to projects when there are resource constraints. Resource levelling forces the amount of work scheduled not to exceed the limits of resources available. This results in either activities being delayed to periods when resources are available. This often results in a longer project duration. It is also known as resource limited scheduling.

Resource management

The acquisition and deployment of the internal and external resources required to deliver the project, programme or portfolio.

Resources

All those items required to undertake work including people, finance and materials.

Resource planning

Evaluating what resources are needed to complete a project and determining the quantity needed.

Resource scheduling

The process of determining the dates on which activities should be performed in order to smooth the demand for resources, or to avoid exceeding stated constraints on these restraints.

Resource smoothing

A process applied to projects to ensure that resources are used as effectively as possible. It involves utilising float within the project or increasing or decreasing the resources required for specific activities, such that any peaks and troughs of resource usage are smoothed out. This does not affect the project duration. It is also known as time limited scheduling.

Responsibility assignment matrix (RAM)

A diagram demonstrating the correlation between the work required by a work breakdown structure element to the functional organisations responsible for accomplishing the assigned tasks (sometimes referred to as the RACI chart).

Re-usable resource

A resource that when no longer needed becomes available for other uses. Accommodation, machines, test equipment and people are re-usable.

Reviews

A review is a critical evaluation of a deliverable, business case or P3 management process.

Risk

The potential of an action or event to impact on the achievement of objectives.

Risk analysis

An assessment and synthesis of risk events to gain an understanding of their individual significance and their combined impact on objectives.

Risk appetite

The tendency of an individual or group to take risk in a given situation.

Risk attitude

The response of an individual or group to a given uncertain situation.

Re-usable resource

A resource that when no longer needed becomes available for other uses. Accommodation, machines, test equipment and people are re-usable.

Risk assessment

The process of quantifying the likelihood of risks occurring and assessing their likely impact on the project.

Risk avoidance

See **Avoid**

Risk evaluation

A process used to determine risk management priorities.

Risk event

An uncertain event or set of circumstances that should it or they occur would have an effect on the achievement of one or more of the project objectives.

Risk identification

The process of identifying project risks.

Risk management

See **Project risk management**

Risk management plan

A document defining how project risk management is to be implemented in the context of a particular project concerned.

Risk owner

The person who has responsibility for dealing with a particular risk on a project and for identifying and managing responses.

Risk reduction

Action taken to reduce the likelihood and impact of a risk.

Risk register

A body of information listing all the risks identified for the project, explaining the nature of each risk and recording information relevant to its assessment, possible impact and management.

Risk response

Contingency plans to manage a risk should it materialise. Action to reduce the probability of the risk arising, or to reduce the significance of its detrimental impact if it does arise.

Risk transfer

A contractual arrangement between two parties for delivery and acceptance of a product, where the liability for the costs of a risk is transferred from one party to the other.

S

Schedule

A schedule is the timetable for a project. It shows how project activities and milestones are planned to occur over a period of time. It is often shown as a Gantt or other bar chart, or as a tabular listing of dates.

Schedule performance index (SPI)

A term used in earned value management. It is the ration of work accomplished versus the work planned, for a specified time period. The SPI is an efficiency rating for work accomplishment, comparing work achieved to what should have been achieved at any point in time.

Schedule variance

A term used in earned value management. The difference between the earned value and the planned cost at any point in time.

Scheduling

Scheduling is the process used to determine the overall project duration. This includes identification of activities and their logical dependencies, and estimating activity durations, taking into account requirements and availability of resources.

Scope

The totality of the outputs, outcomes and benefits and the work required to produce them

Scope change

Any change in a project scope that requires a change in the project's cost or schedule.

Secondary risk

The risk that may occur as a result of invoking a risk response or fallback plan.

S

Schedule

A schedule is the timetable for a project. It shows how project activities and milestones are planned to occur over a period of time. It is often shown as a Gantt or other bar chart, or as a tabular listing of dates.

Schedule performance index (SPI)

A term used in earned value management. It is the ration of work accomplished versus the work planned, for a specified time period. The SPI is an efficiency rating for work accomplishment, comparing work achieved to what should have been achieved at any point in time.

Schedule variance

A term used in earned value management. The difference between the earned value and the planned cost at any point in time.

Scheduling

Scheduling is the process used to determine the overall project duration. This includes identification of activities and their logical dependencies, and estimating activity durations, taking into account requirements and availability of resources.

Scope

The scope is the sum of work content of a project.

Scope change

Any change in a project scope that requires a change in the project's cost or schedule.

Secondary risk

The risk that may occur as a result of invoking a risk response or fallback plan.

Sponsor

The individual or body for whom the project is undertaken and who is the primary risk taker. The sponsor owns the business case and is ultimately responsible for the project and for delivering the benefits.

Stage

A subdivision of a project life cycle phase into a natural subsection with well defined deliverables.

Stakeholder

The organisations or people who have an interest or role in the project or are impacted by the project.

Stakeholder analysis

The identification of stakeholder group, their interest levels and the ability to influence the project or programme.

Stakeholder grid

A matrix used as part of a stakeholder analysis to identify the relative importance of stakeholders to a project, for example, by considering their relative power.

Stakeholder identification

The process of identifying stakeholders in a project.

Stakeholder management

The systematic identification, analysis and planning of actions to communicate with and influence stakeholders.

Start-to-finish

A dependency in an activity-on-node network. It indicates that one activity cannot finish until another activity has started.

Start-to-start

A dependency in an activity-on-node network. It indicates that one activity cannot start until another activity has started.

Statement of work

An annex to the main body of a contract that defines the detail of deliverables, timescales and management procedures.

Steering group

A group, usually comprising the sponsor, senior managers and sometimes key stakeholders, whose remit is to set the strategic direction of a project. It gives guidance to the sponsor and project manager. Often referred to as the project board.

Success criteria

The qualitative or quantitative measures by which the success of the project is judged.

Success factors and maturity

Management practices that, when implemented, will increase the likelihood of success of a project, programme or portfolio. The degree to which these practices are established and embedded within an organisation indicates its level of maturity.

Successor

A successor is an activity whose start or finish depends on the start or finish of a predecessor activity.

Supplier

A supplier is a contractor, consultant or any organisation that supplies resources to the project.

T

Task

The smallest indivisible part of an activity when it is broken down to a level best understood and performed by a specific person or organisation.

Team

A team is made up of two or more people working interdependently toward a common goal and a shared reward.

Teamwork

A group of people working in collaboration or by cooperation towards a common goal.

Team building

The ability to gather the right people to join a project team and get them working together for the benefit of a project.

Team development

Developing skills, as a group and individually, that enhance project performance.

Tender

A document proposing to meet a specification in a certain way and at a stated price (or on a particular financial basis). An offer of price and conditions under which the tenderer is willing to undertake work for the client. *See* Bid.

Termination (phase)

The disposal of project deliverables at the end of their life.

Threat

A negative risk event; a risk event that if it occurs will have a detrimental effect on the objectives.

Three point estimate

An estimate in which the most likely mid-range value, an optimistic value and a pessimistic worst case value are given.

Time limited scheduling

See **Resource smoothing**

Time now

A specified date from which the forward analysis is deemed to commence. The date to which progress is measured. In earned value analysis, this is the actual time expended or ATE.

Tolerance

A permissible variation in performance parameters.

Total float

Time by which an activity may be delayed or extended without affecting the total project duration or violating a target finish date.

Transfer

A response to a threat that reduces its probability, impact or both by transferring the risk to a third party.

U

Users

The group of people who are intended to benefit from the project or who will operate the deliverables.

W

Work

The total number of hours, people or effort required to complete an activity.

Work breakdown structure (WBS)

A way in which a project may be divided by level into discrete groups for programming, cost planning and control purposes. The WBS is a tool for defining the hierarchical breakdown of work required to deliver the products of a project. Major categories are broken down into smaller components. These are sub divided until the lowest required level of detail is established. The lowest level of the WBS are generally work packages. In some instances, work packages are further divided into activities that become the activities in a project. The WBS defines the total work to be undertaken on the project and provides a structure for all project control systems.

Work package

A group of related activities that are defined at the same level within a work breakdown structure.

Z

Zero float

Zero float is a condition where there is no excess time between activities. An activity with zero float is considered a critical activity.

SECTION 16
CASE STUDY

WHIRLWIND BIKES

You work for Whirlwind Bikes, a bicycle manufacturer in the North East of England who has just been awarded a grant of €300,000 from the European Union's 'Cycling for Health Agency' and who wants you to come up with a radical new design for a pedal bike.

The EUCHA believe many people are put off cycling because the current designs are the same, and cycling is perceived as old fashioned and not 'cool'. They hope to get half a million people into cycling with this new design as the focal point for a huge publicity campaign. The award was the result of Whirlwind's successful bid to the EU where they managed to convince them that Whirlwind's status as one of the leading specialist bike designers in the country meant they were ideally placed to carry out this work. Whirlwind won the business in the face of exceptionally strong competition from other EU bike manufacturers including a number of household names.

These competitors are unsurprisingly not best pleased (in fact very annoyed) about Whirlwind's appointment and are actively lobbying the EU to have the agreement cancelled. They see you as inexpert in such a high profile politically charged activity. Also, provided the bike is a success, you will of course license the design and as such enjoy significant revenues in the future, which they would like to get.

Whirlwind is jointly owned by the original founder (James McKee) who is a real traditionalist and is firmly against new technologies, and a venture capitalist (Zak Shallow) who managed to buy into the business a few years ago when times were hard. It is Zak who is driving this piece of work.

Whirlwind is now required to come up with a radical new design for this pedal cycle, one that is light, cheap, with low rolling resistance, extremely adjustable and safe. Whirlwind identified in its submission that a carbon fibre composite would be a good option for the frame, as once in full scale production it will be less expensive for similar specification than aluminium. They have identified a specialist contractor (Carbon Fiber Products) in America who is experienced in the field, but last time you used them they delivered poor quality products. Alternatively, there is a specialist carbon fibre manufacturer just down the road (Carbon Concepts), but they seem expensive.

To satisfy the stringent EU bike safety tests, Whirlwind will have to demonstrate that the new design (once built) has been thoroughly tested on the roads all over Europe in varying conditions. Whirlwind have used the local bike club, The Chain Gang, before (James McKee is Chairman of the club) and they are keen to get involved in the road trials. There is also another firm called Rider Rentals, who have submitted a bid to do the work using unemployed people from mainland Europe. Both will be required to file reports on their experiences and any issues arising. Whirlwind have not worked with either of them before.

Other Information

- Twenty prototypes are to be built based on a design once finished and agreed by the EUCHA.

- Every individual who takes up regular cycling has been shown to save the economy €800 per annum in health costs savings, increased productivity and lower carbon emissions.

- Whirlwind normally keep their product introduction cycle to three main work streams, design, build and integrate and test.

- The main components of the bike are frame, wheels and ancillaries (such as pedals, seat, etc.).

- The bike must be usable by people between 1.4 metres and 2.10 metres in height and up to 160 kg in weight.

- The bike must be demonstrated to have covered over 20,000km of road tests in varying weather and terrain conditions, without any major mechanical failures or any failure-related accidents. Once demonstrated and audited, the design will be awarded type approval for the EU and may be sold for profit in industrial quantities. The test reports will be a vital component in achieving this accreditation.

- Whirlwind have not decided yet whether to build the frame in-house or to get the US contractor to do it. If it is done in the US, the payment will be made in US dollars.

- The decision about whether to use The Chain Gang bike club or Rider Rentals for the testing has not been made. If the European organisation is used, the payment will be made in Euros.

- Exchange rates (both with the US and Europe) are subject to fluctuations.

- Whilst Whirlwind have grant funding to cover the work, all of their design efforts will be consumed on this one job possibly at the expense of other customers (including the British Olympic Cycling Team).

- Health and Safety and Insurance arrangements are a major factor in this type of contract.

- The launch of the campaign when the bike is required is now 12 periods away.

- A successful bike design will earn Whirlwind £200k in profits per annum if market volumes are achieved.

- You are the appointed project manager.

- Whirlwind have received indicative pricing and estimates of durations from the various internal and external suppliers as follows:

WBS Number	Work Package	Time (periods)	Cost	Predecessor	Resource
1.1	Start up and mobilisation	1	£5,000		PM
1.2.1	Design the frame	2	£60,000	1.1	Designer
1.2.2	Design the wheels	1	£10,000	1.1	Designer
1.2.3	Design the ancillaries	1	£10,000	1.1	Designer
1.3.1 (*)	Build the frame	4	£60,000	1.2.1	Carbon Fiber Products
1.3.1 (*)	Build the frame	3	£80,000	1.2.1	Carbon Concepts
1.3.2	Build the wheels	2	£20,000	1.2.2	Builder
1.3.3	Build the ancillaries	1	£20,000	1.2.3	Builder
1.4	Integrate the bike	2	£40,000	1.3.1, 1.3.2, 1.3.3	Builder
1.5 (*)	Testing	2	£20,000	1.4	Rider Rentals
1.5 (*)	Testing	1	£40,000	1.4	The Chain Gang
1.6	Launch event	1	£5,000	1.5	PM
1.7	Project management and administration	The length of the project	£48,000	1.1 (SS), 1.6 (FF)	PM
	Exchange rate info when budgeting: €1 = £1; $1 = £0.67				
	(*) Tasks are alternatives				

SECTION 17

EXAM PAPERS

Sample Exam Paper 2

Question 1

Learning Outcomes   Understand Project Life cycles

Warning   This question has <u>two</u> parts. Answer both parts.

Question Part (a)   Explain the Importance of project reviews.

Marks   10 Marks

Question Part (b)   List and describe <u>four</u> different types of review that may be carried out during a project, and their main purpose.

Marks   40 Marks (10 marks each)

Question 2

Learning Outcomes   Understand project scope management

Question   List and describe <u>five</u> key activities typically performed as part of an effective configuration management process.

Marks   50 marks (10 marks each)

Question 3

Learning Outcomes   Understand planning for success

Warning   This question has <u>two</u> parts. Answer both parts.

Question part (a)   Within the context of Earned Value Management (EVM), explain the term Earned Value (EV)

Marks   10 Marks

Question part (b)   Explain <u>four</u> benefits of using Earned Value Management

Marks   40 marks (10 marks each)

Question 4

Learning Outcomes   Project project procurement

Warning   List and describe <u>five</u> typical stages in the process for selection of a supplier via competitive tender.

Marks   50 marks (10 marks each)

Question 5	
Learning Outcome	Understand schedule and resource management
Warning	This question has <u>two</u> parts. Answer both parts.
Question Part (a)	Explain the following approaches to resource scheduling:

- Resource smoothing
- Resource levelling

Ensure that your answer distinguishes between the <u>two</u> approaches.

Marks	20 marks (10 each)
Question part (b)	Explain <u>three</u> approaches/tactics which a project manager might consider when optimising the resource allocation for a project. Identify in your answer any assumptions made and implications.
Marks	30 marks (10 marks each)
Question 6	
Learning Outcomes	Understand how organisations and projects are structured
Warning	This question has <u>two</u> parts. Answer both parts.
Question Part (a)	List and describe <u>three</u> advantages, to a project manager, of a matrix organisation structure when used in a project environment.
Marks	30 marks (10 marks each)
Question Part (b)	List and describe <u>two</u> disadvantages, to a project manager, of a matrix organisation structure when used in a project environment
Marks	20 marks (10 marks each)
Question 7	
Learning Outcomes	Understand the principles of leadership and teamwork
Warning	This question has <u>two</u> parts. Answer both parts.
Question Part (a)	Explain what is meant by situational leadership in a project environment.
Marks	10 marks
Question Part (b)	List and describe <u>four</u> benefits of adapting leadership styles during a project. Ensure you include at least one beneficiary in each description.
Question 8	
Learning Outcomes	Understand contexts and environments in which projects can be delivered.
Question	List and describe <u>five</u> important environmental legislative requirements which the project manager must take into account when planning a project.
Marks	50 marks (10 marks each)

Question 9

Learning Outcomes	Understand planning for success
Warning	This question is in <u>two</u> parts. Answer both parts.
Question Part (a)	Explain the prerequisites required for each of the following three estimating techniques:

- Comparative
- Bottom up/Analytical
- Parametric

Marks	30 marks (10 marks each)
Question Part (b)	State <u>four</u> practical problems of initial estimates for a project with a protracted timescale.

Question 10

Learning Outcomes	Understand governance of project management and the use of structured methodologies
Learning Outcomes	List and describe five typical contents (e.g. Processes, components, techniques) of a structured project management method.
Marks	50 marks (10 marks each)

Question 11

Learning Outcomes	Understand how organisations and projects are structured
Question	List and describe five activities which the project sponsor performs during the project life cycle.
Marks	50 marks (10 marks each)

Question 12

Learning Outcomes	Understand communication within project management
Question	List and describe a source of conflict arising within each of the following parts of the extended life cycle
Marks	50 marks (10 marks each)

Question 13

Learning Outcomes	Understand project quality management
Warning	This question has <u>two</u> parts. Answer both parts
Question	Explain the difference between continual improvement and project quality planning.
Marks	10 marks
Question Part (b)	List and describe four aspects of project quality assurance.
Marks	40 marks (10 marks each)

Question 14

Learning Outcomes	Understand project scope management
Warning	This question is in <u>two</u> parts. Answer both parts.
Question Part (a)	Explain two reasons why the scope of a project may need to be changed.
Marks	20 marks (10 marks each)
Question Part (b)	Explain three ways that change control can reduce and manage scope creep on a project.
Marks	30 marks (10 marks each)

Question 15

Learning Outcomes	Understand risk management and issue management
Question	List and describe five benefits to an organisation of adopting a formal risk management process.
Marks	50 marks (10 marks each)

Question 16

Learning Outcomes	Understand the principles of leadership and teamwork
Warning	This question is in <u>two</u> parts. Answer both parts.
Question part (a)	Explain the concept of team work
Marks	10 marks
Warning	This question requires <u>four</u> explanations
Question part (b)	From the following team or social roles listed, explain four of these, including how they contribute to an effective team.

- Opponent / Challenger
- Leader
- Team worker
- Completer / finisher
- Collaborator
- Reviewer

Marks   40 marks (10 each)

SECTION 18

MULTIPLE CHOICE ANSWERS

	Section 3.1	
Question	Answer and rationale	
1	Essential, if the relationship between the two is not taken into account then the business may not be properly prepared for the implementation of the products.	
2	True, all projects require a business case	
3	False, projects are unique, there may be similarities with other projects but they will never be the same.	
4	True, projects have a distinct time frame.	
5	False, projects are there to make a difference.	
6	True, there is no point in spending more than you expect to get back.	
7	a) the time it takes, success criteria are those things that are being sought and will be those things that the final result will be measured against.	
8	a) the others are example of operations (or Business as Usual)	
9	True, risk management is arguably at the root of all project management practices.	
10	False, the steering group will approve the business case. The sponsor is nominated as the single point of contact and 'owns' it through the project.	

	Sections 3.2 to 3.4	
Question	Answer and rationale	
1	False, programme managers have a much bigger role than that, they need to be strategic in their approach and heavily focussed on the business and the delivery of benefits.	
2	False, programmes extend beyond the bounds of single projects, they may have multiple projects across a broad range of disciplines with multiple customers.	
3	b) Crucial to the effectiveness of the delivered product.	
4	False, most programmes are multi- year and will have altering customers, stakeholders, focus and scope. The last projects in a programme may be not well understood at the start.	
5	True, portfolio management is very often linked with the implementation of the corporate governance principles.	
6	True, these are all very relevant to programmes.	
7	False, they are continuous and will extend throughout the life of the need for them within the organisation.	
8	False, portfolio management is to do with choosing the appropriate mix of projects and programmes, programmes are vehicles to deliver benefit through multiple projects.	
9	True, these are all within the remit of the portfolio manager.	

	Sections 3.2 to 3.4	
Question	**Answer and rationale**	
10	a) The other two a limited in scope and not strategic.	

	Sections 3.6 to 3.7	
Question	**Answer and rationale**	
1	False, the context considers both internal and external factors	
2	True	
3	True, but not to be confused with the environmental aspects of projects (recycling, energy use, etc.)	
4	Sociological, the human factor.	
5	True, only by exploring the wider aspects of the project can the project team be fully appraised of the potential risks.	

	Section 3.8	page 277
Question	**Answer and rationale**	
1	True, the employer as part of their 'duty of care' are required to make sure that all personal protective equipment is suitable and available.	
2	True, the Health and Safety commission set policy.	
3	d) All of these can cause stress	
4	c) Near misses	
5	a) ISO 14001	
6	a) Intellectual Property Rights	
7	True	
8	c) Whistle blowing	
9	True, not just construction, all projects are governed by the acts	
10	True, they cannot just be imposed.	

	Section 4.1	
Question	**Answer and rationale**	
1	True, it has that characteristic as staff are employed within a given area or department and that will be their professional development home.	
2	True, whilst a matrix organisation does retain skills a purely functional organisation has the most focus on vertical (silo) management structures.	
3	False, a project organisation will form, utilise skills from outside and generally disband losing the skills and knowledge built up..	
4	a) Staff will tend to follow the direction of their line manager.	
5	d) Excessive paperwork doe snot have a home anywhere.	
6	a) The functional managers as they are the only ones with a remit across the business.	
7	False, as more projects are contemplated and run the functional managers role diminishes in authority over the project activities.	
8	True, all resources across the business are visible and potentially able to be deployed across the projects thus avoiding under utilisation	

	Section 4.1	
Question	Answer and rationale	
9	True, the teams are focussed on the delivery of the project	
10	True, they work across multiple lines of business.	

	Sections 4.3 to 4.5	
Question	Answer and rationale	
1	Maybe, there is no particular rule either way.	
2	b) Contract, the project manager would normally be able to steer and guide the contracts in this way.	
3	b) The sponsor owns the business case but it will be approved by the project board / steering group.	
4	a) The project manager owns the PMP but the sponsor will generally approve it.	
5	d) The users generally do not deliver the work itself they are in effect the customers.	
6	a) Yes and the steering group will support them in the execution of their duties.	
7	a) One.	
8	b) The governance framework for the organisation would normally indicate how sponsors are appointed, although in practice they may well be nominated from within a steering group and this decision ratified by the organisation.	
9	a) The sponsor, they approve the business case and must therefore approve changes that may affect it.	
10	True	

	Section 4.6	
Question	Answer and rationale	
1	False, it can be a 'virtual' function spread across different departments in a business.	
2	False. A project office manager may have many projects to look after and cannot therefore report directly to multiple PM's	
3	b) The project office is an administrative function not directly involved in the activities of the teams in their delivery activities.	
4	a) If the project office team report to the sponsor or the steering group they will not be able to deputise for the PM as this will bring them into an area of conflicting interests.	
5	b) Enterprise project management office	
6	True	
7	False, they take direction from the project manager.	
8	True	
9	True, they are a cost that needs to be accommodated within the estimates for the project.	

	Section 4.6	
Question	Answer and rationale	
10	b)	

	Sections 5.1 to 5.5	
Question	Answer and rationale	
1	False, each industry, discipline, company may have a range of life cycles appropriate for the job in hand.	
2	True, the inclusion of operations and termination allow these considerations	
3	True, there is not 'one size fits all' mentality. Building software would be very different in nature to building a power station.	
4	a) During operations the beneficial aspects of the products will become known.	
5	False, they are external to the project.	
6	a) The operations phase.	
7	True, it is too late to wait until the end to record and communicate lessons learned.	
8	False, it is usually for the organisation to avoid bad news being covered up.	
9	False, the plan is normally constructed alongside the business case from the very start of the project.	
10	False, this is a conceptual model and can be adapted to suit local needs.	

	Sections 6.2 to 6.3	
Question	Answer and rationale	
1	a) Methods can only ever help to guarantee success.	
2	False, a method may contain a life cycle.	
3	True, an organisation will usually describe a method to be used by its projects	
4	d) Methods should not be seen as simply more paperwork	
5	False, the method really needs to be consistent across the piece. If a number of methods need to be merged to form a hybrid method that everyone then follows then this will be fine.	

	Sections 7.1 to 7.4	
Question	Answer and rationale	
1	a) The project manager owns the communications plan as it is a component of the project management plan.	
2	True, the communications plan contains the things that the PM must do to ensure communications are properly managed.	
3	False, the PM should try and become part of the project informal networks.	
4	a) The communications plan will be developed from the very start of the project and will evolve to final sign off within the PMP	
5	b) There has to be a feedback mechanism to ensure that communications have been effective.	
6	c) Risk management is not usually considered a barrier to communications.	
7	a) Para-inguistics are normally considered an attribute of body language.	
8	c) Information management overlaps with communications management	

	Sections 7.1 to 7.4	
Question	**Answer and rationale**	
9	True	
10	True	

	Sections 7.5 to 7.6	
Question	**Answer and rationale**	
1	c) Bargaining is not considered to be part of a negotiation process, it may be something done within the steps of a process however.	
2	True, this is a common step when negotiating. You can seek approval from someone who has not been part of the negotiation thus maintaining a good working relationship.	
3	True, a project manger negotiates all the time, it is not limited to formal meetings and quite often involves one to one discussion.	
4	True	
5	c) Accommodating	

	Sections 8.1 to 8.3	
Question	**Answer and rationale**	
1	b) Advancement, this is the only true 'motivator' according to Maslow	
2	False, these are the steps in Situation Leadership from Hersey and Blanchard	
3	c) Salary is not (according to Maslow) a motivator but a hygiene factor.	
4	False, clearly the project manager must play a huge part in motivating their team	
5	d) Sickness, poor quality of work and absenteeism are all potential problems if motivation is not dealt with properly.	

	Section 8.4	
Question	**Answer and rationale**	
1	a) Supporting and directing	
2	False, it is Telling, Selling, participating, Delegating.	
3	False, it is a consideration of how mature they are at being led.	
4	True, the basis tenet of the Hersey Blanchard theory.	
5	c) Leaders are not systems focussed but to exhibit all of the other three attributes.	

	Section 8.5	
Question	**Answer and rationale**	
1	True, the others are Storming, Norming, Performing.	
2	d) Operator.	
3	True, changes or too much negative conflict can cause a team to regress backwards around the Tuckman model.	
4	d) Norming	
5	c) Hopefulness, the others are potential problems while the team is storming.	
6	d) 9 Plant, Completer Finisher, Shaper, Team Worker, Implementer, Resource Investigator, Coordinator, Monitor Evaluator, Specialist.	

	Section 8.5	
Question	**Answer and rationale**	
7	b) Completer finisher	
8	True	
9	False, this would be a performing team in the Tuckman model.	
10	True.	

	Section 9.1	
Question	**Answer and rationale**	
1	a) Organisation Breakdown Structure.	
2	d) Work Breakdown Structure.	
3	True, normally the naming convention will use a numbering structure to achieve this,	
4	Which sites are included. This would steer the work involved whereas the other options are to do with who, when, etc.	
5	True, they may not undertake the detailed work but they will certainly need to make sure the activity is completed.	
6	b) the task and the person involved in it.	
7	True, although it may also appear in the business case.	
8	True	
9	a) Work package.	
10	True	

	Section 9.2	
Question	**Answer and rationale**	
1	False, requirements are the things to be achieved, benefits are the value placed on those outcomes.	
2	True, it is a subsidiary plan in the PMP	
3	b) The governance framework would normally have guidance to accommodate the collection of requirements.	
4	c) Products will be checked as to their suitability throughout the project.	
5	a) Work Breakdown Structures, the others are part of the PICSA components of configuration management.	
6	d) The users specify the requirements of the products in the first place they therefore will need to specify any changes to them.	
7	a) Procurement specialists	
8	c) Reiterate	
9	True	
10	WBS number, it may include the PBS number as it is concerned with products rather than work.	

	Sections 9.3 to 9.5	
Question	**Answer and rationale**	
1	c) Initial investigation and update plans	
2	True, they may be requested by the users but it is the sponsor to determine whether they should be implemented or not.	
3	False, although in most cases they may have tolerance within which to work and act on behalf of the sponsor.	
4	a) Morale, all the others are components that need to be considered.	
5	d) Although there will come a point where it becomes unacceptable.	
6	c) Absorption	
7	d) Generally the WBS number is not appropriate as these relate to the work packages rather than changes.	
8	d) The probability would normally be something to do with risk management.	
9	True	
10	True, they would be able to contribute invaluable information about other products that might be affected or what steps the process requires to be followed.	

	Sections 10.1 to 10.2	
Question	**Answer and rationale**	
1	d) The project sponsor	
2	True, the basic reason for doing a project is that you get more back than it costs	
3	True	
4	a) The benefits are realised during the operations phase.	
5	True, they may add significant new ideas and proposals.	

	Section 10.3	
Question	**Answer and rationale**	
1	a)	
2	True, only in this way can the value of them be recognised in relation to the costs	
3	True.	
4	True	
5	False, it rarely is one monolithic document it usually consists of a number of supporting and associated material.	

	Section 10.4	
Question	**Answer and rationale**	
1	d) It is usually based on current figures without adjusting for how the value of money might vary moving forward.	
2	True, it can be a bit daunting to understand.	
3	True, it is easy to understand.	
4	d) The accountants are much better able to help in this area.	
5	False, the organisation must consider the risk of a project and not jus the return.	

	Sections 10.5 to 10.6	
Question	Answer and rationale	
1	d) Change control	
2	False, there are requirements to make sure that personal information is not kept unless essential.	
3	False, some small projects get by with paper based systems although their ability to transfer data will be limited.	
4	a) The project manager writes all the subsidiary plans	
5	False, even the smallest projects need to consider it especially if they are dealing with public money or personal data,	

	Sections 10.7 to 10.9	
Question	Answer and rationale	
1	b) The project manager	
2	a) The business case is usually considered to be a separate document with a different purpose to the PMP. The business case describes the 'WHY'".	
3	a) The project sponsor as it is they who sign it of fin the first place	
4	True, although you would have to check to make sure it is still appropriate.	
5	c) Just about anyone ought to have sight of the plan if they are involved in the project.	

	Sections 10.10 to 10.11	
Question	Answer and rationale	
1	True	
2	a) At the beginning when high level estimates are most useful	
3	a) WBS, each of the work packages is added up to derive the overall estimate.	
4	d) As many views as possible are helpful to get an accurate a picture as possible.	
5	a) The business case holds the initial figures and estimates	
6	d) PERT is an output of a three point model	
7	True (1 x M) + (4 x 6) + (1xP) all divided by 6	
8	True, as more information is known so this becomes easier.	

	Sections 10.12 to 10.13	
Question	Answer and rationale	
1	a) Power and influence	
2	d) Negotiate	
3	d) Everyone with an interest in the project is a stakeholder	
4	True, everyone will assess things in their own way	
5	c) It will certainly help, as being able to relate and manage the stakeholder community is vital to project success.	

	Sections 11.1 to 11.3	
Question	Answer and rationale	
1	a) Time periods	

282 MULTIPLE CHOICE ANSWERS

	Sections 11.1 to 11.3	
Question	**Answer and rationale**	
2	c) Early finish	
3	True	
4	True	
5	c) Nothing	
6	True	
7	a) The duration	
8	True (either to you from the client or by to you to contractors)	
9	True	
10	a) Total float	

	Sections 11.4 to 11.6	
Question	**Answer and rationale**	
1	c) Resource levelling which may extend the end date and resource smoothing (which will not)	
2	True	
3	False	
4	True, it inevitably will take a number of iterations and the plan must be reviewed all the time to accommodate changing circumstances.	
5	d) Gantt chart	
6	c) Replenishable, the other type is reusable.	
7	a) Mobilisation and demobilisation	
8	d) Time can never be recovered	
9	b) Availability, the first pass of a resourcing model will assume unlimited resources.	
10	True	

	Section 11.7	
Question	**Answer and rationale**	
1	True	
2	c) Actual costs, these are only known when the work has been done.	
3	a) Reduce the time that we are in a deficit situation	
4	c) An accrual is intended to reflect the actual point at which the costs were attributable,	
5	True	
6	True, it becomes the PC curve on the graph.	
7	c) Commitments, the things that have been ordered and cannot be avoided.	
8	b) The project manager	
9	False, they are the backbone baseline for the project and must be calculated with care.	
10	True	

	Sections 11.8 to 11.9	
Question	Answer and rationale	
1	True	
2	True	
3	c) It provides a forecast of outturn, it contributes to cost control but it does not in itself allow efficiencies to be determined within work packages.	
4	c) Actual Costs	
5	d) Budget at completion	
6	True	
7	c) It is as accurate as the quality of the data but is trying to look into the future and provide a forecast.	
8	a) Good, we are producing products and spending less doing it than we expected.	
9	True	
10	True	

	Sections 12.1 to 12.3	
Question	Answer and rationale	
1	d) Probability and impact	
2	c) Share is a response to an opportunity	
3	b) 0.02 - you multiply them together	
4	c) Quantitative, risk assessment is either this or qualitative.	
5	True, it is a subsidiary plan in the PMP	
6	True	
7	False, most people are affected by their own expertise on a particular subject.	
8	False, they need to be continually monitored	
9	d) Guesswork	
10	c) They manage them and are responsible for them being carried out.	

	Sections 12.4 to 12.5	
Question	Answer and rationale	
1	True.	
2	c) The team	
3	d) Probability- this is more to do with risk management	
4	True	
5	True, this is a subsidiary plan in the PMP	

	Sections 13.1 to 13.3	
Question	Answer and rationale	
1	d) Fitness for purpose - does it conform to the specification?	
2	True, they define the acceptability standards for the products produced.	
3	d) Finishing	
4	c) A pareto diagram - 80%of the faults are caused by 20% of the errors.	

	Sections 13.1 to 13.3	
Question	Answer and rationale	
5	True	
6	False, it is a continuous improvement technique.	
7	b) Configuration management	
8	d) Resource management	
9	True, this is referred to the cost of quality	
10	d) Everyone, although the PM will have overall accountability for quality.	

	Sections 14.1 to 14.4	
Question	Answer and rationale	
1	True	
2	Parallel - it is a contract type	
3	False - they follow each others delivery.	
4	c) The project management plan is not a part of the contract although it may be required to be produced under the terms of the contract.	
5	c) Both	
6	a) The client bears the risk and pays more if the effort goes up.	
7	d) All of them are important to pin down.	
8	True	
9	c) Technically there is no limit to the number of parties in a contract. Negotiation may prove more difficult when arriving at the exact terms of it.	
10	d) Usually the PM will need help to complete the procurement strategy.	

INDEX

A

AC. *See* Actual Cost

Acceptance (Contract). 236

Accept (Change) 119

Accept (Risk Response) 219

Accommodating (Conflict) 83

Accountable. 105

Achievement 90

Actual Cost 200

APM. *See* Association for Project Management

APM Body of Knowledge. 10, 222

Association for Project Management. 10, 12

Assumptions 125, 146, 152, 216, 240

Assumptions analysis 216

Attitudes and Emotions 79

Avoid (Risk Response) 219

B

BAC. *See* Budget At Completion

BATNA. 85

Belbin 'Social Roles Model' 94

    Completer Finisher. 95

    Coordinator 94

    Implementer. 95

    Monitor Evaluator. 95

    Plant. 94

    Resource Investigator 94

    Shaper 95

    Specialist 95

    Team Worker 95

Benefits 101

Benefits Management Process 130

Benefits of a Risk Management Process. 214

Benefits of Managing Change 116

Benefits of Programme Management 29

Benefits of Using a Life Cycle 64

Benefits of Using a Project Method 75

Benefits Realisation phase 63

Benefits Realisation Review 66

Body of Knowledge . . . . 11, 12. *See also* APM Body of Knowledge

BoK. *See* Body of Knowledge

Bottom Up Estimating 153

Brainstorming 109, 215

British Standards Institute 11

BS6079 11

Budget at Completion 198, 200

Budgeting and Cost Management 188

Business As Usual 22

Business Case 124
    Evolution Of 126
    Roles (In Preparation Of) 126
    The Need For 124
    Typical Contents Of 125

C

Capacity 236

Cash flows 193

Centre of Excellence 58

Change Control Board 114

Change Control Log 117

Change Control Process 117
    Change Request 117
    Detailed Evaluation 118
    Implement 119
    Initial Evaluation 118
    Recommendation 119
    Update Plans 119

Characteristics of Projects 21

Checklists 216

Clarity 75

Closeout
    See Handover and Closeout 64

Closure 63

Commitments 191

Communication (Barriers to) 79

Communication Plan 77

Communication (Types)
    Formal Written 78
    Informal Verbal 77
    Informal Written 78
    Non Verbal 78

Comparative Estimating 153

Concept 63, 243

Configuration Audit 114

Configuration Control. 113

Configuration Identification 113

Configuration Item Controller. 114

Configuration Items 113

Configuration Management Process 108, 111

Configuration Management Roles
    Change Control Board 114
    Configuration Item Controller 114
    Configuration Librarian 114
    Project Team 114

Configuration Planning 113

Configuration Status Accounting 113

Conflict. 82

Consideration 236

Consistency. 75

Constraints 125

Consulted 105

Context of Programme Management 25

Continuity. 75

Continuous improvement. 59

Contract administration 236

Contract Law 40

Contractual Relationship 233

Cost At Completion 200

Cost Breakdown Structures (CBS) 104

Cost Performance Index 200

Cost Plus. 235

CPI. *See* Cost Performance Index

Critical path analysis 172, 246

Critical Success Factors 130

D

Defer (Change) 119

Definition 63, 246

Delegating 92

Delphi 215

Dependencies 125

Development phase. 63

Different Types of Review 65

Distractions 79

Document Control 112

Document Management System 112

E

EAC. *See* Estimate At Completion

Earned Value 198
      Advantages of using 207
      Disadvantages of using 207

Employment Law 41

Enhance (Risk Response) 219

Environmental issues 39

Environmental Law 41

Environment (Communication) 79

Estimate At Completion 200

Estimates (Difficulties Obtaining) 152

Estimating 151

Estimating Accuracy 151

Exam Format 13

Exploit (Risk Response) 219

Extended Project life cycle 63

External Consultants 126

F

Financial Investment Appraisal 134

Fitness for purpose 225

Fixed Price 235

Formal Verbal 77

Formal Written 78

Format of the Exam 13

Forming 95

Form (Of Contract) 236

Free float 171

Functional Organisation 45

G

Gantt chart 172

Gate Review . . . . 65. *See also* **Phase Gate Review**

GoPM. *See* Governance of Project Management

Governance of Project Management 69

Growth 90

H

Handover 63

Handover and Closure 64

Health and Safety at Work Act 1974 38
Health and Safety Commission 38
Health and Safety Executive 38
Health and Safety Law 38
Health, Safety and Environmental Management Plan 39
Hersey and Blanchard. *See* Situational Leadership
Hertzberg's Two Factor Theory 88, 89
HSC. *See* Health And Safety Commission
HSE. *See* Health And Safety Executive

I

Implementation 64, 250
Informal Verbal 77
Informal Written 78
Information
    Collection 139
    Destruction 140
    Dissemination 140
    Reporting 141
    Reporting Cylce 141
    Storage 140
Information Management Plan 139
Information Management Systems 139
Informed 105
Inspection and Measurement 228
Intellectual Property (Rights) 236
Intent 236
Internal Rate of Return 136
International Project Management Association 11
Interpersonal Conflict 96
Interpreting earned value 204
Interviewing 215
Investment Appraisal 125
Invitation To Tender 236
IPR. *See* Intellectual Property Rights
IRR. *See* Internal Rate of Return
Ishikawa Diagrams 229
Issue management
    Importance of 223
    Issue log 222

K

Key Performance Indicator 17, 18, 20

L

Leadership. 87, 92
Legal Entity 236
Lessons Learned. 67

M

Make or Buy Decision 233
Managerial Judgment 138
Managerial Products 74
Managing Stakeholder Expectations. 158
Maslow's Hierarchy of Needs 88
Method. *See* Project Management Method
Motivation 88

N

Negotiation Process 83
Net Present Value 134
Network Node Relationships. 166
    Finish to Finish. 166
    Finish to Start. 166
    Start to Start. 166
Non Verbal (Communications). 78
NPV. *See* Net Present Value

O

OBS. *See* Organisational Breakdown Structure
Offer. 236
Open and Honest Disclosure. 39
Operations. 63, 64, 252
Opportunities. 219
Options Evaluation 125
Organisational Breakdown Structure. 253
Organisational Roles. 52
    Project Manager. 53
    Sponsor 54
    Steering Group. 53
    Suppliers 55
    Team 53
    User 54
Organisation Structures
    Functional Organisation. 45
    Matrix Organisation 47
    Project Organisation. 46
    (Types of). 45
Outcomes 100

Outputs 100

P

Parallel Contracts 234

Parallel Learning System 3

Parametric Estimating 153

Pareto Analysis 228

Partnering 234

Payback Method 134

PBS. *See* Product breakdown Structure

Perception 79

PERT 154

PESTLE
    Economic (factors) 34
    Environmental (factors) 35
    Legal (factors) 34
    Political (factors) 33
    Sociological (factors) 34
    Technological (factors) 34

PICSA 114

Planned Completion 200

Planned Cost (PC) 164

Plan Response (To Risk)
    Accept 219
    Avoid 219
    Enhance 219
    Exploit 219
    Reduce 219
    Reject 219
    Share 219
    Transfer 219

PMI. *See* Project Management Institute

PMP. *See* Project Management Plan

Post Project Review 64, 65

Potential Impact (Risk) 217

PRAM Process. *See* Risk Management Process

Precedence diagramming 167
    Backward pass 169
    Critical path 170
    Forward pass 168
    Free float 171
    Total float 170

Previous data (Lack Of) 152

Prime and Sub Contracts 234

Prime (Contracts) 234

Prince2™ 10
Process Control Charts 229
Processes 75
Procurement 233
Procurement Strategy
    Contractual Relationship 233
    Feedback and Review 236
    Make or Buy Decision 233
Product Breakdown Structures 103
Programme Management Roles 30
Project Budget 163
Project Life Cycle 64
Project Management Institute 11
Project Management Method 74
    People 74
    Processes 75
    Products 74
    Templates 75
    Tools 75
Project Management Plan
    Contents of 146
    Use Throughout Life Cycle 149
Project Manager 53, 126
Project Method. *See* Project Management Method
Project Organisation 46
Project Reporting Cycle 141
Project Risk
    Causes 213
    Effects 213
    Opportunities 214
Project Risk and Management Guide 75
Project Roles 51, 57
Project schedule 165
Project Scope 146
Project Success
    Benefits 130
    Critical success factors 130
    Key performance indicator 130
    Success criteria 129
    Success factors 130
Projects Versus Programmes 29
Prompt Lists 216

Q

Quality assurance
    Audit 228
    Ishikawa Diagrams 229
    Lessons learned 228
    Process Control Charts 229
    Training 228
Quality (Definition) 225
Quality Management 225

R

RACI Chart 105
    Accountable 105
    Consulted 105
    Informed 105
    Responsible 105
Reduce (Risk Response) 219
Regular reviews 39
Reimbursement Methods 234
Reject (Change) 119
Reject (Risk Response) 219
Requirements (Linkage with Quality) 111
Requirements Management
    Document Requirements 110
    Requirements Analysis 109
    Requirements Capture 109
    Requirements Test 110
Resource histogram 180
Resource levelling 182
Resource Management 179
Resources (Consumable) 179
Responsible 105
Re-usable resources 179
Reviews (types)
    Benefits realisation review 66
    Gate reviews 65
    Post project review 65
Revision tips 20
Risk Assessments (Health and Safety) 39
Risk Event 213
Risk Identification Techniques 216
Risk Management Process 214
Risk Owner 217
Risk Responses 219

Accept 219
Avoid 219
Enhance 219
Exploit 219
Reduce 219
Reject 219
Share 219
Transfer 219

S

Safety equipment 39
Schedule Performance Index 200
Schedule Variance 200
Scope 100
Selective Listening 79
Selling 92
Sequential Contracts 234
Severity (Risk) 217
Share (Risk Response) 219
Single Contracts 234
Situational Leadership Model
    Delegating 92
    Selling 92
    Telling 92
SME. *See* Subject Matter Experts
Software systems 173
    Advantages 174
    Disadvantages 174
SPI. *See* Schedule Performance Index
Splitting tasks 182
Sponsor 22, 54, 126
Stakeholder 54, 77, 157
Stakeholder Management (Process) 157
Steering Group 53
Stress 39
Structured Methods 35
Sub Contracts 234
Subjectivity 152
Subject Matter Experts 126
Success 129
Success Criteria 125, 129
Success Factors 130
Suppliers 55, 126

SWOT 35

T

Target Cost/Price 235
Team 53, 94, 114, 265
Team Development 94
Technical Products 74
Telling 92
Templates 75
Termination 64, 265
Terminology 12
Thomas-Kilman Model 82
    Accommodating 83
Threats 219
Three Point Estimating 154
Time Management 16
Time Zones and Geography 79
Tools 75
Transfer (Risk Response) 219
Tuckman Model (Of Team Development) 95
    Forming 95
Turnkey Contracts 234
Typical questions 17

U

Unit Price 235
Users 54, 266

W

Walkthroughs 228
WBS. *See* Work Breakdown Structure
WIFT 85
Work Breakdown Structure 102, 153
Work Package 103